# Cambridge English
## Advanced
# Result

## Student's Book with Online Practice

Kathy Gude & Mary Stephens

OXFORD
UNIVERSITY PRESS

# Introduction and Exam Overview

## About the course

This fully updated and revised edition provides preparation and practice for candidates who are preparing for the revised *Cambridge English: Advanced (CAE)* exam. The material also provides opportunities for learners to develop their English on a broader level for success in the real world beyond the exam.

The units in this **Student's Book** contain practice of exam-type tasks for each part of the exam. Vocabulary and grammar practice are also an integral part of the course. The *Writing Guide* and *Grammar Reference* at the back of the book provide additional support to consolidate the language and skills covered in the main units.

Interactive online materials help to build on and extend the language and skills covered in the Student's Book and Workbook. The **Online Practice** (your unique access code is on the card at the back of this book) contains additional material which includes:

- exam practice tasks for each part of the exam, including speak-and-record tasks
- skills training exercises
- access to the *Oxford Advanced Learner's Dictionary 8th Edition**
- feedback on your answers*

(*available for self-study use or if your teacher sets assignments from the Online Practice 'with help')

The access code for your Online Practice also gives you access to a **complete online practice test** with feedback on your answers.

A **Workbook** with audio CD provides further exam, language and skills practice, and access to **another complete online practice test**.

We hope that you enjoy using this book to help you prepare for the *Cambridge English: Advanced (CAE)* exam.

## About the exam

*Cambridge English: Advanced (CAE)* is a qualification targeted at level C1 on the CEFR scale. It is proof that a candidate has reached an advanced level of English. It is a high-level qualification used for academic and professional purposes and is officially recognised by a number of organisations around the world, including universities, employers and governments.

In 2015 revisions were made to the *Cambridge English: Advanced (CAE)* exam to ensure that it continues to meet the needs and expectations of candidates, teachers and other users. The revisions also reflect the latest methodological approaches to communicative language testing.

The revised *Cambridge English: Advanced (CAE)* exam consists of four papers:

- **Reading and Use of English** (1 hour and 30 minutes)
- **Writing** (1 hour and 30 minutes)
- **Listening** (approximately 40 minutes)
- **Speaking** (15 minutes)

For more details and the most up-to-date information about the *Cambridge English: Advanced (CAE)* exam, go to www.cambridgeenglish.org.

# Paper 1 Reading and Use of English (1 hour and 30 minutes)

This paper has eight parts and a total of 56 questions.

For Parts 1 to 4, the testing focus is on understanding and controlling elements of language, e.g. grammar, lexis, word formation, lexical and grammatical transformations, and spelling.

For Parts 5 to 8, the test contains a range of texts types which are accompanied by reading comprehension questions.

| Part | Task type | Number of items | What you do | What it tests | How to do it |
|---|---|---|---|---|---|
| 1 | Multiple-choice cloze | 8 | Fill gaps in a text of 150–170 words from multiple-choice options | Fixed phrases, collocations, idioms, phrasal verbs, linkers, etc. used to complete a text with the correct meaning and grammatical context | page 40 |
| 2 | Open cloze | 8 | Fill gaps in a text of 150–170 words with one word per gap | Awareness and control of grammatical and lexico-grammatical items | page 28 |
| 3 | Word formation | 8 | Form appropriate words from the stems of words to fill gaps in a text of 150–170 words | Ability to form parts of speech correctly | page 16 |
| 4 | Key word transformation | 6 | Transform information from one sentence to another using three to six words including the word given | Awareness and control of grammatical structures and lexical items | page 29 |
| 5 | Multiple choice | 6 | Choose the best answer from four-option multiple-choice questions | Understanding of opinion, attitude, tone, purpose, detail and text organisation features | page 10 |
| 6 | Cross-text multiple matching | 4 | Read across four short texts and match prompts to elements in the texts | Understanding of opinion, attitude; comparing and contrasting of opinions and attitudes across texts | page 34 |
| 7 | Gapped text | 6 | Decide where paragraphs belong in a text | Understanding of text structure and development and global meaning | page 22 |
| 8 | Multiple matching | 10 | Match prompts to sections in a text, or several short texts | Understanding specific information, opinion and attitude | page 106 |

Marks

- One mark for each correct answer in Parts 1, 2 and 3.
- Up to two marks for each correct answer in Part 4.
- Two marks for each correct answer in Parts 5, 6 and 7.
- One mark for each correct answer in Part 8.
- All spellings must be correct.

# Paper 2 Writing (1 hour 30 minutes)

This paper has two parts. The Part 1 question is compulsory and is an essay based on input information. In Part 2, you choose one question from three.

Answers for Part 1 and Part 2 should both be 220–260 words in length.

The task types for Part 2 include the following: letters, reports, proposals and reviews.

Examples of Paper 2 question types can be found in the Writing Guide on pages 154–165.

| Part | Task type | Number of items | What you do | What it tests | How to do it |
|---|---|---|---|---|---|
| 1 | Compulsory essay task with a discursive focus | One compulsory task | Read the input information and complete the task given | Ability to evaluate and select information, express opinions and support an argument with subsidiary points and reasons | page 43 page 151 |
| 2 | Contextualised task | One from a choice of three tasks | Select one question from a choice of three and complete the task given | Ability to follow instructions and write in the correct style, layout and register in order to have a positive effect on the reader | page 18 page 79 page 91 |

Marks

* Parts 1 and 2 have equal marks.

# Paper 3 Listening (approx. 40 minutes)

This paper has four parts and 30 questions.

The recorded texts may include the following:

- monologues: radio broadcasts, speeches, talks, lectures, anecdotes, etc.
- conversations between two or more speakers: interviews, discussions, radio broadcasts, etc.

The testing focuses on understanding specific information, gist, attitude, opinion, context, main points and detail.

Each part is heard twice.

There will be a variety of voices, accents and styles of delivery in each listening test.

Candidates write their answers on the question sheet while listening. At the end of the test, candidates are given five minutes to transfer their answers to the separate answer sheet.

| Part | Task type | Number of items | What you do | What it tests | How to do it |
|------|-----------|-----------------|-------------|---------------|--------------|
| 1 | Multiple choice | 6 | Choose the best answer from multiple-choice questions on three unrelated short extracts with interacting speakers | Ability to understand speaker feeling, attitude, opinion and specific information | page 26 |
| 2 | Sentence completion | 8 | Write a word or short phrase heard in the monologue to complete gaps in sentences | Understanding of specific information and stated opinion | page 50 |
| 3 | Multiple choice | 6 | Choose the best answer from multiple-choice questions on conversations with two or more speakers | Ability to understand detail, speaker feeling, attitude and opinion | page 122 |
| 4 | Multiple matching | 10 | Select the correct answer from a list of eight options on five short theme-related monologues | Ability to understand gist, attitude, main points and context | page 14 |

Marks

- One mark for each correct answer.
- In Part 2, spelling must be correct for common words and those considered easy to spell.

# Paper 4  Speaking  (15 minutes)

This paper has four parts.

The standard format is two candidates and two examiners, one acting as interlocutor and assessor, the other acting as assessor only. If there is an odd number of candidates, three candidates sit the test together at the end of the examining session.

| Part | Task type | Length | What you do | What it tests | How to do it |
|---|---|---|---|---|---|
| 1 | Two-way conversation between candidates and interlocutor | 2 minutes | Ask and answer 'personal' questions | Ability to use general interactional and social language | page 15 |
| 2 | Individual long turns and brief responses | 4 minutes | Talk about two out of three pictures based on visual and written prompts for one minute | Ability to describe, speculate, compare and comment during a longer and organised discourse | page 27 page 39 |
| 3 | Two-way interaction between candidates | 4 minutes | Discuss a problem-solving task based on spoken instructions and written prompts | Ability to interact and exchange ideas, express opinions, agree or disagree, evaluate and reach a decision by negotiation | page 51 page 99 |
| 4 | Two-way conversation between candidates and interlocutor | 5 minutes | Discuss topics related to the Part 3 task | Ability to talk about wider issues and express and justify opinions on them | page 63 |

Marks

- Candidates are assessed on their performance throughout the test in the following areas:
  - Grammar Resource – range and control of grammatical structures.
  - Lexical Resource – range and control of vocabulary.
  - Discourse Management – ability to express ideas in coherent, connected speech without undue hesitation.
  - Pronunciation – individual sounds, stress and intonation.
  - Interactive Communication – initiating, responding and developing the interaction.
- The assessor marks according to detailed Analytical Scales, and the interlocutor gives a mark on a Global Scale, which is less detailed.

# What are you like?

## Lead in

**1** What is your ideal job? Make a list of useful qualities for that job, e.g. *imagination*, *sensitivity*. Which do you possess?

**2** Do the personality quiz below, then look at page 153 to discover the best career for you. Do you think the quiz is accurate? Why/Why not?

### Head or Heart?

**1** If your friend started dating someone you disliked and asked what you thought, would you … ?
- a  be brutally honest
- b  be tactful but truthful
- c  tell a lie if necessary

**2** If you are with friends and an argument breaks out, do you … ?
- a  leave them to get on with it
- b  take the side of the person you agree with
- c  try to find a compromise

**3** Which pair of words best describes you?
- a  logical and mature
- b  decisive and motivated
- c  caring and sensitive

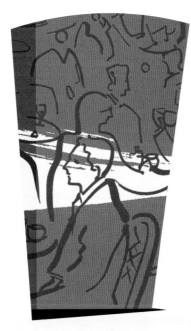

### Extrovert or Introvert?

**4** When out with a group of your friends, how much of the talking do you do?
- a  hardly any
- b  quite a lot
- c  almost all

**5** What do you tend to do when you meet new people socially?
- a  stick with the people you know
- b  worry about how to keep the conversation going
- c  mingle with as many new people as possible

**6** Which pair of words best describes you?
- a  cautious and thoughtful
- b  inquisitive and independent
- c  lively and energetic

### Facts or Ideas?

**7** You buy a piece of furniture which you have to assemble yourself. Do you … ?
- a  follow the instructions exactly
- b  scan the instructions then set them aside
- c  leap in, only referring to the instructions if you get stuck

**8** When giving directions to your home, do you … ?
- a  provide a step-by-step list of instructions
- b  draw a rough map
- c  just give general directions

**9** Which pair of words best describes you?
- a  practical and efficient
- b  realistic and enthusiastic
- c  inventive and imaginative

# Reading Part 5 Multiple choice

## how to do it

- Read the text quickly for general meaning.
- Read the question or stem but not the options.
- Find the part of the text that relates to the question; remember, the questions are in order.
- Read the options and eliminate any that are clearly wrong.
- Choose the option that answers the question fully and accurately.

**1** Read the text opposite and note down the main idea of each paragraph.

**2** Choose the correct answer (A, B, C or D) to questions 1–6, and say why the other options are wrong. Question 1 has been done as an example.

Example

1 What reason is given in the first paragraph for the increased use of personality testing?

   A It is used by 50% of managers. ✗

     ***50% of managers are selected on the basis of these tests.***

   B It has been accepted by educational bodies. ✗

     ***Personality tests <u>may</u> be used by universities in the future.***

   C Research has justified its use. ✓

     ***See lines 3–4.***

   D The tests are now available on the Internet. ✗

     ***This is true but not the reason given for the increased use of personality tests.***

> **tip**
>
> If you are unsure about an item, leave it and come back to it after you have answered the other questions.

2 What does the writer imply about the test she tried out herself?

   A It didn't come up with the right result.

   B It was psychologically challenging.

   C It was a tedious way to spend her time.

   D It wasn't personal enough for her liking.

3 The Myers-Briggs Type Indicator is based on the belief that

   A character traits are largely inherited.

   B certain personality traits are universal.

   C character is largely decided from birth.

   D some personality types are better than others.

4 What is the problem with personality tests, according to Dr Gill?

   A They can have a negative effect on takers.

   B People can easily lie about their true abilities.

   C The results could be counter-productive for employers.

   D Employers often find their results to be unreliable.

5 In Dr Gill's view, how easy is it to change your personality?

   A It's achievable in the short term.

   B It's impossible after the age of 21.

   C It's easy if you have great skill and motivation.

   D It's unlikely because it requires too much energy.

6 What final conclusion does the writer reach about the value of personality tests?

   A They are not really worth doing.

   B They may encourage greater realism.

   C They are of doubtful value to employers.

   D They can strengthen our self-image.

**3** Match a–f with meanings 1–6, using the text to help you.

| | | | |
|---|---|---|---|
| a | indicator (l.2) | 1 | argument |
| b | compulsive (l.18) | 2 | disadvantage |
| c | row (l.24) | 3 | sign |
| d | intuitive (l.31) | 4 | latent abilities or qualities |
| e | downside (l.40) | 5 | instinctive |
| f | potential (l.77) | 6 | irresistible/compelling |

**4** Have you ever taken a test like this? How useful or interesting was it?

# finding the real you

Psychometric testing for recruitment – assessing personality traits as an indicator of performance in a certain role – has mushroomed as studies show their results to be three times more accurate in predicting your job performance than
5 all your previous work experience combined. These tests are now included in virtually all graduate recruitment and are used in the selection of more than 50% of managers. Similar tests may be given to university applicants in future, dating agencies swear by them, and they are used to match
10 pets to owners. Online personality tests are immensely popular, too. So does your personality meet the grade?

I decided to try a test. At one particular site I was informed of my career personality and the job that best matches it. This is the appeal of online tests: the premise that there is
15 a perfect job, a perfect mate and a perfect you. These tests are also the ideal self-discovery vehicle for our alienated hi-tech age: intimate but anonymous. It is incredibly compulsive; when you get hooked on a test you're there for hours. And there is no aspect of life too frivolous to test for.
20 After recording my reaction to a series of ink blots (Is the mood of this picture nostalgic, violent or neutral? Can you find the chicken in this picture? Can you find your wife's/ husband's mother?), I discovered I am mainly motivated by peace. (Somewhat unconvincing as I'd just had a row with
25 my partner!)

The most popular of these personality tests is the Myers-Briggs Type Indicator (MBTI). It is based on the theory that we are born with a predisposition to one personality type which stays more or less fixed throughout life. You answer
30 88 questions and are then given your 'type': Introvert or Extrovert, Thinking or Feeling, Sensing or Intuitive, and Judging or Perceiving. If you're Introverted, Intuitive, Feeling and Perceptive, you'll probably find it harder to do work where you're required to entertain, or persuade lots
35 of people, such as a job in sales or public relations.

Critics of personality testing mutter darkly about 'social engineering'. Psychologist Dr Colin Gill agrees that too many organisations want people with the same traits. But, he warns, these 'popular' personality traits have their
40 downside. 'An extreme extrovert tends to be a selfish "get on" type, who may walk over others. Overly conscientious people are prone to burn out and people who are extremely open to new experiences can be butterflies, going from one big idea to the next without mastering any
45 of them.' Nevertheless, the psychometric test is here to stay – which may be why a whole sub-industry on cheating personality tests has sprung up. 'It's possible to cheat,' admits expert David Bartram, 'but why try to pretend you're an ambitious extrovert if you're a more thoughtful
50 introvert? Having to fake the person you are at work will be exhausting and miserable and probably short-lived.'

So can we change our personality? 'Your basic personality is fixed by the time you're 21,' says Gill, 'but it can be affected by motivation and intelligence. If you didn't
55 have the personality type to be a brain surgeon but desperately wanted to be one and were intelligent enough to master the skills, you could still go ahead. You can overcome certain aspects, but trying to go too much
60 against type for too long requires a huge amount of psychic energy and is actually too draining to be sustained for long. I think it's why we're seeing this trend for downshifting – too many
65 people trying to fit into a type or role that they aren't really suited for.'

Our obsession with personality now invades every aspect of our
70 lives. If you ask an expert for advice on just about anything, you'll probably be quizzed about your personality. But if personality tests have any value to us (rather
75 than employers), perhaps it is to disabuse us of the illusion that all of us are full of potential, and remind us of what we are. As they say in one test
80 when they ask for your age: pick the one you are, not the one you wish you were.

# Vocabulary

## Character adjectives

**1** Match character adjectives a–j with meanings 1–10.

| | | | |
|---|---|---|---|
| a | mature | 1 | curious |
| b | decisive | 2 | outgoing |
| c | motivated | 3 | adult |
| d | sensitive | 4 | aiming high |
| e | inquisitive | 5 | keen |
| f | ambitious | 6 | withdrawn |
| g | independent | 7 | wanting to do things well |
| h | conscientious | 8 | self-reliant |
| i | introverted | 9 | firm |
| j | extrovert | 10 | aware of people's feelings |

**2** Which of the adjectives in 1 are generally positive and which negative? Give examples.

**3** Read the dictionary entry for words similar in meaning to *honest*. Use this information to complete sentences a–c below.

> **WHICH WORD?**
> **Honest** and **frank** refer to *what* you say as much as *how* you say it: *a(n) honest/frank admission of guilt*. They are generally positive words, although it is possible to be *too* frank in a way that other people might not like. **Direct**, **outspoken** and **blunt** all describe sb's manner of saying what they think. **Outspoken** suggests that you are willing to shock people by saying what you believe to be right. **Blunt** and **direct** often suggest that you think honesty is more important than being polite. **Open** is positive and describes sb's character: *I'm a very open person*.

*Oxford Advanced Learner's Dictionary, 8th edition*

a I hope you don't mind me being ........... , but that dress really doesn't suit you.

b Some journalists are deliberately ........... – they don't care who they upset, they just want a good story.

c You should ask Nick's opinion. You can trust him to tell you the truth, he's so ........... .

**4** Discuss questions a and b.

a Which five character adjectives do you think a friend would use to describe you?

b Do you think we are born with certain character traits, or is our character formed as we grow up?

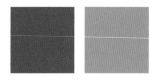

# Grammar

## Review of tenses GR p166–169

**1** Match the verb forms in the sentences below with these tenses.

| | |
|---|---|
| Present simple | Present perfect continuous |
| Present continuous | Past simple |
| Future simple | Past continuous |
| Future continuous | Past perfect simple |
| Present perfect simple | Past perfect continuous |

a Since I moved here, I*'ve been learning* to drive.
Since I moved here, I*'ve learnt* to drive.

b Carla*'s playing* the guitar very well.
Carla *plays* the guitar very well.

c It *started* raining when I left the house.
It *had started* raining when I left the house.

d I*'ll be getting* the dinner ready when you arrive.
I*'ll get* the dinner ready when you arrive.

e When we got to her house, she *cried*.
When we got to her house, she*'d been crying*.

f My brother *always tells* me what to do.
My brother*'s always telling* me what to do.

g We *were having* a party when my sister announced her engagement.
We *had* a party when my sister announced her engagement.

**2** Explain the difference in meaning between the pairs of sentences in 1.

**3** Complete sentences a–i using the correct form of the verbs in brackets.

a His back was aching because he ........... (dig) in the garden all day.

b ........... (your father/work) abroad at present?

c Maria left college early today because she ........... (have) a dental appointment an hour ago.

d As soon as it stops raining, we ........... (take) the dog for a walk.

e My neighbour couldn't stop because his bus ........... (leave) and he didn't want to miss it.

f For the past six weeks, I ........... (have) singing lessons.

g I can't phone you at that time because I ........... (travel) on the underground.

h The photocopy machine ........... (break down) twice already and it's not even lunchtime!

i As a rule, we ........... (spend) part of each summer at my parents' house.

**4** Correct any verbs in a–h which are not normally used in a continuous form.

a These gloves aren't mine – are they belonging to you?

b My girlfriend doesn't like perfumes that are smelling of flowers – she prefers something more exotic.

c Our teacher said we were all deserving a great deal of praise for our exam results.

d Are you thinking what I'm thinking – that this new outfit just doesn't suit me?

e I've always been hating getting up early in the morning, even in the summer.

f This manual is containing all the information you need to run your new computer software.

g At the moment I feel that you really aren't putting in as much effort as you could with your studies.

h The hockey club we're belonging to is always on the lookout for new players.

**5** Say which of these verbs are a) never used in a continuous form, or b) can be used in a continuous form but with a change in meaning.

| like | believe | know | remind |
|------|---------|------|--------|
| detest | hear | understand | belong |
| contain | taste | prefer | mean |

**6** Match a–j with a suitable ending from 1–10 and explain how the context changes the meaning.

a My favourite actor is appearing …

b I'm afraid the DVD player appears …

c The manager is having …

d Celine has …

e Everyone thinks …

f She's thinking …

g Working as a wildlife guide really appeals …

h Our local school is appealing …

i I am seeing …

j I see …

1 … a career adviser tomorrow to get advice on working in IT.

2 … a lot of experience in working with children.

3 … a meeting to discuss the new proposal.

4 … for funds for a new building.

5 … in a new musical in London's West End.

6 … José will get the job.

7 … of buying a car in the near future.

8 … to be broken.

9 … to me.

10 … nothing but fields when I look out of my bedroom window.

**7** Complete sentences a–e with the correct form of the verb.

a If you ........... (feel) that I'm being unreasonable, please say so.

b Sandra ........... (smell) the blossom on her cherry tree when she was stung by a bee.

c Even though you've explained it three times now, I still ........... (not see) what you mean.

d Since I was a young boy, I ........... (have) a fear of heights.

e ........... (you/think) you could give me a hand lifting this equipment?

**8** Read this extract from an email which was sent to an online penfriend agency, and correct any errors in tenses.

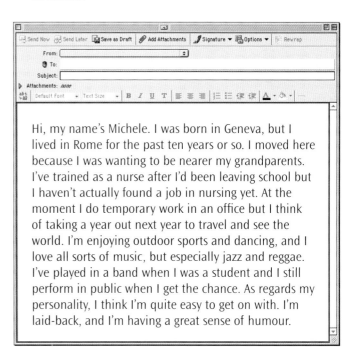

Hi, my name's Michele. I was born in Geneva, but I lived in Rome for the past ten years or so. I moved here because I was wanting to be nearer my grandparents. I've trained as a nurse after I'd been leaving school but I haven't actually found a job in nursing yet. At the moment I do temporary work in an office but I think of taking a year out next year to travel and see the world. I'm enjoying outdoor sports and dancing, and I love all sorts of music, but especially jazz and reggae. I've played in a band when I was a student and I still perform in public when I get the chance. As regards my personality, I think I'm quite easy to get on with. I'm laid-back, and I'm having a great sense of humour.

**9** Write your own email introducing yourself to a penfriend, using the corrected version in 8 as a model.

# Listening Part 4 Multiple matching

**1** Why might someone decide to take up the hobbies and pastimes pictured?

**2** 🎧 In 3 you will hear five people talking about their hobbies. Listen and match the phrases they use (1–7) with the meanings (a–g).

| | | | |
|---|---|---|---|
| 1 | ....b..... | a | We all had different interests. |
| 2 | .......... | b | I became really inspired by it. |
| 3 | .......... | c | I was completely taken aback. |
| 4 | .......... | d | I'd lost my job. |
| 5 | .......... | e | I was chattering away about how busy I was. |
| 6 | .......... | f | I'd had some difficulties with my job. |
| 7 | .......... | g | I didn't have much to occupy myself with. |

## how to do it

- Use the time allowed to read both tasks quickly.
- Remember there are two questions for each speaker.
- On the first listening, answer as many questions as you can for <u>both</u> tasks.
- Use the second listening to answer any questions you missed.

**3** 🎧 Read the how to do it box, then listen twice and do the exam task below.

For 1–5, choose the people's reasons for taking up their new interest (A–H).

A  to recover from an accident
B  to please a relative
C  to be more independent
D  to broaden their horizons
E  to fill in time
F  to take some exercise
G  to express their feelings
H  to relieve the pressure of work

Speaker 1 ☐ 1
Speaker 2 ☐ 2
Speaker 3 ☐ 3
Speaker 4 ☐ 4
Speaker 5 ☐ 5

For 6–10, choose the outcome of the speakers' new interests (A–H).

A  It's enabled me to win an award.
B  It's inspired me to be more competitive.
C  It's turned out to be quite profitable.
D  It's become a kind of obsession.
E  It's restored my faith in human nature.
F  It's made me more critical of myself.
G  It's revealed a new aspect of my personality.
H  It's made me feel less dejected.

Speaker 1 ☐ 6
Speaker 2 ☐ 7
Speaker 3 ☐ 8
Speaker 4 ☐ 9
Speaker 5 ☐ 10

**4** Tell a partner about your hobbies and interests and why you enjoy them.

# Speaking Part 1

**1** In pairs, take it in turns to answer questions a–f. Try to use some of the phrases below.

a Where were you born?
b How long have you been studying English?
c Have you always been interested in languages?
d What's your favourite time of the year?
e How would you describe your character?
f What are your plans for the future?

### Answering personal questions

Well, actually …
That's a difficult question, but …
I've never given it much thought, but …
As a matter of fact, …

**2** 🎧 Listen to five students answering an examiner's questions. What different mistakes with tenses do they make?

**3** In pairs, ask each other about the subjects in a–e. Use the phrases below to help you.

a your favourite TV programme
b your ideal job
c a day out you have enjoyed
d subjects you enjoyed learning at school
e the kind of music you listen to

### Asking for personal information

So, tell me what … is.
Could you tell me about … ?
I'd like to know what … is/would be.
What would you say … is/would be?
Could you describe … ?

**4** 🎧 Listen to two candidates answering the same Part 1 question. Suggest three ways in which they could improve their performance.

### how to do it

In Speaking Part 1 you may be asked to talk about a variety of topics, e.g. your past experiences, present circumstances or future plans, travel, education. Make sure you use the appropriate tenses.

**5** In pairs, answer questions a–d, giving reasons. Use the phrases below to help you.

a Would you like to spend some time working in another country?
b Do you think that having a lot of free time is a good or a bad thing?
c How necessary is it to have good friends?
d Which is more important: money or health?

### Expressing personal views

In my opinion, …
I think it's essential to …
I strongly believe that …
As far as I'm concerned, …

**6** 🎧 Listen to a candidate expressing a personal view and decide if her attempt is successful. Explain why.

# Use of English Part 3 Word formation

1 Look at the title of the text below. Do you think it is possible to be 'born lucky'? Why/Why not?

2 Read the text and the how to do it box. Decide which part of speech belongs in gaps 1–8 in the text.

3 Complete the text using the words in CAPITALS in the correct form. Use the tip box to help you.

4 Do you agree with what the writer says in the text? Why/Why not?

## how to do it

- Decide what parts of speech you need.
- You may need to form words with negative meanings, or plurals.
- You may need to make more than one change to the word given.
- Check your spelling carefully.
- Read your completed text for overall sense.

# Born lucky?

## tip

The eight missing answers in this text include:
- two singular nouns
- three adjectives
- two plural nouns
- one adverb

Research shows some **0** ...noticeable... differences in the **1** ..................... attitude and behaviour of lucky and unlucky people. If genes affect personality and behaviour, then you can indeed be born lucky.

Lucky people create opportunities for good fortune by being extrovert, sociable and using open body language. They are relaxed and **2** ..................... , and more receptive to new opportunities. They also like change and **3** ..................... , and this brings about new **4** ..................... and the prospect of new friends.

Lucky people also have positive **5** ..................... of life. In one famous experiment psychologists told American high school teachers certain school children were especially **6** ..................... . In fact, there was nothing exceptional about them. The teachers, however, showered them with praise and **7** ..................... , and the children responded by producing better schoolwork.

The converse is also true. Finnish researchers divided 2,000 men into 'negative', 'neutral' and 'positive' groups, depending on their personalities. Over a six-year period, those in the 'negative' group were **8** ..................... more susceptible to illness and accidents.

**0** NOTICE
**1** PSYCHOLOGY

**2** APPROACH
**3** VARY
**4** POSSIBLE

**5** EXPECT

**6** GIFT

**7** ENCOURAGE

**8** DENY

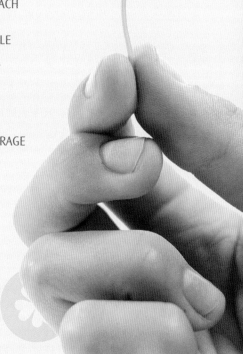

# Vocabulary

## Expressions with *luck*

**5** Write the related verbs for nouns a–i below.

|   | noun | verb |
|---|------|------|
| a | behaviour | |
| b | personality | |
| c | creation | |
| d | reception | |
| e | production | |
| f | praise | |
| g | response | |
| h | division | |
| i | dependency | |

**6** Write negative adjectives made from the verbs a–i. More than one answer may be possible. Then use the negative adjectives in sentences of your own.

|   | verb | negative adjective |
|---|------|--------------------|
| a | notice | |
| b | expect | |
| c | legalise | |
| d | mature | |
| e | socialise | |
| f | offend | |
| g | exist | |
| h | guide | |
| i | respect | |

**1** Discuss the meaning of these expressions and match them with 1–8, then use them to complete a–h.

with any luck     beginner's luck
the luck of the draw     push your luck
take pot luck     no such luck
be out of luck     by a stroke of luck

1  rely on continuing good luck
2  fortunately and unexpectedly
3  success at your first attempt
4  risk the outcome
5  decided by chance
6  unfortunately not
7  if things turn out well
8  not be lucky this time

a  'Did you manage to fix your car?'
   '.......... . It's a complete write-off.'
b  You shouldn't .......... . You haven't been caught speeding yet but you might be!
c  You may win the lottery – you may not. It's quite simply .......... .
d  The only problem with this cheap package holiday I've arranged is you can't choose your accommodation; you just have to .......... .
e  You .......... , I'm afraid. I've just sold the last copy of that particular book.
f  I've just realised I've forgotten my house key, but .......... my wife might be at home.
g  Jane missed the last bus but .......... a friend was passing and gave her a lift.
h  Robert won his first professional tennis match but modestly said it was just .......... !

**2** When was the last time you were very lucky or unlucky? What happened?

# Writing  Part 2  A formal letter or email  WG p158

**1** Read the writing task below and answer questions a and b.

a Who are you going to write to? For what purpose?

b What are the three things you must include?

A friend of yours is applying for a job as a holiday representative with an international holiday organisation. The company has asked you to provide a character reference for your friend. The reference should indicate how long you have known the person. It must also include a detailed description of the person's character and the reasons why he or she would be suitable for the job.

Write the **reference** in 220–260 words.

**2** Make notes on questions a–c.

a What sort of things might a holiday representative have to do?

b What skills might be needed?

c Which personal qualities might be needed for the job?

**3** The two references opposite, A and B, were written by two different people. Read them and decide which person did not make a plan before starting to write. Give examples of the effect this has had on the organisation of the reference.

**4** Read the references again and do tasks a–c.

a List the linking words in A and B (, , etc.). Which writer makes better use of them?

b Identify the purpose of each paragraph in B.

c Identify any useful phrases for references in general.

**5** Read the question below, then write your reference. The how to do it box and tips will help you.

One of your friends has applied for a job teaching English abroad. The job involves teaching pupils aged 10–16 and organising games and activities for them. You have been asked to provide a character reference for your friend.

You should say how long you have known your friend and include a detailed description of their character. You should also give reasons why he or she would be suitable for the job.

Write your **reference** in 220–260 words in an appropriate style.

## tip

Describe two or three things the person has done which show the qualities/abilities that make them right for the job.

## tip

Start a new paragraph for each complete change of topic but avoid one-sentence paragraphs.

Try to include a topic sentence summarising the main idea of the paragraph. Expand on that idea and/or give examples in the rest of the paragraph.

## how to do it

■ Read the task carefully and underline the key words.

■ Brainstorm ideas and select the best ones.

■ Organise your ideas and make a paragraph plan.

■ Link sentences and paragraphs where appropriate.

## A

Dear Sir or Madam

I am writing to you on behalf of Juan Fernández.

I have known Juan for three years. We're in the same tutorial group at college.

He is very popular at college and certainly knows how to enjoy life.

Juan is very fit and healthy. He's good at sports.

Juan doesn't lose his temper very often. He'd be good at dealing with difficult customers and their complaints.

Juan's a complete extrovert. He loves being the centre of attention. He'd enjoy entertaining people in your resorts. In his free time, Juan likes to keep fit. He goes down to the gym most evenings and he swims and plays football. He's got lots of friends. He won't have a problem getting on with his clients.

Juan speaks fluent English. He will deal easily with different nationalities in the holiday destination. He's quite a laid-back person and he doesn't panic in difficult situations. You can rely on him to stay cool, calm and collected.

Juan works in a local bar on Saturdays and knows how to deal with difficult people. He doesn't lose his temper. He's prepared to listen, but he can be quite firm when it's necessary, too.

I am sure Juan will be a good holiday representative. I have no hesitation in recommending him for the post.

Yours faithfully,

Sylvia Garcia

## B

To whom it may concern

### Reference for Paola Gianni

I have known Paola for approximately six years. She is a very bubbly, down-to-earth character and gets on well with people of all ages, so she would be very popular with holiday groups. Paola helps run the local youth club in our area, so she is very used to dealing with young people. The organisational and leadership skills she has learnt in this work should serve her well as a holiday representative. In times of crisis, Paola is an excellent person to have around because she is dependable and not inclined to panic or lose her temper. Although never bossy, she can take control of difficult situations without upsetting anyone. For this reason, I believe she would definitely be able to cope if things went wrong in a holiday situation.

When it comes to entertaining people, Paola is very talented, which might come in very useful in her role as a holiday representative. As well as singing and dancing, she plays the guitar and often takes part in performances at the youth club.

In addition to performing, Paola is an accomplished sportswoman. She is a strong swimmer and a qualified lifeguard. Her favourite sports include scuba-diving, windsurfing and waterskiing, at which she has reached competition level. With her enthusiastic, common-sense approach, she would ensure holidaymakers have safe access to a full range of beach activities.

In my opinion, Paola would make an excellent holiday representative. I have no hesitation in recommending her to your company.

Yours faithfully

Antonio Calanducci

# Review

**1** Match character adjectives a–h with their opposite meanings 1–8.

| | |
|---|---|
| a introverted | 1 uninterested |
| b decisive | 2 careless |
| c sensitive | 3 outgoing |
| d inquisitive | 4 thick-skinned |
| e mature | 5 unmotivated |
| f independent | 6 childish |
| g conscientious | 7 helpless |
| h ambitious | 8 vague |

**2** Complete the adjectives defined in a–h.

a diplomatic about what you say    ta _ _ _ _ _
b rational and reasonable    lo _ _ _ _ _
c concerned or interested in others   ca _ _ _ _
d helpful and considerate    th _ _ _ _ _ _ _ _
e hesitant about your actions    ca _ _ _ _ _ _
f excited or passionate    en _ _ _ _ _ _ _ _ _ _
g sensible and realistic    pr _ _ _ _ _ _
h creative and imaginative    in _ _ _ _ _ _

**3** Write these words in the form indicated in brackets. There may be more than one possible answer.

a depend ............... (adjective)
b broad ............... (verb)
c able ............... (verb)
d obsess ............... (noun)
e criticise ............... (adjective)
f inspire ............... (noun)
g represent ............... (noun; person)
h press ............... (noun)
i capable ............... (noun)
j psychology ............... (adverb)

**4** Use one of the words in 3 in the correct form to complete sentences a–d.

a James couldn't have stolen the money. He's ............... of doing anything dishonest.
b The government came in for a lot of ............... when the new tax laws were introduced.
c This painting is a very good ............... of the kind of scenery found in this area.
d My aunt is quite ............... about cleaning her house – everything has to be spotless!

**5** Complete the expressions with *luck* in a–h.

a I broke my grandmother's favourite vase but, by a ............... of luck, I found an identical one in a shop down the road.
b Some things in life you have no choice about – it's just the luck of the ............... .
c Sorry, you're ............... of luck! We sold the last newspaper five minutes ago.
d We aim to set out early and, ............... any luck, we should arrive before dark.
e I thought I might get the job but ............... such luck. They gave it to someone else.
f Let's just ............... pot luck and see where we can book a last-minute holiday to.
g Helen managed to get a film part after her first audition but she said it was just ............... luck!
h I know everything seems to be going swimmingly at the moment but just remember – you shouldn't ............... your luck!

**6** Fill in missing words 1–14 in this job reference.

I am writing to you on **1** ................ of Belinda Morris, who has **2** ................ to be a trainee manager in your restaurant. Belinda is a very lively, **3** ................-to-earth character who **4** ................ on well with people of all ages. She has worked as a waitress during the summer holidays in our hotel, so she's **5** ................ to dealing **6** ................ all kinds of customers. The organisational skills she has learnt should **7** ................ her well **8** ................ a restaurant manager. In **9** ................ of crisis, she is an excellent person to **10** ................ around because she doesn't panic. When it **11** ................ to making people feel at ease, Belinda is an expert. What's **12** ................ , she has a great sense of humour. In my **13** ................ , she would make an excellent manager. I have no **14** ................ in recommending her.

# Customs and traditions

## Lead in

**1** Discuss the following questions.

a   What annual festivals or celebrations take place in your country?

b   When do they happen and what do they involve?

c   What do you know about their origins?

**2** What do you imagine happens at the festivals shown in the photos?

**3** 🎧 Listen to two people talking about the two festivals shown and choose the best answer to questions 1–4.

1   The Kattenwoensdog festival dates back to a time when

a   local people began to breed cats in the town's Cloth Hall.

b   local cats had been unsuccessful in ridding the town of rodents.

c   local people decided that the town cats had outlived their usefulness.

2   What happened when the speaker visited the Kattenwoensdog festival?

a   Everyone taking part in the parade was dressed as a cat.

b   The bad weather failed to spoil the carnival atmosphere.

c   Spectators rushed to buy a toy cat from the jester.

3   What is one of the rules of La Tomatina?

a   You must be a member of a team to join in.

b   The tomatoes must be crushed before you throw them.

c   Tourists are not allowed to hit locals.

4   What happens at the end of La Tomatina?

a   Trucks arrive to clear away all the mess.

b   Free tomato juice is given away.

c   You can wash in specially provided showers.

**4** Tell a partner about any festivals that you have been to or would like to go to.

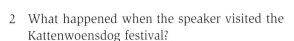

La Tomatina

# festival in the deser

There's little beyond the Malian town of Timbuktu but a vast expanse of unwelcoming desert. Yet each January, a host of musicians and tourists gather in the market place, preparing to head north into the Sahara. As people fill their jeeps with diesel and supplies, it's hard not to get swept up in the excitement and anticipation of the *remotest* music festival on Earth.

**1** ☐

The Tuareg, a nomadic group who inhabit the Sahara, *have more appropriate transport*, arriving on white camels. There are 1,800 of them at the festival, which isn't surprising, *because the event grew out of an annual Tuareg get-together*.

**2** ☐

As the Tuareg cook over campfires, the tourists settle into their tents. The sun goes down and charcoal braziers light up the dunes. Then bands from all over Mali and neighbouring countries take the stage, playing lutes and talking drums. There's a group of dancers from Niger decorated with beads and covered in body paint. There are Western performers too. As one group hit their electric guitars and yell into the microphones, an old Malian lady claps her hands over her ears.

**3** ☐

Maybe that's because when I visit, the festival is still in its infancy as a tourist attraction. There are no more than 500 foreigners present, most of whom feel lucky to be witnessing something 'authentic'. And indeed, there is *little sign of the profit motive* that underpins most World Music festivals.

**4** ☐

A music festival may seem an odd mechanism for kick-starting tourism, but this is the intentio In the eyes of Mali's minister of tourism, Malian music is one of the country's main draws. She is convinced that the north, the poorest part of the country, could support year-round tourism. Until recently there have been few opportunitie for the Tuareg. They need tourists to bring employment and development to the region.

**5** ☐

But *this sort of envy* only exists between the Tuareg because the festival is seen to be a good thing. In fact, for now, *it enjoys almost universal support. And similar events are springing up in neighbouring countries* too, with the Tuareg organisers of the Festival in the Desert fast becoming consultants.

**6** ☐

The Tuareg dance and sing, Dicko explains, and afterwards they talk about their problems. He is studying to be a doctor in Timbuktu and his village is far away. At the festival he can meet family and friends for the first time in two years Perhaps it's to people like Dicko, who've given u the nomadic lifestyle, that the festival brings the greatest pleasure.

## Reading Part 7 Gapped text

**1** What music festivals are there in your country? Who goes? What happens?

**2** Read the article about a music festival in the Sahara, and match paragraphs A–G with gaps 1–6. There is one extra paragraph. Find links in the text and use the words in italics to help you.

### how to do it

- ☐ Read the main text for general meaning.
- ☐ Look for grammar and vocabulary links before and after each gap and in the paragraphs.
- ☐ Fill the easiest gaps first to reduce the number of options.
- ☐ Try the extra paragraph in each gap again.
- ☐ Read the complete text again for grammar and overall sense.

**A** *With such obvious popularity*, who knows what the future may hold for the Timbuktu festival. But for now, at least, it still retains its original purpose as a get-together for the Tuareg people themselves.

**B** But *despite this lack of commercialism*, the benefits of tourism are there for local people. The Tuareg stroll between the tents offering camel rides or selling their handicrafts. Dicko, my Tuareg friend, explains that cash spent by tourists is used to buy foodstuff in Timbuktu, which is then taken back to the villages.

**C** In fact, as the event's organiser explains, *Tuareg have been meeting at this oasis for centuries*. Here they have traditionally swapped news, raced camels, made music and even arranged marriages. They started the festival because they felt it was time to get in touch with the outside world.

**D** *Meanwhile*, the sustainability of the festival has been called into question. Westerners say that if the festival gets too big, it will lose its authentic feel. And it appears to have reached capacity already.

75 **E** To get to Timbuktu, I spent three whole days driving. As the convoy of *four-wheel drives* headed into the dunes, it became clear that the final stretch of the journey was the trickiest, and the track was soon lined with *jeeps* stuck in deep sand, some almost within 80 earshot of the music.

**F** There are few concerns about the environmental impact of the festival. But conflict between Tuareg could be more of a problem. An elderly man complains that the festival started out as a moveable event with 85 a different site each year, bringing benefits to different parts of the Sahara. But for several years it has been held in the same place because it is easier to build a permanent stage here. *'Why can't we have a festival where I come from?'* he asks.

90 **G** But *while rock groups might not produce the desired effect on everybody*, Tuareg bands do. Their Tuareg fans watch from the seats of their camels. This is clearly a Tuareg event, but there is little sense of being an outsider. As I shovel sand to try to gain some height, my 95 Tuareg neighbours usher me forward for a better view. The sense of intimacy and respect among the small crowd is remarkable.

**3** Complete the phrases in a–h with 1–8, then rephrase the sentences in your own words.

a  The claim that the festival will remain authentic has been *called into* .......... .     1  draws
b  We sat at the back of the crowd but just *within* .......... *of* the music.     2  impact
c  Traditional festivals can become a *mechanism for* .......... tourism.     3  earshot
d  As the bands began to play, we all *got* .......... *up* in the excitement.     4  kick-starting
e  The rock music did not produce the *desired* .......... *on* everyone.     5  question
f  As a tourist attraction, the festival is still *in its* .......... .     6  effect
g  Traditional music is *one of the country's main* .......... .     7  swept
h  *The environmental* .......... of the festival is not currently a major concern.     8  infancy

**4** What positive and negative effects might tourism have on traditional festivals like this?

# Vocabulary

## Easily confused words (1)

**1** Choose the correct verbs in a–h to complete the collocations.

a  I wasn't enjoying myself so I .......... *an excuse* and left. (did/put/made)

b  The director promised my sister a part in the film – he'd better .......... *his word.* (keep/hold/take)

c  We're planning to .......... *a party* to celebrate Tina's good news. (make/throw/do)

d  He .......... *a lie* when the police interviewed him and now he's in big trouble. (told/said/spoke)

e  The first chapter of a book usually .......... *the scene* for what happens later. (lays/puts/sets)

f  Everyone else was furious when one man .......... *the queue* for tickets. (overtook/jumped/missed)

g  That film was so complicated – I didn't .......... *a clue* what was going on! (follow/get/have)

h  It's very hard to .......... *a living* as an actor. (earn/get/gain)

**2** Read the dictionary entry below to find the adverb that collocates best with *disappointed*. Then choose the most suitable word in sentences a–c. Check your ideas in a dictionary.

> **dis·ap·point·ed** 0-ᴡ /ˌdɪsə'pɔɪntɪd/ *adj.*
> upset because sth you hoped for has not happened or been as good, successful, etc. as you expected: ~ **(at/by sth)** *They were* **bitterly disappointed** *at the result of the game.* ◇ *I was disappointed by the quality of the wine.* ◇ ~ **(in/with sb/sth)** *I'm disappointed in you—I really thought I could trust you!* ◇ *I was very disappointed with myself.* ◇ ~ **(to see, hear, etc.)** *He was disappointed to see she wasn't at the party.* ◇ ~ **(that...)** *I'm disappointed (that) it was sold out.* ◇ ~ **(not) to be...** *She was disappointed not to be chosen.*

*Oxford Advanced Learner's Dictionary, 8th edition*

a  Amanda's (highly/fully) competitive with her more successful older sister.

b  It was (immediately/clearly) obvious that there was no way we could reach the airport in time.

c  She is an extremely strict teacher and expects (whole/total) obedience from her pupils.

**3** Complete questions a–c, using your answers from 1 above, then discuss each question.

a  Do you generally queue in your country? What happens if you .......... the queue?

b  How would you most like to .......... a living?

c  Has anyone ever not .......... their word to you? What happened?

# Grammar

## Gerunds and infinitives GR p171–172

**1** Put these verbs into three columns as shown below.

| avoid | want | like | deny | promise |
| enjoy | expect | fancy | hope | risk |
| offer | prefer | deserve | begin | continue |
| practise | threaten | manage | miss | love |
| refuse | | | | |

| followed by gerund | followed by infinitive + *to* | followed by gerund or infinitive |
| --- | --- | --- |
| *avoid* | *expect* | *like* |

**2** Which of the verbs in 1 can also be immediately followed by a *that* clause?

**3** Complete these sentences with an appropriate verb in the correct form.

a  Our football team deserves .......... because they have trained so hard.

b  One of the suspects has denied .......... part in the robbery.

c  My sister is hoping .......... a job as a stewardess with our national airline.

d  We lost the car keys but we managed .......... the car by turning a piece of wire in the ignition!

e  I'm disappointed that my favourite group have refused .......... at the festival.

f  Since my grandmother moved to another town, I really miss .......... her every day.

g  What time is the President expected .......... at the airport?

h  Armed police threatened .......... the gunmen if they did not release the hostages.

**4** Match each verb (in both the gerund and infinitive form) with definitions a–j.

　　stop　try　remember　regret　mean

a  do something to see what happens as a result

b  be sorry for something you've done

c  intend to do something

d  not forget that something must be done

e  stop something you've been doing

f  involve or require something

g  be sorry about something you're going to do

h  stop one thing to do something else

i  not forget something which has already happened

j  see if it's possible to do something

**5** Use the verb in brackets to complete a–d in two ways: first with the gerund and then the infinitive.

a I didn't remember (invite) my neighbour to my barbecue so …

b I wish for once you'd stop (think) about …

c I like our neighbours, but I regret (say) that …

d My six-month-old nephew has just tried (eat) …

**6** Complete sentences a–h with one of the prepositions below and an appropriate gerund.

| on | at | for | to | of | in |

a I'm not very keen ……… when the sea is this rough but I'll come if you insist.

b Are you looking forward ……… school and getting a job?

c In trying to take a shortcut across the fields, we only succeeded ……… completely lost.

d I apologise profusely ……… you waiting in the cold for so long.

e My classmates insisted ……… me a birthday present even though I said I didn't want one.

f If you carry ……… about people behind their backs, you'll soon end up with no friends.

g I've never been very good ……… letters but I regularly telephone my grandparents in Australia.

h My brother is thinking ……… abroad, maybe as a tour guide.

**7** Cross out *to* where it is not needed with the infinitives in these sentences.

a I don't think politicians should be allowed to get away with the lies they tell.

b If you let that boy to do whatever he wants, you'll really live to regret it.

c Adults can rarely be made to do what they don't want to, but you can often make someone to do something through persuasion.

d That looks like a nasty cut – I'd advise you to get medical attention at once.

e My parents helped me to buy a small flat in the suburbs.

f You had better not to tell anyone what we've just been discussing.

g It's just typical that when someone's watching you to do something, you make a right mess of it.

**8** Complete these sentences with an object and an infinitive with or without *to* as appropriate.

a When I was a child, my parents wouldn't let …

b The water in the resort wasn't clean enough to drink so our holiday rep advised …

c I woke up suddenly and thought I heard …

d I know it may sound unreasonable but I'd rather …

e I love sitting by the lake watching …

**9** Complete 1–13 with an appropriate form of the verb in bold.

I've always wanted ……… **1 do** something really adventurous, so when, in my final year at university, I was invited ……… **2 join** a wildlife expedition to the Amazon, I didn't stop ……… **3 think**. I just said 'yes'! I looked forward to ……… **4 explore** the forests and dreamt of ……… **5 discover** a species new to science. I also hoped ……… **6 film** a jaguar as these animals are of special interest to me. The trip would mean ……… **7 struggle** through thick jungle and I knew we risked ……… **8 be** bitten by insects and snakes. My girlfriend was so worried about me that she threatened ……… **9 burn** my plane ticket! In the event, I managed ……… **10 avoid** any kind of disaster. I watched a giant snake ……… **11 catch** a monkey, but that was the nearest I came to any danger. I really enjoyed ……… **12 see** such a huge variety of wildlife and I would like ……… **13 go back** to the Amazon again one day, that's for sure.

# Listening   Part 1   Multiple choice

**1**   Read this quote and discuss how far you agree with these ideas.

> We want to preserve our identity, history, land, language and values for our children. Our children, who are our future, must understand our history so no one can say our culture is gone. If we do not preserve this, our lives won't belong to us any more.

**2**   Read questions 1–6 below before you listen to the three different extracts. Then listen and choose the best answer (A, B or C) for each question. The how to do it and tip boxes will help you.

**extract one**   **You hear part of an interview with a tour operator discussing a museum dedicated to Native Americans.**

1   What criticism does the man make about the museum?
   A   Native Americans were not consulted enough when setting it up.
   B   Some exhibits do not capture the impact of Native American culture.
   C   The museum project took far too long to conceive and set up.

2   The museum aims to
   A   ensure that it will attract large numbers of local visitors.
   B   demonstrate the lifestyle of Native Americans to visitors.
   C   display objects originally in the possession of local communities.

**extract two**   **You hear two people talking about a town fair.**

3   What did the two speakers learn about the town fair from the newspaper?
   A   Attendance was down on last year.
   B   It had managed to attract a lot of outsiders.
   C   There was a lack of atmosphere.

4   The two speakers agree that
   A   the best thing about the town fair was the evening concert.
   B   the quality of the items on sale at the town fair was excellent.
   C   the town fair greatly benefits the local community.

**extract three**   **You hear part of an interview with a woman who is a museum curator.**

5   The woman disagrees with the interviewer about
   A   what kinds of historical objects should be displayed in museums.
   B   the role of historical objects in educating young people.
   C   whether historical objects should be returned to where they came from.

6   How does the woman see her responsibilities as a museum curator?
   A   She believes we should be aware of the history of our ancestors.
   B   She is determined to preserve the past for future generations.
   C   She wants to encourage people to read more about history.

**how** to do it

■   Read the context and both questions for each extract to familiarise yourself with the topic.

■   Try to answer both questions for each extract the first time you listen.

■   In the second listening, check your answers carefully.

**tip**

Remember that the extracts will be on <u>different</u> themes in the exam.

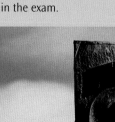

# Speaking Part 2

**1** Answer questions a and b about photos 1–3.

a What are the ceremonies shown?
b What do ceremonies like these have in common?

**2** Underline the key words in the exam task below.

> • How might the people taking part in the ceremonies be feeling?
> • How memorable might these occasions be for them?

**3** 🎧 Read the how to do it box below, then listen to someone doing the task in 2 and answer these questions.

a Which adjectives does she use to describe the people's feelings?
b Does she answer the whole task?

## how to do it

Choose the two photos you want to talk about.

Make sure you answer both parts of the task.

Use a variety of words to show your range of vocabulary.

Remember to compare, not simply describe the photos.

**4** Fill the gaps in a–h with 1–8 below to form sentences about the photos.

a It looks as if these people are ............ in a degree ceremony.
b The ............ in this ceremony appear to be feeling very proud.
c This ceremony is ............ in a huge stadium.
d I think the degree ceremony would be ............ than the opening ceremony.
e You would probably have lasting ............ of all these occasions but for different reasons.
f People ............ occasions like these for the rest of their lives.
g Photos like these ............ us of important events.
h Some occasions in our lives are simply ............ .

| | |
|---|---|
| 1 more memorable | 5 remind |
| 2 taking place | 6 unforgettable |
| 3 remember | 7 taking part |
| 4 memories | 8 participants |

**5** In pairs, do the task in 2. Student A compares photos 1 and 3, and Student B compares photos 2 and 3. The phrases below will help you.

## Speculating

It looks like/looks as if it is ...
It seems to be/appears to be ...
They probably/perhaps/may ...
They might be/could be ...

# Use of English  Part 2  Open cloze

**1**  When do young people 'come of age' in your country? How do you celebrate this event?

**2**  Read the text below quickly and answer these questions.

  a  Who are the Xicrin?
  b  Who takes part in the ceremony?

**3**  Read the text again and think of the word which best fits gaps 1–8. The how to do it and tip boxes will help you.

**4**  Do you think the Xicrins' traditions will survive? Why/Why not?

## how to do it

- Read the text once for overall meaning, then again sentence by sentence, ignoring the gaps.
- Look at the words before and after each gap.
- Don't always choose your first idea – consider some other options.
- Check your completed text for sense and grammar.

## tip

The eight answers in this text include:
- one possessive adjective
- two prepositions
- one relative pronoun
- one auxiliary verb
- three words from part of a phrase

# AN UNUSUAL COMING-OF-AGE CEREMONY

Living in the heart of the Brazilian Amazon, the Xicrin are a small tribe who have retained their traditional customs and rites. 0 ...One... such ritual is part of an age-old ceremony young men have to endure in 1 ............ to prove their manhood and become warriors. This entails attacking a wasps' nest with their bare hands. It is one of the many ceremonies 2 ............ mark the maturation of the young men and reflect the tribe's relationship 3 ............ the natural environment.

I was invited to witness this ceremony 4 ............ of my support for the Indians over many years as they tried to 5 ............ to terms with outside culture.

6 ............ a period of several days and nights, the villagers had prepared for the event. The young men, aged fourteen to eighteen, had been listening to stories of the tribe's history, as well as 7 ............ taught hunting and survival skills. The final ordeal, which always results in wasp stings, proves 8 ............ willingness to face dangerous situations.

## Part 4 Key word transformation

**5** Look at the example key word transformation exercise below. Which part of the first sentence has been replaced by the key word? Do both sentences have a similar meaning?

**Example**

*Do you think I could disturb you for a moment?*
*WONDERING*
*I **was wondering if I** could disturb you for a moment.*

**6** Read the answers given to a–f and say which ones are correct. Then correct the ones that are wrong. The how to do it box will help you.

### how to do it

- Find which part of the first sentence needs to be replaced by the key word.
- Think carefully how this will affect the grammar of the second sentence.
- Write between three and six words, including the key word given.
- Never change the key word.
- Read your completed sentence and check it has a similar meaning to the first sentence.

a The actor's autobiography was published last week.
CAME
This is the actor whose autobiography comes out last week.

b I'm so sorry we have to endure this weather.
PUT
If only we did not put up with this weather.

c Pam will never accept the fact that what she believed was a lie.
TERMS
Pat will never come to terms with the fact that what she believed was a lie.

d Mosquito bites are nowhere near as painful as wasp stings.
FAR
Mosquito bites are less painful than wasp stings.

e Will the elections be a massive victory for the opposition party?
RESULT
I wonder if the results will be a massive victory for the opposition party.

f The course teaches students to act independently.
CAPABLE
Without the course, students would not be capable of act independently.

# Grammar

## Relative clauses GR p172–173

**1** Complete sentences a–j with clauses 1–10.

a You may decide to enrol on our courses online, … .

b My grandfather, … , kept chickens in the garden.

c Paris is a city … .

d The house was full of famous paintings, … .

e We ventured further afield to explore the remote, uninhabited islands, … .

f I eventually finished writing my essay at midnight, … .

g The popular foothills … were often cut off in winter.

h Have you ever had one of those days … ?

i Give me one reason … .

j Initially, you'll be in a class of ten students, … .

1 by which time I'd missed that TV programme

2 all of which were worth a small fortune

3 none of whom has ever studied art before

4 where we went climbing in the summer

5 about which very little is known

6 when everything seems to go wrong

7 who loved nature

8 whose art galleries are one of its biggest attractions

9 in which case, the following instructions must be followed

10 why you don't want to go out tonight

# Writing Part 2 A proposal WG p164

**1** Look at the photos and answer questions a–c.

   a  Which country do the photos represent?
   b  What different aspects of culture are shown?
   c  What else do you know about this country's culture?

**2** Read this exam task and answer questions a–c.

> You are on the planning committee representing your country for an international cultural festival in London. Write a proposal for the festival organiser suggesting what should be included in the festival to represent the culture of your country and explaining why you think the aspects you have chosen would be of special interest.
>
> Write your **proposal** in **220–260** words in an appropriate style.

   a  Who is your target reader?
   b  What type of text should you write?
   c  What two main points should you include in your answer?

**3** Read the model answer and decide if statements a–g about proposals are true or false.

  a They begin in the same way as a letter.
  b They focus on a future event.
  c They are informal in register.
  d They are divided into sections with clear headings.
  e They aim to inform and persuade the target reader.
  f They do not need an introduction or conclusion.
  g They give suggestions and/or recommendations.

**4** List the different ways the writer suggests for showing his ideas, e.g. *a live performance*.

**5** Which verb forms cannot be used in a–d? Read the proposal to check your answers and find other ways of making suggestions.

  a I suggest *we show/to show/show/showing* a film about our national history.
  b It would be a good idea *teach/teaching/to teach/ that we teach* people one of our local dances.
  c I recommend *invite/to invite/inviting/we invite* one or two of our national celebrities to appear.
  d I propose *putting on/put on/we put on/us to put on* a special display for children.

**6** Find phrases in the model answer which mean the same as a–e below. Why is each equivalent phrase in the model more suitable?

  a Nobody else has a culture like theirs.
  b a group of people from our past
  c make our past seem more real
  d Visitors would think the animals were great.
  e Why don't we go for Kylie Minogue?

**7** Write your proposal. Plan your answer first by doing a–c.

  a Think of all the aspects of your country that are culturally significant.
  b Choose the ones you could show at a festival, and decide how you would show them.
  c Decide on three main headings, and select the best items from your ideas in b. Remember to include a separate introduction and conclusion.

### Introduction

This proposal contains my suggestions for our country's contribution to the international festival in London.

### Our national history

Aboriginals were the only inhabitants of Australia and their culture is unique. I recommend a live performance of traditional dances and music. Visitors might also enjoy a photographic display of aboriginal cave and rock paintings and of Uluru, their sacred red rock. We could follow that with a procession of historic characters in costume, which should bring our history alive.

### Outdoor life

I suggest we show a DVD so visitors can appreciate how thrilling it is to surf and swim off our fabulous beaches. Scuba-diving is very popular too, so I suggest having a display showing people diving at the Great Barrier Reef. We could also have photos showing people trekking in the rainforest. Visitors would be amazed and captivated by the huge variety of wildlife to be found.

### Contemporary arts

The Sydney Opera House is world famous and I am sure visitors would enjoy a live performance by one of our celebrated opera singers. I propose we also ask singers from our thriving pop music scene to contribute. Kylie Minogue would be an obvious choice. Another aspect of the arts scene that would definitely interest visitors is our film industry, so we could show clips and stills from films featuring our most famous actors, such as Russell Crowe and Nicole Kidman.

### Conclusion

My proposal would give visitors a real taste of Australian culture, past and present, and I hope it meets with your approval.

# Review

## 1
Rearrange the words in bold so that they fit the correct definitions a–e.

a  **Parades** are days or periods of celebration.
b  **Traditions** are formal public occasions celebrating a particular event.
c  **Rituals** are public processions.
d  **Ceremonies** are customs and beliefs handed down to future generations.
e  **Festivals** are a prescribed order of performing rites.

## 2
Rewrite the second sentence in a–c keeping the meaning the same. Use three to six words including the word given.

a  There have been serious doubts about Sam's professionalism after his recent behaviour.
**QUESTION**
Sam's professionalism .......................................... after his recent behaviour.
b  We don't want any criticism to be overheard by the event's organisers.
**WITHIN**
Be careful not to say anything ........................... the event's organisers.
c  Everybody is affected by the excitement of a carnival.
**UP**
It's impossible not ............................................. in the excitement of a carnival.

## 3
Complete the following sentences with a suitable verb or adverb to match the meaning of the words in brackets. The first letter of the word is given.

a  One of the main motivations in many people's lives is to e............ a living (make money).
b  If you read the programme, you will find a paragraph at the beginning which s............ the scene (gives the background) brilliantly.
c  A first child can often be f............ (extremely) competitive with younger siblings.
d  Ted's p............ (strongly) interested in archaeology. He's been on hundreds of digs.
e  I would like to say how d............ (very) grateful I am for all that you have done.
f  One thing politicians rarely admit to is b............ (going back on) their word.
g  We were a............ (completely) furious to hear that Paula had missed the train again.
h  Would you be b............ (terribly) disappointed not to be offered the job?

## 4
Use the verbs in brackets in their correct form to complete sentences a–f.

a  We would like to thank you for your invaluable ............ (contribute) to the event.
b  At the entrance to the museum, there is an impressive wooden ............ (carve) of a buffalo.
c  The ............ (reveal) that someone had robbed her of her most treasured possession was devastating.
d  You should let the airline know of any special dietary ............ (require) in advance.
e  After the initial ............ (form) of the company, the business rapidly went from strength to strength.
f  Clearly confused, she looked at me with no sign of ............ (recognise) on her face.

## 5
Complete the sentences with a word connected with remembering. The first letter of the word is given.

a  Which do you think is more m............ as you grow older – your childhood or your teenage years?
b  Souvenirs can bring back happy m............ of special events.
c  The chairman has asked to be r............ in good time about the annual meeting.
d  My first day at work was u............ for a number of very interesting reasons.
e  Please don't f............ to phone your aunt. It's her birthday tomorrow.

## 6
Number sentences a–e in the best order (1–5) to form a proposal suggesting what to include in an international exhibition about France.

a  To accompany this, we could also have a small gallery of photographs showing the many islands off the French coast. ............
b  Another aspect would, of course, be an exhibition outlining the country's history. I am sure this would be popular with visitors. ............
c  As well as showing people the geography of France, it would be an excellent idea to have a section devoted to traditional French cuisine, as well as a section with examples of traditional crafts. ............
d  My suggestions would give visitors a taste for French culture, and I hope they meet with your approval. ............
e  I would recommend initially showing a video of France's impressive mountains. ............

# Looking ahead

## Lead in

1 Answer these questions.

a Look at the photos and talk about different situations in which people make predictions.
b What kinds of jobs involve people making predictions?
c Who relies on the information provided by their predictions?
d What can happen if the predictions turn out to be inaccurate?

2 What changes are you likely to see in the following areas in your lifetime? The expressions in the box below will help you.

- work
- holidays
- transport
- entertainment

> ### Making predictions
>
> There's no likelihood of …
> It's unlikely that …
> There's absolutely no way that …
>
> As likely as not, …
> There's a good chance that …
> The chances are that …
>
> … seems inevitable.
> … is bound to …
> There's no doubt that …

3 If you could find out any three things about the future, what would they be?

# DESTINATION MARS!

Four writers comment on reasons to explore space and to journey to Mars.

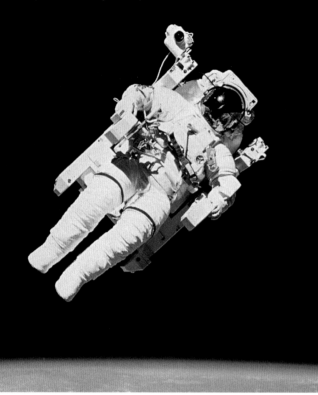

**A** Mars has long been a focus for those who dream of space exploration. Unmanned missions have recently found evidence of water, so humans can now build upon this discovery and look for signs of life. Clearly, investigating Mars' geological evolution will
05 be an important factor in this search. A mission to our nearest planetary neighbour also provides the perfect opportunity to demonstrate that humans can live for extended stays beyond Earth's orbit, which is without doubt the prime concern of those involved in space exploration. Besides these commendable aims,
10 the research methods and insights that result from exploring Mars will have long-lasting benefits, driving innovation and encouraging scientists to think of creative ways to address challenges here on Earth. Finally, the challenge of travelling to Mars and learning how to live there will encourage nations to collaborate, providing a
15 global sense of community.

**B** There are many reasons to explore space – among them, scientific discovery and economic benefits. These are 'acceptable reasons' because they can be defended logically; we tend to dismiss reasons that are emotional or value-driven. But in space exploration
20 the latter are the most important. We all know that people strive to accomplish great things for 'real reasons' that are intuitive and compelling but not necessarily logical. First, most of us want to excel in some activity. We want to stand out. Second, we are curious. Who doesn't yearn to explore? Finally, we humans have,
25 since the earliest civilisations, wanted to leave something to show later generations. This is the impulse behind cathedrals, pyramids and museums. The products of our space programme are today's cathedrals. The space programme satisfies the desire to compete and does so in a safe and productive manner. It speaks to our
30 sense of awe at the unknown, and it addresses our need to leave something for future generations.

# Reading Part 6 Cross-text multiple matching

how to do it

- Read all the texts through carefully before looking at the questions.
- Try and identify places in the text where there is agreement or disagreement between the writers. Underline these, or make a note in the margin.

**1** Quickly read the four texts A–D. Which basic idea do all the writers agree on?

**2** Read the texts again and the how to do it box. For questions 1–4, choose from the texts A–D. The texts may be chosen more than once.

Which writer, A, B, C or D:

shares writer A's opinion of the opportunities space exploration offers for co-operation? 1 ....

has a different opinion from the others regarding the advisability of space exploration at this time? 2 ....

takes a similar view to C on the top priority for space exploration? 3 ....

has a different opinion from the others regarding what inspires people to undertake space exploration? 4 ....

**C** No planet has inspired us as much as Mars. Scientists have sent robotic spacecraft there, lured by the prospect of discovering life. These missions have proved that Mars may
35 once have been a hospitable cradle for life, meaning that the chances of life existing on suitable planets elsewhere are much higher. The quest to discover if we are unique in the universe and the possibility of giving humanity a foothold in other worlds is the foremost justification
40 for investing in space exploration. But Mars is also a useful comparative laboratory for studying climate and geophysics on Earth. Space exploration has always been the ultimate status symbol but it can also act as an incentive to countries to work together peacefully. The wisdom of
45 focusing so intently on a single planet is debatable though, given our current pressing needs back home.

**D** A common argument against investment in space exploration is that the money could be used here at home. That would constitute a very short-sighted strategy. The
50 satellites we have orbiting the Earth help us understand and better manage everything from weather, to floods, to crops and even pollution. They also provide us with services we use every day, such as global communications. Some may see waste in studying the surface of Mars with robots,
55 or sending humans into space, however many discoveries made in deep space have practical benefits. Understanding planetary geology by studying the surfaces of other planets, for example, has helped us improve the models we have for problems such as global warming. Without
60 improved modelling, we risk making poor choices about how to manage the future. The modest investments we make in space exploration are far more than just inspirational; they are of practical use to improve life on Earth.

3 Complete sentences a–h with an appropriate preposition. You can find examples to help you in the texts.

  a  They have found evidence .......... water on Mars.

  b  Scientists hope to build .......... this discovery.

  c  It's an important factor .......... the search for life on Mars.

  d  Who doesn't want to excel .......... their profession?

  e  We all want to stand .......... from the crowd in some way.

  f  Are we unique .......... the universe?

  g  Should we invest so much money .......... space travel?

  h  We must make choices .......... the best way to manage the future.

4 Explain what the five highlighted words refer to in the texts.

5 Do you think the vast sums of money spent on space exploration would be better used here on Earth? Why/Why not?

# Vocabulary GR p182–183

## Phrasal verbs with *up* and *down*

**1** Complete a–e with phrasal verbs formed from these verbs plus *up* or *down*.

> break   set   put   bring   turn

a If you haven't got enough room, we can ..................... your relatives for the night.

b His intention is to use the inheritance to ..................... his own business.

c Protesters are threatening to ..................... the government if their demands aren't met.

d Police ..................... the demonstration by firing tear gas into the crowd.

e It was the thought of commuting every day that made me ..................... the job offer.

**2** Use a dictionary to answer these questions.

a In which phrasal verbs in 1 could you put the object between the verb and the particle?

b Turn the objects of the phrasal verbs in a–e into pronouns. Then rephrase the sentences.

**Example**

*a If you haven't got enough room, we can put them up for the night.*

**3** Replace the underlined verbs in a–d with new phrasal verbs formed from the verbs in 1 plus *up* or *down*. Check your answers in a dictionary.

**Example**

> *It's best if you don't <u>mention</u> the subject of Mark's resignation, as it's a rather sensitive matter.*
>
> *bring up* ..........................................................

a The key witness <u>lost control and started crying</u> in court.

......................................................................

b You shouldn't have <u>made him look stupid</u> in front of his friends – no wonder he was upset.

......................................................................

c Could you <u>increase the volume of</u> the radio a bit – I can hardly hear what the newsreader's saying.

......................................................................

d Students are expected to respect the college rules as <u>written down</u> in the official handbook.

......................................................................

# Grammar

## Future forms GR p167–169

**1** Name the verb forms used to express the future in a–g, then match them with functions 1–7.

a Our train leaves at four o'clock tomorrow morning.

b I'm having my hair cut tomorrow at 10 a.m.

c By this time next year, I'll already have left school and found a job.

d I'm tired. I think I'll go to bed.

e I'll be lying on a beach this time next week.

f We're going to move house next year.

g By the end of this week, they'll have been travelling for a year.

1 an appointment/definite arrangement

2 a spontaneous decision

3 a timetable or travel plan

4 an action completed before another future time

5 an action happening for a continuous period before a future point

6 a personal plan

7 an action that will be in progress at a certain future time

**2** Choose the correct verb forms to complete the dialogue.

A: Have you heard? Anna and Mark (1) *are going to get/will get* married.

B: Surely not! Anna (2) *will start/is starting* university next week.

A: Well, she must have changed her mind. Her parents (3) *are going/will go* crazy when they find out.

B: You're not joking! Are you absolutely certain?

A: Quite certain. I'll tell you what, (4) *I'm going to/I'll ring* her right now and she can tell you herself. She (5) *will have/is having* some friends over for dinner tonight so she should be at home.

B: Good idea! I hope it's not just a rumour. I think (6) *they'll make/they're making* a perfect couple.

**3** Put the verbs in brackets into an appropriate future form.

a Do you think most office workers .......... (work) from home by 2025?

b .......... space tourism .......... (become) widespread within the next five years, in your opinion?

c How likely is it that ordinary people .......... (use) robots to do domestic tasks in their houses in the very near future?

d Do you think scientists .......... (clone) a human being by next year?

e Where do you think most people in your country .......... (live) in 50 years' time: in rural or urban areas?

**4** Discuss your opinions of the completed questions in 3.

**5** Underline the time conjunctions in a–c and match the verb forms which follow them with 1–3.

a We'll be going to the beach as soon as the rain has stopped.

b When space flights become cheaper, we'll all want to try them.

c News reporters will be taking photos while the President is speaking.

1 emphasises the continuous nature of the action

2 emphasises that one action will be finished before another begins

3 simply states a fact

**6** Complete sentences a–e with your own ideas and say which tenses could follow the time conjunctions.

a Make sure you phone me from the airport as soon as …

b I'm sure you will be in a better mood once …

c I usually feel really tired after …

d Do you think you'll still enjoy clubbing by the time …

e One of our assistants will help you the minute …

**7** Correct the tense errors in a–d. There may be more than one possible answer.

a My brother is planning to travel round Europe with his girlfriend next year, but now she's changed her mind.

b The celebrity who is to open the new hospital has pulled out at the last minute.

c She is about to take a mouthful of juice when she noticed the wasp in her glass.

d I hadn't realised my mother-in-law will stay until the end of the month.

**8** Complete the sentences in an appropriate way.

a They were going to order dessert …

b We were about to leave the house …

c If I had known my boss was going to …

d I knew that my decision would …

**9** Ask a partner or partners about a–e.

a What they're doing for a holiday this year.

b Whether they hope to be living in the same place in five years' time.

c Whether they think that something significant will have happened to them by this time next year.

d Which film they think they'll see next.

e What the next big purchase they're about to make is.

# Listening  Part 3  Multiple choice

**1** What connection do you think there might be between these two photos? What can be done to preserve places like the one in the picture on the left for future generations?

**2** 🎧 Read quickly through the questions, then listen twice to two conservationists, Bob and Carrie, talking about plans for the future of ancient monuments, and choose the best answer for 1–6.

1 What does Bob say about building visitor centres near ancient monuments like Stonehenge?

  A Facilities like these are essential for encouraging tourism.

  B It's difficult to find architects willing to take on projects like these.

  C Finding the right design for centres like these is problematic.

  D The cost of building projects like these is incredibly high.

2 What suggestion does Carrie make regarding Stonehenge?

  A Existing visitor facilities should be updated.

  B The standing stones should be removed from the site.

  C There should be a maximum number of visitors allowed.

  D The site should go back to how it looked in the past.

3 Bob feels that Carrie's plan for Stonehenge

  A would not be environmentally friendly.

  B would result in a huge loss of income.

  C might be popular with the authorities.

  D might lead to an increase in tourism.

4 What comment does Carrie make about the visitor centre at Petra?

  A It has been designed to blend in with the landscape.

  B The building destroys the atmosphere of the place.

  C It has been welcomed by many local people.

  D It restricts the entrance of large groups of tourists.

5 In Bob's opinion, the Petra building project

  A proved to be too ambitious.

  B went over budget.

  C is educational.

  D makes Petra even more beautiful.

6 According to Carrie, many people believe that places like Stonehenge and Petra should

  A be visited by as many people as possible.

  B provide a relaxing experience for tourists.

  C receive more publicity in the future.

  D be allowed to keep their air of mystery.

**3** Match a–e with 1–5 to make phrases about the future from the recording.

| | | | |
|---|---|---|---|
| a | on the | 1 | in store |
| b | in the | 2 | cards |
| c | what lies | 3 | run |
| d | you never know | 4 | pipeline |
| e | in the long | 5 | what's around the corner |

**4** Use some of the phrases in 3 to talk about things you expect to happen in the future where you live.

# Speaking Part 2

1 Talk about your ambitions for the future using some of the phrases below.

> ### Talking about the future
>
> I'm not really sure what …          I doubt if I'll …
>
> I wouldn't be surprised if …     It's unlikely that I'll …
>
> I think I'll probably decide to …

2 Put these expressions into three groups: 'success', 'failure' or 'making an effort'.

a  come up with something original
b  lack the talent to do something
c  have the determination to do something
d  make it to the top
e  beat the competition
f  make your mark
g  put your heart and soul into it
h  make (a lot of) sacrifices
i  lack the necessary ambition
j  give it everything you've got

3 Look at the two pairs of photos and the Part 2 exam task above them and make some notes about how you could answer these questions.

4 🎧 Read the how to do it box, then listen to how one candidate began the task in 3, and say how suitable their answer is and why.

## how to do it

▪ In the exam you will be given three photos. You must choose two to talk about.

▪ Begin talking immediately and keep talking for a full minute.

▪ Speak clearly enough for both examiners to hear you.

5 Now do the exam task in 3 with a partner.

6 Take it in turns to look at your partner's photos and answer this follow-up question:

* Which of these ambitions do you think would be the most difficult to achieve?

### tip
For the follow-up task, give only a brief answer (no longer than 30 seconds) for the question about your partner's photos.

* What ambitions might the people have for the future?
* How difficult might it be to fulfil their ambitions?

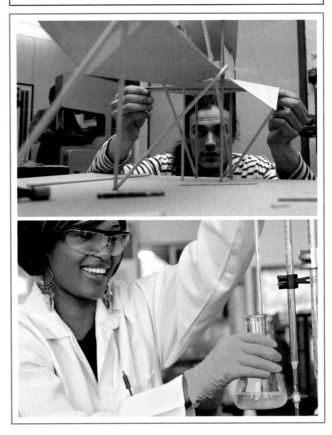

# Use of English Part 1 Multiple-choice cloze

1 How accurately can you tell someone's age by looking at them? What else gives you clues to how old people are?

2 What do you think the difference is between your 'calendar age' and your 'biological age'? Read the text in 3 quickly to check.

3 Read the how to do it box then complete gaps 1–8 with the best option (A, B, C or D).

how to do it

- Read the text quickly for general sense, ignoring the gaps.
- Read the text again and think of a possible answer for each gap before you look at the options.
- Try each option in the gap to check your choice.

## As old as you feel

It might be true that you are only as old as you feel. A British clinic is carrying 0 ....A.... tests to calculate the 'real' biological age of patients based on their rate of physical deterioration. Information on every 1 .......... of a patient's health is fed into a computer to establish 2 .......... they are older or younger than their calendar age suggests.

The availability and increasing accuracy of the tests has prompted one British gerontologist to call for biological age to be used to determine retirement age. He 3 .......... that if an employee's biological or 'real' age is shown to be 55 when he reaches his 65th birthday, he should be 4 .......... to work for another decade. Apparently most employers only take into 5 .......... a person's calendar years.

A doctor offering these tests claims their 6 .......... will be to motivate people to improve their health. Although the concept of 'real age' seems set to become big 7 .......... , many believe that looks will always be the best 8 .......... of age.

| | | | | |
|---|---|---|---|---|
| 0 A | out | B forward | C over | D on |
| 1 A | position | B prospect | C attitude | D aspect |
| 2 A | unless | B in case | C so that | D whether |
| 3 A | debates | B argues | C discusses | D enquires |
| 4 A | encouraged | B supported | C incited | D promoted |
| 5 A | interest | B detail | C account | D importance |
| 6 A | desire | B reason | C purpose | D project |
| 7 A | business | B pursuit | C trade | D concern |
| 8 A | notice | B indicator | C example | D token |

4 Complete sentences a–g with one word. You can find examples to help you in the text.

a Our conclusions are .......... on extensive research.
b We are going to .......... the data into a computer and analyse it.
c The delicacy of this situation .......... for an immediate but effective response.
d I'm trying to .......... what the significance is of all these figures.
e Many people retire when they .......... the age of 65.
f Apparently a well-known pharmaceutical company .......... to have found a cure for the common cold.
g We only wish to recruit people who are highly .......... to work for our company.

Try these tests to find your biological age. How accurate do you think they are?

**A** Stand on your left leg, with your right leg bent behind at 45 degrees and hands on your hips. Close your eyes. Time how long it is before you lose your balance. Take the best score from three.

| biological age: | 20 | 30 | 40 | 50 | 60 |
|---|---|---|---|---|---|
| seconds: | | 70+ | 60 | 50 | 40 |

**B** Hold a ruler out below your eye. Hold a business card at the end of the ruler, and slowly move it towards you until it blurs. Measure the distance at which you can still read it.

| biological age: | 20 | 30 | 40 | | 50 | 60 |
|---|---|---|---|---|---|---|
| centimetres: | 10 | 20 | 30 | 40 | 50 | 60 |

**C** Get someone to hold a 45-cm ruler above your open dominant hand. Catch the ruler as quickly as possible when dropped. Measure where you catch it and take the average of three scores.

| biological age: | 20–30 | 30–40 | | 40–50 | 50–60 | |
|---|---|---|---|---|---|---|
| centimetres: | 5 | 10 | 15 | 20 | 25 | 30 | 35 |

# Vocabulary

## Expressions connected with age

**1** Match the expressions in italics in a–h with the meanings 1–8.

a My 90-year-old grandfather has only recently begun to *feel his age*.

b The children shouldn't have acted so irresponsibly. They are *old enough to know better*.

c Some people say that the secret of staying young is to remain *young at heart*.

d *The youth of today* seem so different from when I was a youngster.

e My aunt may be 60 but she certainly *doesn't look her age*.

f When I was a lad, anyone over 40 seemed *as old as the hills*.

g Tim's only 14 but very mature. He *has an old head on young shoulders*.

h We should take every opportunity because we're *not getting any younger*.

1 be mature enough to act in a more sensible way
2 young people
3 be more mature than is expected for someone so young
4 growing older
5 look as old as you really are
6 still feeling and behaving as you did when you were younger
7 extremely old
8 be physically aware of your real age

**2** Discuss the following questions.

a Do you have similar expressions about age in your language?

b Do you agree with the saying 'You're never too old to learn'? Why/Why not?

# Writing Part 1 An essay  WG p154

**1** Do you travel everywhere by car or try to use public transport whenever possible? Why? How could the government persuade people to use their cars less often?

**2** Read the exam task and input text opposite and answer these questions.

   a  How many of the methods do you need to choose?
   b  Do you need to compare the methods in any way?
   c  If you use opinions from the seminar, what must you avoid?
   d  Do you need to give reasons for all your opinions?
   e  How many words should you write?

**3** Match a–f with six of the areas often tested in the writing paper, and discuss how you could achieve good marks in each.

   1  content        4  register
   2  format         5  organisation
   3  cohesion      6  range

   a  use of formal/informal language
   b  use of connectors/linking words
   c  the way the text is divided up into paragraphs
   d  the variety of vocabulary and structures used
   e  the layout, e.g. a title, headings, etc
   f  the writer's coverage of the topic

**4** Read the model essay on page 43 and using the assessment areas in exercise 3, discuss how well the task has been completed.

You have just attended a seminar on the subject 'Transport and the Environment'. The discussion focused on the methods governments should use to discourage car use and encourage more environmentally friendly forms of transport, such as cycling or travelling by bus. You have made the notes below.

> Methods governments could use to discourage car use and encourage environmentally friendly forms of transport:
>
> • transport planning
> • campaigning
> • fuel prices

> Some opinions expressed in the discussion:
>
> 'If environmentally friendly forms of transport were better organised, people might choose to use them more often.'
>
> 'It would be good if governments could help environmental groups to get the message across.'
>
> 'Maybe people would drive less if petrol and diesel were more expensive.'

Write an essay discussing **two** of the methods in your notes. You should **explain which method you think is more important** for governments to consider, **giving reasons** in support of your answer.

You may, if you wish, make use of the opinions expressed in the discussion, but you should use your own words as far as possible.

Write your **essay** in **220–260** words in an appropriate style.

## The Future of Transport

There has been a huge increase in car ownership in recent years. We now know that petrol and diesel fumes pollute the environment and contribute to climate change. So what should governments do to curb the use of cars?

I believe the most important step is to provide better public transport. Unless this is made affordable and easy to use, people will turn their backs on it. Buses and trains also need to be a lot more regular and reliable than they are now. There is a need for more pedestrian walkways and designated cycle lanes too, and these must be safe and convenient.

A good transport system is therefore a top priority, but once this is in place the government has to persuade people to use it. The best strategy would be to campaign in the newspapers, on TV, and with street advertising. Environmental groups are already engaged in this kind of work but they lack resources. If governments were willing to fund them, campaigns could reach far more people than at present.

To sum up, both of the above measures are important but the first and greatest need is to improve transport. Educating the public about using it comes next. By following this strategy, governments stand a good chance of persuading the public out of their cars and into more environmentally responsible ways of travel.

### how to do it

- Note down ideas for the main paragraphs of your essay.
- Decide which ideas belong together, and in which paragraph.
- If there are too many ideas, delete the less important ones.
- Remember to state which of the two points is more important, and why.
- Decide what to put in your introductory and concluding paragraphs.

**5** Find a sentence in the essay which is used to compare two ideas. Then use the prompts below to make more comparative sentences.

a Increasing fuel prices is / important / any other measure / because / it / discourage / motorists / use / cars
b I believe / top priority / to provide / good public transport system / than / have now
c While / raise / fuel prices / not as effective / campaigning / it / still / important role / play
d I think nothing / as important / make people aware / we need / stop / rely / cars so much

**6** Look at the steps the writer followed when making a plan for the model essay and say whether you think you would find them helpful yourself.

– I underlined key words in the question so I was very clear about what I had to do.
– I decided how many paragraphs I needed.
– I looked at the word limit and made a note of roughly how many words to include in each paragraph.
– I brainstormed all my ideas for the essay on rough paper.
– I grouped together ideas on the same topic.
– I evaluated my ideas and decided which to include in each paragraph. (I remembered there's a limit to how many ideas I can develop in 220–260 words.)
– I decided which method was the most important and why.
– I thought about what to write for a good introduction and conclusion.

**7** Plan your own answer to the exam task in 2. Use the steps in exercise 6 and the how to do it box to help you. To ensure that your answer is different from the model, write about the last two points from the task:
- campaigning
- fuel prices

**8** Now write your essay.

# Review

## 1 Correct the mistakes with the phrasal verbs in a–g.

a On hearing the sad news, Sally broke up and wept.

b It's an international organisation helping those in crisis, and it was set off last century.

c If you get more guests than you bargained for, we have plenty of space, so we can easily put up some.

d Who finally put up the subject of money during the negotiations?

e It's extremely unprofessional to turn someone down in front of their colleagues.

f The rules and regulations for the procedure are set up in this document.

g Only after several shops had been robbed did the authorities break down the riot.

## 2 Write the missing words in the phrases in a–e.

a Following a spell of poor weather, forecasters say that high temperatures are just .......... corner.

b Although I've applied for a number of jobs, I have nothing definite .......... pipeline yet.

c Initially, this may seem an expensive investment, but .......... run, it will prove good value for money.

d If we'd known what .......... store for us that day, we would never have gone on the excursion.

e Everyone hopes it won't happen, but it's .......... cards that the factory will close.

## 3 Correct any mistakes in the underlined expressions in a–h.

a Despite <u>putting it everything we'd got</u>, we still lost yesterday's match.

b Only by analysing their strengths and weaknesses can we hope to <u>knock the competition</u>.

c It seems that nowadays you need very little talent to <u>do your mark in life</u>.

d After years without success, John finally accepted that he <u>wanted the talent</u> to become a star.

e Few celebrities realise the pressures involved in <u>getting it to the top</u>.

f You could see from the children's faces that they were <u>putting their head and soul</u> into the performance.

g At the end of the day, I wasn't prepared to <u>create the sacrifices</u> needed in my personal life for the sake of my job.

h To be a successful inventor, you've got to <u>come up to</u> something original at the right time.

## 4 Choose the correct word to complete sentences a–f.

a Employees who work hard are often *incited/ promoted*.

b Many senior citizens have contacted us to *enquire/ discuss* about the new tax.

c We always take an *interest/account* in a prospective employee's ambitions.

d Most doctors are motivated by a *reason/desire* to help people.

e Campaigners against the international arms *trade/ concern* have presented a petition.

f We can't help you *unless/so that* you are prepared to confess to the robbery.

## 5 Circle the correct word in sentences a–g.

a We should make the most of life because none of us are *coming/going/getting* any younger.

b Some people stay young at *head/soul/heart* all their lives.

c For many people, it isn't until they hit retirement that they begin to *be/seem/feel* their age.

d The *young/youth/younger* of today don't know how lucky they are!

e What outrageous behaviour! You're old enough to know *well/better/best*.

f It's amazing how some elderly famous people don't *seem/look/appear* their age!

g Teenagers consider anyone over 30 to be as old as the *valleys/rivers/hills*.

## 6 Use the prompts to complete these sentences from an essay.

a educating the public is far / important / any other measure / because / make / motorists / aware / the environmental costs / driving

b I believe / top priority / raise petrol prices

c while / raising fuel prices / not as effective / running an education campaign / it / still / important role / play

d I think nothing / as important / make people think about / damage / cars / cause / the environment

# Into the wild

## Lead in

**1** For each part of the body below, name two creatures which have them.

| | | | |
|---|---|---|---|
| mane | scale | beak | hide |
| flipper | antenna | hoof | tusk |
| fin | claw | horn | paw |
| wing | shell | | |

**2** Name a creature which:

a is generally feared.
b might be found repulsive.
c has human characteristics.
d is thought of as man's friend.
e has sinister associations.
f is exotic.
g is endangered.

**3** Say which creatures are described in a–d and explain the words in italics.

a Most members of this species are very *agile* climbers and swing through the trees at great speed. They are highly *sociable* and spend hours *grooming* each other.
b They're *intelligent*, playful creatures with fins but no scales, and are a favourite with sailors.
c They're tall, extremely *graceful* animals with long necks and very small horns.
d They're *fierce* hunters with large paws. They *stalk their prey* and can run faster than all the other big cats.

**4** Write brief descriptions of three more wild animals and see if a partner can guess what they are.

# Reading Part 7 Gapped text

**1** Do you know any stories, real or fictional, in which animals help humans?

**2** Quickly read the main text and summarise what it says about the relationship between humans and dolphins.

**3** Look at lines 1–8 and lines 9–12. Which of a–c below is most likely to summarise the first missing paragraph?

   a   other similar incidents about dolphins
   b   a theory of animal behaviour
   c   what led up to this situation

**4** Match a–c in 3 with paragraphs from A–G.

**5** Complete the text with the remaining paragraphs, using the highlighted words and the tip box to help you find links. There is one extra paragraph.

**6** Say how the clues helped you match the paragraphs.

Example

*The word* drama *in paragraph G summarises the events of the first paragraph.*

**7** Do you agree that humans are purely motivated by self-interest? Can you think of any examples of people acting unselfishly?

## tip

For this task think about
- lexical links, e.g. nouns and pronouns
- time references, e.g. *earlier, later*
- the order of events in the story

# saviours of

As the dolphin hurtled through the water straight at him, Rob Howes, a burly 38-year-old lifeguard, wondered if he was about to be killed. A stone's throw from him across the choppy ocean waters, his 15-year-old daughter Niccy and her friend Karina were
5 terrified. The girls had been surrounded by six highly agitated dolphins and were being held hostage in a maelstrom of flashing fins and swerving bodies. The seventh dolphin was charging at Howes, seemingly intent on driving him back to the other captives.

**1**

Believing the advancing dolphin was going to ram him from
10 beneath, Howes turned to his right. But as he turned, what he saw in the water was not a dolphin but something much worse – a great white shark.

**2**

So were the dolphins really trying to protect their human 'hostages'? It isn't the first time these creatures have apparently
15 saved humans from disaster. Greek mythology tells how Arion, a musician, was carried to land on the backs of dolphins after sailors had thrown him from their ship. The fact that the myth centres on dolphins indicates that, even then, humans believed this species to be brighter and possibly kinder than other beasts.

**3**

20 The near-fatal attack was witnessed by diver Matt Fleet. He and his crew were anchored nearby when he saw the dolphins circling. He grabbed his camera and jumped into the water, hoping to get some pictures. But the first thing he saw as he surfaced was not a dolphin but the vertical fin of a great white. Had it not been for
25 his boat's underwater rescue team, he too might have come under attack.

**4**

Such questions are extremely difficult for scientists to answer. In fact, biologists have argued for years over whether even humans are capable of altruism – many believing that every 'kind' act has
30 some self-interest behind it.

**5**

According to these scientists, all the apparently benevolent acts seen in nature – wolves sharing their kill with the rest of the pack and primates feeding the offspring of others in their group – are explained by the idea of kinship. The theory is that kindness is
35 offered only to relatives of the same species who carry many of the same genes as the giver. By helping them, it is suggested, the giver is improving the chances of his or her own genes surviving.

_the seas_

**6**

Whatever the answer, these creatures have little reason to be thankful to humans; thousands are killed each year by tuna fishermen using drift nets. And Howes is still uncertain whether two dolphins found slaughtered by poachers near Whangarei harbour were members of the group that saved him. The thought leaves him distraught. 'This is how we repay them for their help,' he says. 'I'd like to give the men responsible a taste of their own medicine.'

**A**
The modern version of this debate has its origins in the 1975 publication of Edward O. Wilson's book _Sociobiology_ and, published a year later, of Richard Dawkins's _The Selfish Gene_. Wilson believed animal and human behaviour is rooted entirely in our genes. Dawkins described humans and animals as 'lumbering robots', whose minds and bodies are entirely controlled by selfish genes.

**B**
So do incidents like that witnessed by Fleet prove that dolphins really are the good guys of the deep, always ready to extend a flipper to humans in distress? And if they are genuinely altruistic, what makes them that way?

**C**
Such a belief would appear to be justified by other, real-life events. In 1996 Martin Richardson, a 29-year-old traveller, was mauled by a shark while swimming in the Red Sea. He credited bottlenose dolphins with chasing away the predator as it closed in for the kill.

**D**
This may explain altruism within species but why should dolphins help humans, as in the Whangarei incident? Were they following an ethical code? Or had they simply mistaken the human swimmers for other dolphins?

**E**
Howes had often spotted these fearsome predators in the course of his work, but this was one of the biggest he had ever seen. Had the dolphin not intentionally diverted the shark with its charge, he contends, he would almost inevitably have been attacked and killed.

**F**
It could be that they mistook the shape of a human in the water for a sick dolphin. The dolphin's sonar system can create a three-dimensional picture of any living object and the air spaces, internal organs and other human features may have looked very similar to those of a dolphin.

**G**
The drama had started some minutes earlier. Howes and the girls were swimming in Whangarei harbour, off New Zealand's North Island. They had been diving from rocks, and were swimming across open water when the group of dolphins appeared and started herding them up, circling tightly. This is very unusual behaviour for dolphins, which normally show little aggression to humans.

# Vocabulary

## Expressions with animals

**1** Complete sentences a–f with these words. Explain the meanings of the expressions with animals.

water    dinner    work    time    grass    bag

a Although we didn't think we'd enjoy ourselves, we ended up having a whale of a .......... .

b I can't believe I did my homework so badly – I made a real dog's .......... of it!

c Next week's party was meant to be a surprise but Sonya's just let the cat out of the .......... .

d Tom had always lived in the country and felt like a fish out of .......... in the city.

e My last boss was a real snake in the .......... – you couldn't trust a word he said.

f When we decorated our house, my husband helped me choose the paint but left me to do the donkey .......... .

**2** Complete sentences a–e appropriately to illustrate the meaning of the expression. Use a dictionary to look up any expressions that are new to you.

a I wish you'd stop rabbiting on about football – you know I ... .

b I've got butterflies in my stomach because this time tomorrow, I ... .

c Brian usually eats like a horse but ... .

d Poor David's going to be in the doghouse. He's just ... .

e If Jane's having a hen party, it must mean ... .

**3** Answer these questions.

a When was the last time you were in the doghouse? What had you done wrong?

b Can you remember the last time you felt like a fish out of water? How did you cope?

c Do brides-to-be in your country usually have a hen party? What do they do?

d Have you ever let the cat out of the bag about something important? What happened?

# Grammar

## Past tenses GR p166–167

**1** Name the tenses in italics in a–i.

a After the football match, we *went* to a bar, *had* a few drinks and *celebrated* our win.

b By the time the fitness trainer finally turned up, we *had been waiting* for half an hour.

c So you*'ve been on* the Atkins Diet? How was it?

d Inspector Lomas looked out the window. It *was snowing* and the streets *were becoming* icy.

e Karen*'s put* on a lot of weight recently.

f That's the best film *I've seen* in a long time.

g As the skier *was racing* downhill, his ski hit a stone and threw him off balance.

h Heavy fog delayed us, and by the time we reached the airport, our plane *had taken off*.

i Farmers *have been campaigning* for more support from the government for years.

**2** Look again at the verbs in 1 and complete the grammar description below.

a .past simple. : for a series of separate past events.

b ................ : for events in the recent past, which are not completed, or connect to the present.

c ................ : for an event that finished before another past event or time.

d ................ : for a continuous past action that finished before another past event or time.

e ................ : for an interrupted past event or a background event.

f ................ : for the first, second, etc. time we do something, and with superlatives.

**3** Put the verbs in brackets in a–g into the past simple or present perfect simple. Identify any time expressions or other clues that help.

a I .......... (study) in Paris for six years until my parents moved to Rome.

b This isn't the first time I .......... (taste) shark meat.

c As a child, I .......... (excel) at sports.

d Ouch! I .......... (twist) my ankle.

e It was a long time before I .......... (dare) tell my parents I had a tongue stud.

f I .......... (resist) eating a single piece of chocolate for the past six weeks.

g Many of the plays that Shakespeare .......... (produce) have been made into films.

**4** Put the verbs in brackets into the present perfect simple or continuous.

a He .......... (play) for the national football team three times so far this season.

b I .......... (work) on the computer since 8 a.m. but I'm going to have a break in a minute.

c So far I .......... (phone) Jim five times this morning but I haven't managed to catch him yet.

d If you .......... (read) the book I lent you, can I have it back now?

e Pop singer Rihanna .......... (travel) round the country all summer giving performances.

**5** Write two sentences about yourself for each of a–c, using the present perfect simple, present perfect continuous or the past simple, as appropriate.

a challenging things at work or school

   Example

   *I've been working on a fascinating project./I gave an important presentation last week.*

b disappointing/exciting experiences

c free-time activities

**6** Explain how the sentences in each pair below differ in meaning.

1a A policeman stopped the motorist because he was breaking the law.

 b A policeman stopped the motorist because he had been breaking the law.

2a Most students were taking their exam when the fire alarm rang.

 b Most students had taken their exam when the fire alarm rang.

**7** Correct any errors with tenses in these sentences.

a I knew she had cried because her eyes were red and puffy.

b Last week they were killing a great white shark which had been menacing swimmers for weeks.

c I was washing my car and my flatmate repaired his motorbike when our landlord turned up.

d As our plane had been landing, one of the engines caught fire and we had to make an emergency landing.

e When I last saw Bill he sat on the riverbank, throwing stones into the water.

f The reason the DVD player wouldn't work was because you weren't plugging it in!

**8** Put the verbs in bold (1–17) into the correct form.

Most of us .......... 1 **see** gorillas on TV but few people .......... 2 **ever/observe** one in the wild. I .......... 3 **be** fascinated by these creatures since I .......... 4 **be** a child. So imagine my delight when, a few weeks ago, I .......... 5 **get** the chance to go to Rwanda to track wild mountain gorillas. The trip was not without danger. An armed soldier .......... 6 **accompany** us to scare off the buffalo which .......... 7 **attack** a previous group. Our guide .......... 8 **cut** a path through the undergrowth and we .......... 9 **follow**. When we .......... 10 **find** what looked like claw marks in some trees, we realised that gorillas .......... 11 **feed** there recently. Suddenly, we .......... 12 **catch** sight of them – a whole family of gorillas! The adults .......... 13 **sit** in the sun watching the youngsters, who .......... 14 **play** in the trees. One of the adults .......... 15 **stare** at me, .......... 16 **scratch** his head, and .......... 17 **yawn**. For me, it was love at first sight!

**9** Using your imagination, make up a story about the events that led up to this scene, using a variety of tenses.

# Listening

## Part 2 Sentence completion

**1** Look at the three photographs and answer these questions.

a What do wildlife photographers do?
b What skills and training do you think they might need?
c What would some of the advantages and disadvantages be of this job?

**2** 🎧 You will hear Clare Martin talk about wildlife photography. Read the how to do it box and as you listen, correct the wrong answers given for 1–8.

## how to do it

Use the sentence context and structure as clues to the answers.

Don't be too quick to put an answer; it may be a distractor.

You usually only need to write one or two words.

You listen twice, so if you miss an answer, concentrate on finding it the next time.

Check your answers for spelling, grammar and sense.

## Wild about animals!

Clare has just returned from an assignment in
1 ......*South Africa*......... .

Most of her correspondence comes from
2 ..*young schoolchildren*.. .

Earning a living as a wildlife photographer isn't easy because of the many 3 ..*really good quality pictures*.. operating in the field.

The bird photographer Arthur Morris was originally a
4 ...........*teaching*........... by profession.

One university in Britain offers a degree in
5 .........*Biography*.......... Imaging.

Clare suggests working as a travel guide or
6 ......*conversationist*...... to establish yourself.

You need to bring in 7 ........*compensation*........ to cover your expenses.

She recommends studying 8 .....*creative subjects*..... if you want to become a full-time photographer.

# Speaking Part 3

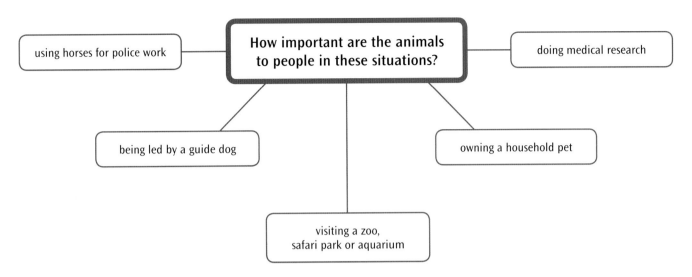

How important are the animals to people in these situations?

- using horses for police work
- doing medical research
- being led by a guide dog
- owning a household pet
- visiting a zoo, safari park or aquarium

**1** 🎧 Listen to an examiner giving instructions for the first part of the exam task above. Use the information to complete the sentences below.

> - You are going to talk about something **1** ............... for about **2** ............... .
> - You have about **3** ............... to look at the task.

**2** Complete the gaps a–e with the words below. Then talk about the situations in which animals are important to people by finishing the sentences appropriately.

> companionship    resource    independence
> experimentation    entertainment

a   Horses are a valuable ......... for the police. They can be used …
b   Older people probably like having pets for .......... . I expect they …
c   If you're blind or partially sighted, a guide dog can be vital for your .......... . Without one, …
d   Animals are an essential part of medical .......... and research. Without them, …
e   An aquarium is a form of .......... . It attracts visitors because …

**3** 🎧 Listen to two students as they begin to do the Part 3 task and answer these questions.

a   What initial mistake does the female student make?
b   What does the male student do right?
c   What does he do wrong?

**4** Do the first part of the task in 1 in pairs, using the how to do it box and phrases below to help you.

### how to do it

■   Give reasons for your ideas to show your range of language.
□   Keep talking for the full two minutes.
■   Disagree politely with your parter, if you wish.

■   Inviting your partner to speak

Do/Don't you think this one … ?
Personally, I (don't) think this one … . What about you?
I believe … , don't you?
Would(n't) you agree that … ?
What do you think about this one?

**5** 🎧 Listen to two students responding to the instructions for the second part of the task and complete the notes.

> **Task the examiner outlines:**
> Now you have about a minute to decide in which situation the animals ............................................... .
> **The main problems which the students identify:**
> 1   ............................................. .
> 2   ............................................. .
> 3   ............................................. .
> 4   ............................................. .
> **The decision the students reach:**
> ...............................................

> **tip**
> Consider more than one situation when making your final decision in Part 3.

**6** With a partner, do the exam task in 5.

# Use of English

## Part 2  Open cloze

**1** Look at these pictures of imaginary creatures and discuss which real creatures they resemble.

**2** Read texts a–d, ignoring the gaps, and match them with the pictures and these names.

The Toraton      The Ocean Flish
The Snowstalker      The Megasquid

**a**   This fearsome creature will be one 1 ............ the most ferocious predators of the next Ice Age. In order to adapt to the blizzards that will bury northern Europe 2 ............ several metres of ice, it will have a thick coat, and sturdy legs with large, flat paws. It will travel 3 ............ miles in pursuit of its prey – sheep-size rodents called 'shagrats'.

**b**   This amazing creature will be like no other. Heavier than an elephant and almost as large, it will push its way 4 ............ the dense forest on eight tree trunk-size legs. It will walk 5 ............ elongating each of its legs in turn, and then compressing them again.

**c**   This will be the largest animal ever to walk the planet but will evolve 6 ............ something as small as the humble tortoise. Grazing on more than half a ton of vegetation every day, it will be 7 ............ home in the huge swamps formed when the east coast of Africa collides 8 ............ the southern parts of Asia. These massive creatures won't have many predators to fear.

**d**   These creatures, so called because they can fly and swim, will replace the birdlife which will previously have been wiped 9 ............ . They will develop from cod-like creatures and grow elongated fins that serve as wings, enabling them to make their escape from predators in the sea 10 ............ the safety of the birdless sky.

**3** Read texts a–d again and complete gaps 1–10 with these prepositions and particles.

with    for    out    into    under
through    by    of    from    at

**4** Read the text below to find out more about these creatures, and complete gaps 1–8 with one word each. These questions will help you with 1–6.

1 Which word can collocate with *to* to mean *in their opinion*?
2 Which word is missing from this conditional sentence?
3 What collocates here to mean *helped by*?
4 What can collocate with *as* to mean *like* or *similar to*?
5 What can collocate here to mean *plenty of*?
6 What collocates with *look* to mean *resemble*?

## OUt OF thiS WOrld?

Humans pride themselves on **0** ..being.. the masters of the Earth, but we have only been around for the past 200,000 years. And **1** ........... to many scientists, our long-term outlook isn't rosy. **2** ........... our tendency to get rid of each other doesn't finish us off, our propensity for destroying the environment could. So what might replace us? Here, **3** ........... the aid of computer graphics, are some fantastic creatures experts believe could emerge as our inheritors. Creatures **4** ........... as these appear to be from a science-fiction film, but experts claim there are **5** ........... than enough clues to predict what future inhabitants of the Earth might look **6** ........... .

We know the continents are moving, so with the right computer modelling, we can calculate **7** ........... they will end up and predict what types of creatures might exist. The good news is that this species upheaval is millions of years away, so there is **8** ........... need for us to lose sleep over it just yet!

**5** Use your imagination to think of other creatures which might evolve in the future, taking characteristics from two or more of these creatures.

| kangaroo | leopard | eagle | snail |
| giraffe | shark | chameleon | swan |

# Writing Part 2 A report WG p162

**1** What sorts of activities do teenagers tend to enjoy in the countryside? How can they be encouraged to learn about wildlife? What problems might you encounter if you were responsible for taking a group of teenagers on a trip to the countryside?

**2** Discuss which of a–f are true.

A report:
a should begin and end like a letter
b usually focuses on the past and/or present
c should be chatty in style
d is usually divided into sections with clear headings
e may contain bullet-pointed lists
f doesn't need an introduction or conclusion

**3** Read the writing task below and underline the key words that tell you who you are, who the report is for and what information you must include.

> You work for an international organisation based in the UK that organises trips for children. Your boss recently put you in charge of a group of teenagers on a wildlife holiday, led by professional guides.
>
> Your boss has now asked you to write a report on the holiday, saying whether it had sufficient educational value for teenagers, outlining any problems and saying whether it would be suitable for other age groups.

**4** Now read what one student wrote in answer to the exam question and say which of a–e the writer has done correctly.

a used the correct layout for a report
b used the correct register
c included all the required information
d organised ideas into clear paragraphs
e used appropriate linking words

Dear Mr Stone

1 ...............................

I am writing this report to give you my assessment of our recent wildlife holiday and to advise about its suitability for other age groups.

2 ...............................

The educational element of this trip exceeded our expectations. We encountered some iconic species, including bears, whales and eagles, and learnt about the threats they face, such as habitat destruction and climate change. In addition, our guides taught us a great deal about geology and the local environment. In fact, our teenagers commented that they had learnt more than would be possible in any classroom.

3 ...............................

Not only were our guides knowledgeable, they were also very helpful. However, given the age of our group, I suggest that in future we have one more guide, for safety's sake.

**5** Complete a–f with one of the prepositions below and say whether a–f introduce or conclude a report. Then rewrite the first sentence in paragraphs 1 and 6.

| in | into | up |
|----|------|----|
| to | of | on |

a The aim .......... this report is to …
b .......... conclusion I would say …
c To sum .......... , our group felt that …
d The following report relates .......... …
e Taking everything .......... consideration, …
f .......... balance, I am of the opinion that …

**6** The layout of a report is important and should use distinct sections with clear headings. Delete the opening and closing features of a letter from the model report in exercise 4. Then write these headings above the correct paragraphs.

Accommodation
Activities
Conclusion
Educational value
Guides
Introduction

**7** Choose the correct verb form in a–d to complete the recommendations.

a I would not recommend *take/to take/taking* very small children on the holiday.
b I suggest *we book/us to book/us booking* with a different company in future.
c I have no hesitation in recommending *us to go/ us go/that we go* again.
d I would suggest *try/trying/to try* a different destination next year.

**8** Make a short plan for your own answer to the exam task in 3. Use your ideas from exercise 1 to help you. Then write your **report** in **220–260 words** in an appropriate style.

**4** ...........................................

While the focus of our holiday was on wildlife, getting to places involved hiking or climbing, while our whale-watching day included sea-kayaking. These pursuits offered adventure and excitement without being too dangerous. However, they would not be suitable for very young children.

**5** ...........................................

Camping was a great success. The tents were surprisingly roomy and we had modern conveniences on site. Our group enjoyed the freedom and the opportunity this gave them to learn new skills, such as making a fire and cooking over it.

**6** ...........................................

The wildlife trip was very suitable for our teenagers. Provided we request the changes I have mentioned and put a lower age limit on our group of perhaps fourteen, I have no hesitation in recommending that we repeat the holiday.

Yours sincerely

...................

# Review

**1** Match the parts of the body in 1–12 with creatures a–f.

| | | | | |
|---|---|---|---|---|
| a | fish | 1 | flipper | 7 scale |
| b | bull | 2 | hide | 8 hoof |
| c | eagle | 3 | beak | 9 fin |
| d | lion | 4 | shell | 10 horn |
| e | tortoise | 5 | wing | 11 mane |
| f | dolphin | 6 | claw | 12 paw |

**2** Complete the dialogues in 1–5 with suitable phrases based on these animals.

■ rabbit   butterfly   dog   hen   horse

1  A  Are you going to go out to celebrate with your friends before the wedding?
   B  Yes, my bridesmaid's organising a …….. for me.

2  A  How did you feel about performing in front of such a large audience?
   B  I have to confess I …….. in my stomach just thinking about it!

3  A  I can't believe I forgot to go to that meeting this morning.
   B  You'll be …….. for the rest of the week then!

4  A  Do you fancy watching the new chat show on television tonight?
   B  No way. I can't stand programmes with so-called 'celebrities' …….. about themselves.

5  A  Do you think I've bought enough food to go round at the barbecue?
   B  However much you buy, it will get eaten – everyone we know eats ………. .

**3** Circle the correct animals to complete the phrases in a–e.

a  The ageing president felt like a *fish/whale* out of water when he attended the music awards.
b  I don't mind doing all the *goat/donkey* work as long as I get paid for it.
c  We had a *butterfly/whale* of a time on the last night of the sales conference last year.
d  I once tried my hand at painting but the result was a real *cat's/dog's* dinner.
e  The controversial new traffic scheme was supposed to be kept under wraps, but someone let the *rat/cat* out of the bag.

**4** Complete gaps 1–8 in these newspaper extracts using suitable prepositions or particles.

It is a widely held theory that the dinosaurs were wiped ………. 1 by a giant meteor which collided ………. 2 Earth. It is possible, however, that there is another explanation for what finished ………. 3 the dinosaurs.

Some ……….. 4 the most well adapted creatures on Earth can survive in extremely inhospitable places. For example, the camel is so ………. 5 home in the desert that it can journey ………. 6 miles without water.

According ………. 7 experts, the pace at which global warming is developing might be more serious than we thought. It seems that the world is warming up ………. 8 an alarming rate.

**5** Rewrite this paragraph in a more formal style for part of an information leaflet about toucans.

You can find toucans in South and Central America. There aren't any wild ones in the UK, but you can see lots of them in zoos. You can recognise these creatures easily. They've got a really big beak. Their beaks have very bright colours. Their body is about twice as long as their beak. They really like fruit, seeds and insects. They don't like being on their own. In fact, they live in groups.

# Health matters

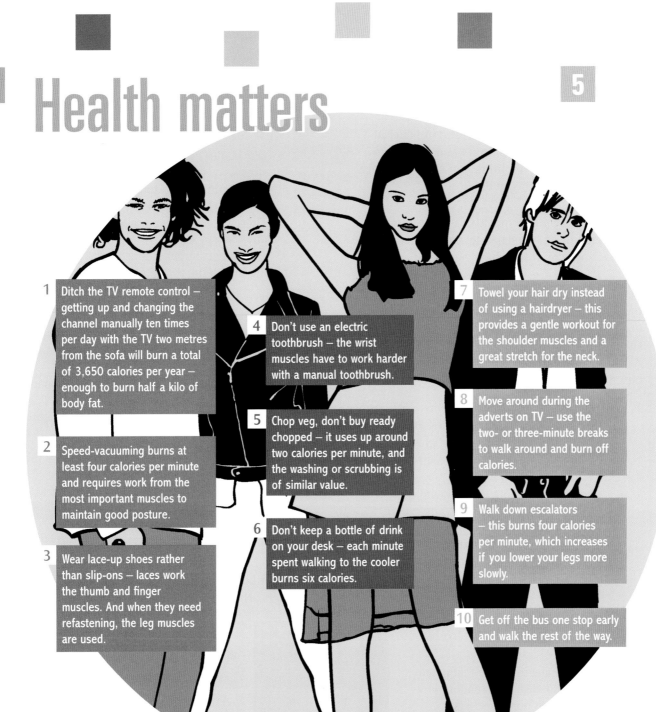

1  Ditch the TV remote control – getting up and changing the channel manually ten times per day with the TV two metres from the sofa will burn a total of 3,650 calories per year – enough to burn half a kilo of body fat.

2  Speed-vacuuming burns at least four calories per minute and requires work from the most important muscles to maintain good posture.

3  Wear lace-up shoes rather than slip-ons – laces work the thumb and finger muscles. And when they need refastening, the leg muscles are used.

4  Don't use an electric toothbrush – the wrist muscles have to work harder with a manual toothbrush.

5  Chop veg, don't buy ready chopped – it uses up around two calories per minute, and the washing or scrubbing is of similar value.

6  Don't keep a bottle of drink on your desk – each minute spent walking to the cooler burns six calories.

7  Towel your hair dry instead of using a hairdryer – this provides a gentle workout for the shoulder muscles and a great stretch for the neck.

8  Move around during the adverts on TV – use the two- or three-minute breaks to walk around and burn off calories.

9  Walk down escalators – this burns four calories per minute, which increases if you lower your legs more slowly.

10  Get off the bus one stop early and walk the rest of the way.

## Lead in

1  Read the ten simple ways to get fit. Which three do you think would be most effective? Which three could you build into your daily routine?

2  Can you add any similar simple suggestions for getting fit? Think about:

    shopping     housework     getting ready for school/work     getting around

3  What advice would you give to a teenager and an elderly person for leading a healthy lifestyle? Think about:

    diet     sleep     physical exercise

# Reading Part 5  Multiple choice

**1** What do you think is the best form of physical exercise? What is the minimum and maximum amount of exercise you think you should do each week? How much do you do?

**2** Read the text opposite quickly to find out what unexpected thing happened to explorer Ranulph Fiennes and why it may have happened.

**3** Read the text again and use the clues to help you with question 1. Ask yourself similar questions for options A–D to help you choose the best answer to questions 2–6.

tip

Make sure <u>all</u> the information is correct in the option you choose.

1 What does the writer say in the first paragraph about Fiennes' obsession with diet and health?

  A It was unreasonable even for an explorer.
*What does the phrase 'comes with the territory' in line 10 tell us?*

  B It had become more intense with time.
*How long has Fiennes been 'fine-tuning' his body?*

  C It contributed to his collapse.
*Does the writer state this in the first paragraph?*

  D It makes subsequent events hard to believe.
*What 'came as something of a surprise' to the writer?*

2 On the question of who will live longest, it seems that

  A genetic make-up is the main factor.
  B there is no clear explanation why some people outlive others.
  C lifestyle choices play little part.
  D family history is not as significant as once thought.

3 According to the text, one of the positive effects of taking regular exercise is that it

  A speeds up the heart rate.
  B strengthens blood vessels.
  C quickens the pulse.
  D reduces heart exertion.

4 What does health expert Len Almond imply?

  A Our bodies can cope with intense physical stress.
  B We should allow a long period of recovery after any physical exercise.
  C There is more to learn about the effects of physical stress.
  D Taking part in endurance sports is harmful in the long term.

5 Experts in sports medicine have

  A studied the effects of altitude on various types of athletes.
  B questioned the wisdom of taking part in extreme sports.
  C found a common factor among participants in extreme sports.
  D discovered an enzyme which causes heart attacks in cyclists.

6 What final conclusion about exercise does the writer reach?

  A It makes life more enjoyable.
  B It may not be worth the effort.
  C It should be done in moderation.
  D It ought to be a priority.

**4** 'It's not how long life is, but how good it is, that matters.' How far do you agree?

The *Guinness Book of World Records* describes Ranulph Fiennes as the world's greatest living explorer. His expeditions include the first polar circumnavigation of the Earth and the first unsupported crossing of the Antarctic continent on foot. He has been up the White Nile in a hovercraft, and parachuted onto Europe's highest glacier. An obsession with diet and fitness comes with the territory, and for years Fiennes has fine-tuned his body

A healthy diet with plenty of fruit and vegetables helps prevent obesity and stops fatty deposits forming in the arteries and blocking them. Smoking, incidentally, has the opposite effect, as nicotine increases the heart rate and makes the blood clot more easily. Exercise is highly beneficial as it reduces both the pulse rate and blood pressure so minimising strain on the heart as it pumps blood round the body. It also

condition? 'It could have had an effect, or there may be genetic predisposition and an event could have made it worse,' says Almond. 'We haven't done enough research in this area.'

This is changing though. There is growing interest in sports medicine, a field that arguably began as long ago as 490 BC, when the first person to run the marathon ran 26 miles from the town of Marathon to Athens with news of a

# an unhealthy obsession

to cope with the most inhospitable of environments and the most stressful situations of physical hell. So when I read that this model of physical fitness had suffered a heart attack – not while planting a flag in a no-man's-land, but while boarding a plane – it came as something of a surprise.

Given what happened, lesser mortals like myself might be forgiven for wondering whether the benefits of following a healthy lifestyle are all they're cracked up to be. Why bother exerting all that effort if in the end survival turns out to be a lottery? Of course, fitness and diet are only part of the story. 'Some people live a healthy lifestyle and still succumb to heart problems,' health expert Alison Shaw explains. Genetics and family history also play a crucial role in determining who will achieve longevity. 'It could all be a question of genes', she says, 'but then some people never have a trace of the disease, even though their family history would seem to make them prime targets.'

Whether or not some people are genetically programmed to have a higher chance of heart disease, there are steps they can take to reduce their risks.

helps to keep the artery walls more elastic. 'Whether you've got a family history of heart disease or not, everybody should be living a healthy lifestyle,' Shaw says. 'We wouldn't want people to stop looking after themselves.'

But can you look after yourself too much? On the subject of exercise, the standard recommendation is to take five sessions of 'moderate' exercise a week, where moderate is a little more than brisk walking. 'We need to be very careful when we're doing extreme sports or endurance events,' says health expert Len Almond. 'Extreme physical stress can impose almost impossible demands on the body's ability to recover. The strain of endurance events forces biochemical changes in the human body. The physiological response to that kind of activity will be extreme … and how the body overcomes that is bound to leave some kind of legacy.' So could Fiennes' love for exploration and endurance events have contributed to his

victory. The man collapsed as soon as he arrived, and the cause of his sudden demise is not known. However, scientists are using athletes like him to answer questions about the effects of extreme exercise on the heart. One group of researchers studied cyclists on a one-day race in Austria that covers 230 km with an altitude change of 5,500 m. They were interested in one particular enzyme, high concentrations of which are found in those who have suffered a heart attack. The scientists found that levels of this chemical increased in thirteen of the 38 cyclists who completed the race. The largest increases were seen in the youngest, fastest cyclists who had trained the hardest. Similar increases in the chemical have been found in cross-country skiers.

Most of us will never put our bodies to such severe tests. But if, when you hear about someone like Fiennes, you ask whether exercise is worth it, I advise you to consider your own priorities. Personally, I subscribe to this adage: 'Run not to add years to your life but to add life to your years.'

# Vocabulary

## Health and fitness

**1** Put the parts of the body in a–p under the appropriate headings.

| | | | | | | | |
|---|---|---|---|---|---|---|---|
| a | thigh | e | rib | i | hip | m | ankle |
| b | elbow | f | chin | j | wrist | n | calf |
| c | shoulder | g | skull | k | palm | o | cheek |
| d | heel | h | thumb | l | waist | p | shin |

**arm and hand**

**leg and foot**

**face and head**

**torso**

**2** Which of a–p in 1 can you harm in these ways?

| | | | |
|---|---|---|---|
| a | break/fracture | c | sprain |
| b | twist | d | dislocate |

**3** Read the dictionary entry below for synonyms of *disease*. Use this information to choose the correct word to complete sentences a–d.

> **Disease** is used to talk about more severe physical medical problems, especially those that affect the organs. **Illness** is used to talk about both more severe and more minor medical problems, and those that affect mental health: *heart/kidney/liver illness* ◇ *mental disease*. **Disease** is not used about a period of illness: *she died after a long disease*
> **infection** an illness that is caused by bacteria or a virus and that affects one part of the body: *a throat infection*
> **condition** a medical problem that you have for a long time because it is not possible to cure it: *a heart condition*
> **ailment** (*rather formal*) an illness that is not very serious: *childhood ailments*
> **bug** (*informal*) an infectious illness that is usually fairly mild: *a nasty flu bug*

*Oxford Advanced Learner's Dictionary, 8th edition*

a There's a nasty *condition/bug* going round college. I had it last week, but I'm feeling much better now.

b My sister has always been prone to chest *infections/ailments* and seems to catch them quite often.

c Whilst there appears to be no cure for his heart *condition/infection*, he can still lead an active life.

d More *conditions/ailments* are reported during the winter months than at other times of the year.

# Grammar

## Direct and indirect speech GR p173–175

**1** Rewrite statements a–e as direct speech.

**Example**

*Explorer Ranulph Fiennes said he'd been preparing for his trip for months, so he was feeling optimistic.*

'*I've been preparing for this trip for months, so I'm feeling optimistic.*'

a Critics said it was likely that the new film would break box-office records.

b My doctor told me I'd feel much better if I did some exercise.

c The manager told them they could all play in the final but that they had to attend all the practice sessions the next day.

d The boss told me that I didn't need to work over the weekend.

e My physiotherapist says my shoulder is responding well to treatment.

**2** Use the sentences in 1 to help answer these questions about direct speech.

a What do you normally need to change when rewriting reported statements as direct speech?

b When do you not need to change the verb tense?

c Which modal verbs change form, and which stay the same?

**3** Choose the most appropriate reporting verb to complete the sentences in a–h as shown.

| | | | |
|---|---|---|---|
| admit | boast | complain | explain |
| mention | protest | realise | warn |

a 'This beach isn't safe for swimming today.'
One of the lifeguards .......... us that …

b 'Oh no! I've left the car keys in that café.'
John suddenly .......... that …

c 'By the way, Alice and I are thinking of trading in our motorbike and buying a car.'
My brother .......... that …

d 'The reason I want this job so much is because it will allow me to travel.'
At his interview he .......... that …

e 'Yes, it's true. I've been lying.'
The prime suspect .......... that …

f 'I'm a million times better than anyone else in the team.'
Our club's top scorer .......... that …

g 'It's ridiculous – there's never anyone at the reception desk when you need them.'
Some of the hotel guests .......... that ...

h 'But honestly, I really didn't cause the accident!' The driver .......... that ...

4 Correct any mistakes in the reported questions in a–g.

a Reporters asked the climber how long had he been training to climb Everest.

b Fans wanted to know whether Kylie is playing at last night's concert.

c In the interview Fiona was asked had she ever worked abroad.

d Our neighbours were keen to find out when were we going on holiday.

e Union leaders enquired whether the deal would go ahead or not.

f The taxi driver asked would I like a hand with my luggage.

g Mum wanted to know did the postman deliver the package she'd been expecting.

5 For a–g circle the word in italics which correctly completes the sentence.

a My boss *suggested/begged* me to reconsider.

b Health experts *advise/recommend* us to eat five portions of fresh fruit and vegetables daily.

c The celebrity model has *denied/refused* selling her story to the press.

d Haven't your parents ever *forbidden/warned* you not to do something?

e Are you *proposing/threatening* going to the police about this?

f Your boss shouldn't *ask/promise* you to do something that's impossible!

g Sergeant Smith *ordered/reminded* his soldiers that they had to polish their boots every day.

6 Rewrite the sentences in 5 using the word in italics not circled.

7 Complete a–e with your own ideas.

a Parents should always warn teenagers ...

b Recently, my friend foolishly suggested ...

c Politicians always promise ...

d My dad once threatened ...

e I usually need to be reminded ...

8 Complete sentences a–f, using one of the prepositions below and an appropriate gerund.

on     from     of     for

a Staff are blaming one of the pupils ...

b Maria accused her boyfriend ...

c Bystanders praised the heroic firefighter ...

d The accident wouldn't have happened if you hadn't insisted ...

e An effective way of discouraging children ...

f The millionaire footballer has apologised ...

9 Underline the correct structure in a–f from the pairs in italics.

a My mother suggested *my friends and I going/that my friends and I should get* away for the day.

b Enrico rang and asked if *we were going/we are going* to last night's birthday celebrations.

c I was shocked when the policeman accused me *to shoplift/of shoplifting.*

d Mark wanted to know what *was I planning/I was planning* after work.

e His wife proposed *they go out/them to go out* for dinner.

f Terrorists threatened *blowing up/to blow up* major government buildings.

# Listening Part 1 Multiple choice

**1** Look at the photographs and discuss these questions, which relate to the extracts in 2.

   a  How can you ensure a good night's sleep?

   b  Besides crosswords, what other kinds of activities can help to keep your brain active?

   c  Which do you think are better: contact lenses or glasses? Why?

**2** 🎧 Read questions 1–6 below before you listen to the three different extracts. Then listen and choose the best answer (A, B or C) for each question.

**3** Answer these questions, which all contain expressions from the recording.

   a  How do you put yourself *in the right frame of mind* to relax after a busy day?

   b  What types of things do you do to *stimulate muscle activity*?

   c  What types of health remedies would you *treat with caution*?

 **You hear part of an interview with a health expert.**

**1** What does the interviewer say happens to people after a bad night's sleep?
A  They wake up feeling exhausted.
B  They often sleep badly the next night as well.
C  They lack energy later on in the day.

**2** Some children fail to sleep well because they
A  use their computer too much.
B  read for too long before going to sleep.
C  have too many late nights.

 **You hear two people talking about how to improve brain power.**

**3** What do they disagree about?
A  whether the size of the brain can be increased
B  how easy it is for some people to forget things
C  the usefulness of doing activities like crosswords

**4** What does the woman suggest the man can do to improve his brain power?
A  take some physical exercise once a week
B  try to think more about what he's doing
C  take up a hobby like dancing

 **You hear a doctor and a patient talking about laser eye surgery.**

**5** How does the doctor feel about laser eye surgery?
A  It has had a very low success rate to date.
B  It works better if your eyesight is very poor.
C  It has dramatically changed the treatment of poor eyesight.

**6** What warning does the doctor give the patient?
A  Even after surgery, eyesight will still get worse with age.
B  He may never be able to wear ordinary glasses again.
C  An experienced eye surgeon could still make mistakes.

# Speaking Parts 3 and 4

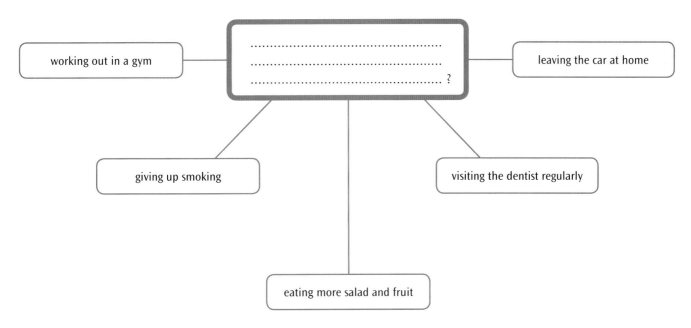

working out in a gym

leaving the car at home

giving up smoking

visiting the dentist regularly

eating more salad and fruit

1 Look at the different things above that people can do to stay fit and healthy. What might the question in the first part of this exam task be?

2 🎧 Listen to the first part of the exam task and write the question in the space above. How does it compare with your ideas in 1?

3 Read some of the things two students said when doing the task in 2, and correct any mistakes.

a I believe that working out in a gym is a great way to making sure you get enough exercise.
b There's no doubt that people who smoke put themselves at risk later on in life, so stopping when you're young would be an effective way of avoid smoke-related diseases.
c It's been prove that if you eat around five portions of fruit and vegetables every day, you'll see the benefits health-wise.
d Well, they say you should to visit a dentist every six months or so, but it's very expensive and not everybody can afford it.
e I'm not thinking that this is a very effective way of staying fit and healthy. I mean – some people don't live anywhere near an efficient public transport system, so they really do need their car.

4 With a partner, do the task in 2. Allow yourselves two minutes, then compare your ideas with another pair of students.

5 🎧 Now listen to the instructions for the second part of the task. What decision do the students have to make?

6 With a different partner, do the task in 5. Allow yourselves one minute.

7 Answer these Part 4 questions using the prompts in brackets and how to do it box to help you.

a How else can you keep fit and healthy?
*(What do your friends and family do?)*
b Should smoking be banned in all public places?
*(How would you feel as a smoker and a non-smoker?)*
c Some people say that fast-food restaurants promote an unhealthy diet. Do you agree?
*(Don't be afraid to say if you don't agree, but do so politely and explain why.)*
d People are healthier nowadays and live much longer than they did in the past. What kinds of problems does this create for society?
*(Think about looking after an ageing population and the age at which people retire.)*

## how to do it

- Quickly correct any mistakes, but don't interrupt your flow of talking.
- Don't give one-word answers; try to develop the discussion as much as possible.

# Use of English  Part 3 Word formation

**1** Read the text quickly, ignoring the gaps, and choose the best heading (a, b or c).

  a  Life-threatening illnesses
  b  Looking after your health
  c  A disease we can avoid

**2** Read the text again carefully and decide which part of speech belongs in each gap. Check your ideas with the tip box opposite, then complete gaps 1–8 with words formed from those in capitals.

**tip**

The eight missing answers in this text include:
- two plural nouns
- two singular nouns
- one adverb
- two adjectives with a suffix
- one adjective with a prefix and a suffix

Rising temperatures and a hotter climate? Well, if you are 0 .....*unfortunate*..... enough to live in a country with a 1 ..................... climate, it sounds great. But there is a dark side. This climate might bring visitors of a particularly 2 ..................... kind – Anopheles mosquitoes, 3 ..................... of malaria. No one has caught malaria from a British mosquito for several decades, but 4 ..................... believe that this may become more widespread.

It seems that malaria in our modern world would be more endemic if any 5 ..................... by the authorities were to occur. There are many parts of the world where malaria would exist were it not for 6 ..................... by the authorities. Despite their warm climate, places such as Italy and Spain do not have problems with malaria because they have 7 ..................... managed their medical resources.

Malaria is not 8 ..................... , providing that it is dealt with promptly. So if you should come back from the tropics feeling ill, make sure you get medical treatment as quickly as possible.

| 0 | FORTUNE |
| 1 | MISERY |
| 2 | HAZARD |
| 3 | CARRY |
| 4 | SCIENCE |
| 5 | MANAGE |
| 6 | INTERVENE |
| 7 | EXPERT |
| 8 | CURE |

# Vocabulary Word formation (1)

**1** Change the form of the words in bold to complete the second sentence in a–d.

a Jane's work is always **perfect**.
Jane is a ........................ .

b I don't really **believe** in alternative medicine.
I'm not a strong ........................ in alternative medicine.

c The college has to **provide** career advice.
The college is responsible for the ........................ of career advice.

d You are required to **attend** the event.
Your ........................ at the event is compulsory.

**2** Fill in the missing parts of speech in the table below. There may be more than one possible answer.

| verb | noun (thing) | noun (person) | adjective | adverb |
|------|-------------|---------------|-----------|--------|
| | product | | | |
| | | perfectionist | | |
| | | authority | | |
| —— | medicine | | | |
| provide | | | —— | —— |
| | management | | | |
| believe | | | | |
| —— | | expert | | |
| —— | fortune | | —— | |
| attend | | | —— | —— |

**3** Look up *product* and *perfect* in a dictionary. How does the word stress change with the different parts of speech?

**4** Write adjectives ending in *-able* to match definitions a–h.

a for _ _ _ _ _ _ _ _   (something you're unlikely to remember)
b avo _ _ _ _ _ _   (something you can prevent)
c tol _ _ _ _ _ _   (something you can bear)
d acc _ _ _ _ _ _ _   (something satisfactory)
e des _ _ _ _ _ _   (something wanted)
f pre _ _ _ _ _ _ _ _   (something you are sure will happen)
g agr _ _ _ _ _ _   (something pleasant)
h ex _ _ _ _ _ _ _ _   (something you can explain)

**5** Add prefixes to the words in 4 to give an opposite meaning, then use the words to talk about things that have recently happened to you.

# Writing

**1** How often do you exercise each week? What kind of exercise do you do? Do people in your country take enough exercise in your opinion? How might they be encouraged to take more?

**2** Read the writing task and input text opposite and underline the key points that you must cover in your essay.

**3** Decide if statements a–f are true of the writing task in 2.

a You must write about all three bullet points.
b You need to compare two things and say which is best.
c You must use at least one of the opinions given in the task.
d You can quote opinions word for word in your essay.
e You must justify your views.
f There is no word limit for your essay.

Your class has attended a panel discussion on the measures that could be taken to encourage people to take more exercise. You have made the notes below.

> Ways in which people could be encouraged to take more exercise:
>
> • subsidised gyms
> • education
> • compulsory sport at work and school

> Some opinions expressed in the discussion:
>
> 'People might use gyms more if governments subsidised them all.'
>
> 'Doctors and teachers need to advise people about the importance of exercise.'
>
> 'They should persuade companies to make exercise classes compulsory in the workplace.'

Write an essay discussing **two** of the methods in your notes. You should **explain which method you think is more important** for governments to consider, **giving reasons** in support of your answer.

You may, if you wish, make use of the opinions expressed in the discussion, but you should use your own words as far as possible.

Write your **essay** in **220–260** words in an appropriate style.

4  Read the task in 2 again and decide which two methods you are going to write about. Read the reasons one student noted down for choosing 'education', and make similar notes for your two choices. Then decide which of your choices is more important and why.

Why education is important:

– it makes people aware of the health benefits, e.g. enables you to concentrate better/good for heart

– it encourages people to take responsibility for their own health and make sensible decisions, e.g. go by bike instead of driving

– it teaches children good habits connected with exercise and these habits will last for life

5  Put the linking words and expressions a–j into groups 1–3.

1  similar or extra information
2  contrasting information
3  expressing a result

a  although
b  as a consequence/result
c  so that
d  therefore
e  while
f  which is why
g  however
h  what is more
i  in spite of/despite
j  furthermore

6  Read the introduction one student wrote for this writing task and fill each gap with a linking word. There is one extra word.

| therefore | as a consequence |
| while | however |

Nowadays a lot of time is spent on pursuits such as watching television or playing video games. **1** .......... of this inactivity, many people consider physical exercise too exhausting or difficult. **2** .........., failure to exercise can lead to obesity and other health problems. It is **3** .......... extremely important that governments encourage people to get fit.

7  Expand your notes from 4 into full sentences using your own words. Organise the sentences into two paragraphs, each with a topic sentence and a range of linking words.

8  Read one student's concluding paragraph and complete it using the words and phrases below. Use each word or phrase once only.

| by | to sum up | however |
| although | therefore | so that |
| which is why | along with | |

**1** .......... , many people do not realise the importance of exercise, **2** .......... governments should definitely make education their top priority. **3** .......... , that is not the end of the matter. **4** .......... some people may prefer to choose their own form of exercise, many would benefit from going to a gym. It is important, **5** .......... , that governments should make sports venues like these cheaper to join **6** .......... people can get help and advice, **7** .......... the chance to meet like-minded people. **8** .......... doing this, governments will ensure we are all a great deal healthier than we are now.

9  Write your own answer to the exam task in 2. Remember that you need to compare two methods and give reasons why one is more important than the other.

# Review

## 1
Match parts of the body a–j with explanations 1–10.

a   rib      f   thumb
b   chin     g   waist
c   wrist    h   shin
d   skull    i   palm
e   cheek   j   thigh

1   the bony casing that protects the brain
2   the joint that gives flexibility to the hand
3   the narrower middle part of the human figure
4   young children often suck this
5   used as a verb with *up*, it means 'climb quickly'
6   the fleshy part at the front of the jaw
7   parts of the face that blush if you are embarrassed
8   one of the curved bones that protect the lungs
9   the top part of the leg
10  the flat surface of the inside of the hand

## 2
Complete sentences a–h with suitable words in the correct form.

a   Most of the children in school were off last week with a nasty stomach .............. .
b   The lead singer had picked up a chest .............. , so the opera had to be cancelled at the last minute.
c   I fell down a step and .............. my ankle. Thankfully, it's not too bad so I should be fine tomorrow.
d   The team's top striker will be out of action for weeks because of his .............. leg.
e   Lung .............. is one of the major health risks associated with smoking.
f   One of the Olympic gymnasts .............. her shoulder in a fall and had to have it put back into place.
g   If you suffer from a heart .............. , you should not take this medicine.
h   Although the top tennis seed's wrist wasn't broken, it was so badly .............. that she had to withdraw from the championship.

## 3
Use words 1–8 below in the correct form to complete sentences a–h.

1   survive     4   predict      7   threat
2   mechanic   5   technology   8   prevent
3   manage     6   intervene

a   It's true to say of most illnesses that .............. is better than cure.
b   .............. in the affairs of others is usually inadvisable.
c   I'm afraid I'm not ..............-minded enough to be able to fix the DVD player!
d   Several supporters of the visiting football team were arrested for .............. behaviour.
e   Do you think this amount of work is .............. in such a short space of time?
f   Although the ship sank without trace, a rescue boat managed to pick up all the .............. .
g   What are your .............. for the next general election? Who would you say is going to win?
h   My motorbike's at the garage as it's recently developed a serious .............. fault.

## 4
Read this newspaper extract about a demonstration, then replace the words in brackets with adjectives ending in *-able*.

Yesterday's mass demonstration was **1** (likely to be remembered) .............. for many reasons. The large turnout was **2** (not a surprise) .............. and the atmosphere could be described as **3** (pleasant) .............. at the start of the day, with the level of policing **4** (satisfactory) .............. . Unfortunately, for some **5** (impossible to explain) .............. reason, events took a turn for the worse. Violence previously thought to have been **6** (possible to prevent) .............. broke out and several incidents of vandalism took place which local residents found **7** (impossible to put up with) .............. . It was therefore considered **8** (wanted) .............. to bring the demonstration to a halt before it reached its intended destination.

# Would you believe it?

## Lead in

**1** Discuss whether these statements are true or false. The answers are on page 153.

a To see a full-length reflection of yourself in a mirror, it must be at least half as tall as you.

b The word 'news' is formed from the first letters of north, south, east and west.

c Of any group of 23 people, there is a 50% possibility that two of them will share a birthday.

d Chewing gum takes seven years to pass through the digestive system.

e The number of people alive today is greater than the number of people who have previously lived and died.

f Eating celery makes you lose weight.

**2** Complete these sentences with *true* or *false*.

a I hope all your wishes come ........... .

b The tourist brochure had given a ........... impression of the resort; our hotel was only half built.

c Obtaining money under ........... pretences is a criminal offence.

d I'm sure something fishy's going on – Tim's explanation just doesn't ring ........... .

e The newspaper was sued for making accusations that weren't strictly ........... .

f Buying a cheap car is usually a ........... economy, as you often end up spending more on it than you paid in the first place.

g Winning the lottery is a dream come ........... for some and a nightmare for others.

h Installing smoke alarms can give a ........... sense of security, as people forget to check them regularly.

**3** Discuss the following.

a What things did you believe as a child that you now know aren't true?

b Do you wish any of them were true?

c Are there any you're glad aren't true?

d Is it right to let children believe things that aren't true?

# Reading   Part 8  Multiple matching

**1** What special abilities do the superheroes in the pictures have?
Quickly read sections A–D to check your ideas.

**2** Read the text again and the tip box. In which section (A–D) are 1–10
mentioned? The underlined words will help you find links to A–D.

a <u>substance</u> that <u>speeds up</u> a natural process   1 ....
a <u>substance</u> that <u>looks weaker</u> than it is   2 ....
<u>someone</u> who takes refuge <u>away from his home</u>   3 .... 4 ....
a <u>substance</u> that enables <u>creatures</u> to <u>secure themselves</u> in place   5 ....
a <u>selfless act</u> with unforeseen consequences   6 ....
<u>someone</u> given a <u>new identity</u> from a <u>young age</u>   7 ....
a <u>creature</u> that hides itself by <u>changing the way it looks</u>   8 ....
<u>someone</u> whose powers are the principle behind a <u>form of transport</u>   9 ....
<u>substances</u> that make physical <u>discomfort</u> <u>less noticeable</u> to the sufferer   10 ....

**3** Discuss the meaning of these
phrases from the text.

a  crime-ridden streets (l.5)
b  nooks and crannies (l.13)
c  weight for weight (l.18)
d  one thing's for sure (l.36)
e  driven by fury (l.60)
f  great feats of strength (l.64)
g  mask the pain (l.68)

> **tip**
>
> Try concentrating on one section at a time
> and finding which questions refer to that. It
> may be quicker than skimming through A–D
> for every question.

**4** If you had the capability to
do <u>one</u> of these things, which
would you choose and why?

- become invisible at will
- fly
- see in the dark
- breathe underwater
- change your appearance at will

# *super*

## A SPIDER-MAN

Spider-Man acquired his superhuman abilities when, during
a demonstration of radiation technology, a spider crept into
the beam of radiation and bit his hand. As Peter Parker he
works as a photographer for *The Daily Bugle*, but as Spider-
Man he fights evil in the crime-ridden streets of New York.   5
Spider-Man shoots and spins webs from small jets attached
to his wrists and can stick to almost any surface, scaling
skyscrapers with his bare hands. So how far can real science
go in explaining his powers? Like our superhero, spiders
can adhere to almost any surface. Many do this by secreting   10
sticky silk onto their feet, which anchors them in position.
Others have millions of specially shaped microscopic
hairs on their legs, that slip into nooks and crannies. As
for Spider-Man's traps, anyone who has ever walked into
a spider's web knows that the silk is deceptively strong,   15
despite its gossamer appearance. Dragline silk, which spiders
use to crawl down from ceiling to floor, is the strongest of
all; weight for weight it is actually stronger than steel.

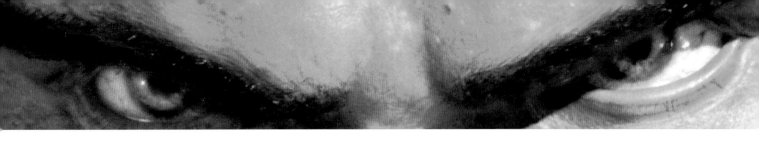

## B SUPERMAN

As a child, Superman was forced to flee his doomed
20 planet, Krypton, eventually landing on Earth where he was
adopted under the name Clark Kent. He now works as a
mild-mannered newspaper reporter, but whenever danger
calls he's a quick change away from saving the world … as
Superman. He is faster than a speeding bullet, can fly, has
25 superhuman strength, can leap over tall buildings and has
X-ray vision. Superman's cells convert the sun's energy into
incredible superpowers – but can scientific fact explain this?
While animals have to eat plants (or each other) to survive,
plants can harvest their energy directly from the sun's
30 light by photosynthesis. Plants are full of a chemical called
chlorophyll that accelerates this reaction. It traps all of the
energy we need to live, storing it inside plants until the
energy is released inside our bodies after eating. So perhaps
Superman is using some form of photosynthesis to build
35 up the tremendous reserves of energy that he needs for his
superhuman feats of strength. One thing's for sure – he's not
using chlorophyll, because it would turn him bright green!

## D THE INCREDIBLE HULK

As a nuclear physicist, Bruce Banner developed a new gamma
bomb for the military. When a reckless teenager strayed onto
the bomb test site, Banner saved him – but was caught in the
middle himself and transformed into a huge green monster,
enormously strong and driven by fury. When angry, Banner 60
now changes into the Hulk, acquiring superhuman strength
– and turning green – but with decreased intelligence and an
inability to control his temper. At times of stress, humans do
sometimes perform great feats of strength. This may be caused
by the release of certain hormones in the body which boost the 65
levels of oxygen and fuel available to muscles. Over time, they
can even increase muscle bulk. Other natural chemicals can
mask the pain that over-stretching muscles may cause, allowing
individuals to push their body beyond its natural limits. The
Hulk's colour changes may be related to the way animals use 70
colour cells to alter their appearance; the cuttlefish uses this for
camouflage, and may even be able to communicate using waves
of colour.

# heroes

## C MAGNETO

Hunted by the X-Men, Magneto was born a mutant
in a world that feared and despised his kind.
40 In response he isolated himself from humanity
on Asteroid M, preparing for the time when
mutants would rule the Earth. Magneto can create
electromagnetic fields and control them so that he can
levitate all objects made of metal, project force fields and
45 generate electricity. So can science explain his abilities?
Iron and steel are magnetic, and are attracted to either
the north or south poles of a magnet. Electromagnets
are used to make trains that float over the rails; these are
easier to move forward than a conventional train, which
50 loses a lot of energy through friction between the rails and
wheels. Most materials, including water, are 'diamagnetic',
meaning that they are always repelled by both magnetic
poles. Since animals are mostly water, scientists have found
that if they use a strong enough magnetic field, they could
55 levitate a live frog without hurting it at all.

# Vocabulary

## Verbs of moving and looking

**1** Decide which word in each group a–e is not a verb of movement.

| | | |
|---|---|---|
| a | creep | glance | stumble |
| b | hobble | totter | gaze |
| c | limp | plod | glimpse |
| d | glare | stagger | limp |
| e | peep | trip | crawl |

**2** Which verbs of movement in 1 have similar meanings? Choose the best verbs to complete a–e below.

a It was such a low tunnel into the cave that we had to .......... on our hands and knees.

b We got completely lost on our walk and had to .......... through lots of wet, muddy fields.

c I got home after midnight and slowly .......... upstairs so I wouldn't disturb anyone.

d Despite .......... slightly after the first fence, the horse quickly recovered and won the race.

e My grandmother is extremely prone to accidents and is always .......... over things.

**3** Read the dictionary entries for synonyms of *look*. Which verbs of looking from 1 are being defined?

a ......... a quick look: *She stole a ....... at her watch.*

b ...... a long steady look at sb/sth: *She felt embarrassed under his steady ..... .*

c .......... a look at sb/sth for a very short time, when you do not see the person or thing completely: *He caught a ........ of her in the crowd.*

d ....... a long angry look at sb/sth: *She fixed her questioner with a hostile ..... .*

*Oxford Advanced Learner's Dictionary, 8th edition*

# Grammar

## Modals GR p175–176

**1** Underline the modal verbs in a–g and match them with their functions 1–7 below.

a I could ride a bike by the time I was five years old.

b Passports must be shown at the border.

c We might arrive in time for the conference, but I doubt it.

d The stewardess said we can unfasten our seat belts now.

e You should put on overalls if you plan to paint the bedroom.

f We don't need to get a ticket to park here.

g Clare must be allergic to bananas – they always bring her out in a rash.

| | | | |
|---|---|---|---|
| 1 | obligation | 5 | possibility |
| 2 | absence of obligation | 6 | ability |
| 3 | permission | 7 | strong advice |
| 4 | assumption/deduction | | |

**2** Look at the picture and decide whether the assumptions and deductions in a–g on page 73 are justified, giving reasons. Then make other deductions from the clues in the picture.

Example

*The owners of the house can't be well off.* ✗
*The owners of the house must be well-off because they've got a safe.*

a   The safe can't be burglar-proof.
b   The burglars must have had a key for the flat.
c   A neighbour might have called the police.
d   There could have been more than one burglar.
e   The burglars can't have taken any valuables.
f   The police might have found a clue.
g   The owners couldn't have gone out for the evening.

**3** Use modal verbs of assumption or deduction, and the verbs in brackets, to complete the dialogue.

A: Oh no! I put my bag down by the door and it's gone! Someone .......... (1 steal) it!
B: Don't be ridiculous. There's nobody here but us!
A: Yes, but we've been busy talking. Someone .......... (2 come) in quietly, picked it up and slipped out with it. It's possible, you know.
B: Are you sure you didn't leave it on the bus? I saw you put it down on the seat next to you. You .......... (3 leave) it behind when you got off.
A: No, I .......... (4 do), because I remember looking in it on the way here. I wanted to check I'd got my mobile.
B: Well, it's not here now.
A: Oh dear, I .......... (5 be) more careful with it, I know. Thank goodness there wasn't much in it.
B: That's a relief! Let's just check at the police station anyway. You never know, someone .......... (6 hand) it in there.

**4** Complete a–g with an appropriate form of *can/able to.*

a   Sorry I .......... get out to meet you last night but I had to babysit for some friends.
b   One day, we .......... cure many common illnesses.
c   It took a lot of work but in the end the mechanic .......... get the car going.
d   I .......... go ice skating for the past few weeks because I've injured my leg.
e   Tom .......... come to the phone at the moment but I'll take a message if you like.
f   A child genius, he .......... solve difficult fractions by the time he was three years old.
g   I love .......... stay in bed on Sunday mornings.

**5** Complete a–f with an appropriate form of *don't need to* or *needn't* and the verb in brackets.

a   Look, there's no one else on the tennis courts. We .......... (bother) to book one in advance.
b   Apparently there are still plenty of tickets left for this year's festival, so we .......... (worry) about getting hold of some.
c   My work colleagues kindly took me out to dinner to celebrate my promotion, and I .......... (pay) a penny.
d   My husband and I bought a dishwasher yesterday, so we .......... (do) the washing-up ever again!
e   You .......... (apply) for a visa to travel round this country, as far as I know.
f   It was much too cold to go swimming when I was on holiday, so I .......... (pack) my bikini after all.

**6** Correct the modal verbs in these sentences.

a   Surely you mustn't be retiring this year? You look so young!
b   You mustn't make up your mind about the job offer yet if you don't want to.
c   How lovely to see you, Bill! And this should be your wife, Betty?
d   After many failed attempts, they could rescue the trapped miners.
e   I've just seen the weather forecast and it could not be warm enough for a barbecue after all.

**7** Match modals a–e with their meanings 1–5. Then explain to a partner the rules of a game or sport you know well, using a–e.

a   You don't have to/need to …
b   You shouldn't …
c   Everyone has to  …
d   You ought to …
e   You mustn't …

1   It's forbidden to do it.
2   The rules say so.
3   It isn't necessary to do it.
4   It's advisable to do it.
5   It isn't advisable to do it.

# Listening Part 4 Multiple matching

**1** Who would you include in a top five of today's best live performers? Discuss your choices.

**2** 🎧 Listen to part of a radio programme about a singer called Beyoncé to find out:

a what Beyoncé was accused of.
b whether the accusation was true.
c what effect her performance had on the audience.
d why she did not perform live.
e what action she performed that was misleading.

**3** 🎧 You will hear five short extracts in which people are talking about pop stars miming or 'lip-synching'. While you listen, complete tasks 1 and 2 below. The tip box will help you.

> ### tip
> Remember that questions 1–5 and 6–10 refer to the <u>same</u> five speakers, so scan across both tasks while you listen.

**TASK ONE**

For questions 1–5, choose from the list A–H what each speaker feels about the music industry today.

A The only thing that matters nowadays is talent.
B The industry creates music that follows what's fashionable.
C Tickets for live shows should be offered to fans first.
D The industry's too concerned about what artists look like.
E It's not only professionals who can perform well.
F It's a pity that a lot of talent is going to waste.
G It's not always easy to obtain tickets for live concerts.
H Many singers are second-rate live performers.

Speaker 1 [ ] 1
Speaker 2 [ ] 2
Speaker 3 [ ] 3
Speaker 4 [ ] 4
Speaker 5 [ ] 5

**TASK TWO**

For questions 6–10, choose from the list A–H each speaker's attitude towards artists lip-synching.

A It would be unwise for some performers not to lip-synch.
B No professional musician should need to lip-synch.
C Most singers who lip-synch simply look awkward.
D It's better to watch a recorded performance than artists lip-synching.
E The press should give more coverage to the fact that artists lip-synch.
F Lip-synching is acceptable if you know it's going to happen.
G Lyrics aren't important any more so it doesn't matter if artists lip-synch.
H If artists lip-synch, this is an insult to the audience.

Speaker 1 [ ] 6
Speaker 2 [ ] 7
Speaker 3 [ ] 8
Speaker 4 [ ] 9
Speaker 5 [ ] 10

**4** Are there any occasions when you think artists should lip-synch?

# Speaking Part 2

**1** Match phrases a–e with the photos.

  a  (in) fancy dress     d  (in) costume
  b  make-believe       e  dressed up as
  c  putting on

**2** Which of the people in the photos might be experiencing these feelings? Explain why.

- excited at the thought of something
- lost in a world of their own
- committed to what they are doing
- apprehensive about what might happen
- self-conscious about their appearance

**3** With a partner, each choose a pair of photos to compare. Talk for a minute each about why the people have changed their appearance in these ways, and how they might be feeling.

> **tip**
> Remember that in the exam you will be given three photographs. You must choose two and talk about them.

**4** Look at your partner's photos and tell your partner, in no more than 30 seconds, which change of appearance would cause the greatest reaction.

■ Making decisions and giving reasons

I'd go for this one because …
It has to be this one because …
Definitely this one because there …
It's difficult to decide between these two, but …
I'm torn between them, but …

# Use of English Part 1 Multiple-choice cloze

**1** Discuss any tricks you have played on someone, or any good ones you have heard about.

**2** Read the newspaper article below quickly, ignoring the gaps, to find out what trick a fast-food chain played and who was fooled by it.

## THE LEFT-HANDED BURGER

A well-known fast-food chain recently published a full-page advertisement announcing that they were 0 ....*B*..... a new item to their menu – a 'Left-Handed Burger', 1 ............ specifically for their left-handed customers. According to the advertisement, the dimensions of the new burger were identical to those of the original burger, 2 ............ were the ingredients. The difference was that the ingredients had been rotated by 180 degrees to 3 ............ left-handed people to handle the burger without 4 ............ .

The following day, April 2nd, the fast-food store 5 ............ that the story had been invented as an April Fool's trick and the left-handed burger didn't exist. Nevertheless, restaurants reported that they had been visited by several thousand customers 6 ............ the new burger. Simultaneously, there were many other concerned customers who insisted that staff should provide them with their own right-handed 7 ............ . It just proves how readily people can be 8 ............ , even on April Fool's day.

**3** Decide which answer (A, B, C or D) best fits each gap in the text in 2.

| | | | | |
|---|---|---|---|---|
| 0 | A establishing | B introducing | C initiating | D organising |
| 1 | A created | B imagined | C obtained | D generated |
| 2 | A while | B as | C since | D because |
| 3 | A enlist | B endure | C entitle | D enable |
| 4 | A difficulty | B issues | C problem | D damages |
| 5 | A conflicted | B confessed | C confided | D conformed |
| 6 | A requesting | B calling | C attracting | D appealing |
| 7 | A figure | B form | C version | D adaptation |
| 8 | A trapped | B disappointed | C betrayed | D deceived |

## Part 4 Key word transformation

**4** Match phrasal verbs a–f with the similar meanings in 1–6.

- a to take someone in
- b to come up with (an idea)
- c to get hold of (something)
- d to own up
- e to set up
- f to bring out

1 confess
2 obtain
3 deceive
4 invent
5 publish
6 establish

**5** Rewrite the second sentence in a–f keeping the meaning the same. Use three to six words including the word given. Your answers from 4 will help you.

- a Do you know whose invention this gadget was?
  **CAME**
  I wonder ............... the idea for this gadget.

- b Have you any idea where I can obtain a cheap, second-hand car?
  **HOLD**
  Where ............... a cheap, second-hand car?

- c The thief should have confessed to the crime when he had the chance.
  **OWNED**
  If only ............... the crime when he had the chance.

- d Bob deceived me with his promises to invest capital in the business.
  **TAKEN**
  I ............... Bob's promises to invest capital in the business.

- e We regret not publishing the novel sooner.
  **BROUGHT**
  We wish ............... the novel sooner.

- f The government formed a committee to oversee the changes.
  **SET**
  A committee ............... the government to oversee the changes.

# Vocabulary

## Expressions with *right* and *left*

**1** Choose the best explanation for the expressions with *right* in a–g below.

- a I thought that film we saw last night was really violent.
  *Too right* – not my kind of film at all.
  (I completely agree/I think you're being unfair)
- b John's just popped out to get a paper but he'll *be* right back.
  (return eventually/return soon)
- c *By rights*, the children should be in bed by now.
  (according to what is proper/only if necessary)
- d The company started distributing advertisements for their products *left, right and centre*. (in three locations/everywhere)
- e My colleagues in my new job were so friendly that I felt at home *right away*. (completely/immediately)
- f Apparently our new manager is very friendly – if you manage to *get* on the right side of him!
  (get him to realise you exist/get him to like you)
- g Paul didn't need to apologise because he knew he *was in the right*.
  (got answers right/had justice on his side)

**2** Match the expressions with *left* with the most suitable sentence in 1–4 and discuss their meaning.

- a The *left-luggage office* is on platform three.
- b David's *got two left feet*!
- c There were a lot of *leftovers* from our meal.
- d Sam *doesn't know his left from his right*.

1 So I don't need to cook anything new tonight.
2 He's the worst dancer I've ever seen.
3 We can leave our suitcases there.
4 That's why he's no good at giving directions.

**3** Look up *left* and *right* in a dictionary. Which one has more idioms? How many new words can you find that derive from each one?

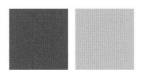

# Writing Part 2 A review WG p160

**1** Name your favourite website and explain what sort of website it is and why you like it. What are the elements of a good website, in your opinion?

**2** Which of the following features might a well-written review of a website contain?

a clear, useful information
b a lively style to involve the reader
c some present tenses
d a good range of vocabulary
e comments on any special features
f well-formed paragraphs containing topic sentences
g section headings
h good sentence and paragraph linkers
i an interesting introduction that catches the reader's attention
j a conclusion that recaps and gives a recommendation

**3** Read the writing task below and the model answer opposite and answer these questions.

a Does the answer address all parts of the task?
b Does the answer include appropriate items from a–j in 2 above? Give examples.

You see the announcement below in an international magazine.

**Reviews wanted: useful websites**

We want to publish reviews of websites that may be new to our readers. Send in a review describing a useful website you have used recently, explaining what makes it stand out from similar websites, and saying who it would appeal to most and why.

Write your **review** in **220–260** words in an appropriate style.

Men often find choosing presents for women really difficult. As for me, I used to go blank, and would then end up buying my partner something boringly predictable, like flowers. Then I discovered ManBuysPresent.com!

So how does it work? You type in who the present is for, their age, what the occasion is, the price you want to pay and when the gift must be delivered and simply click 'search'. You are then offered three ideas, together with a helpful description telling you why each product would appeal to a woman. If the choices are not suitable, you just hit the 'Spin' button. It works a bit like a fruit machine – press the button and different gift choices spin up on the screen.

This website takes all the stress out of choosing a present. Instead of wandering round a department store for hours, you have an online personal assistant with the perfect suggestion. There's even a 'Get out of jail' option in the form of a next-day delivery service for last-minute purchases. The price quoted for the ideal gift includes fancy wrapping – what man wouldn't appreciate that service?

ManBuysPresent.com is cooler, more user-friendly and more intuitive than any other e–commerce site around at the moment, and far more original. No wonder it's a hit – not just with men either! Due to popular demand, the site now offers similar gift advice to women buying for the men in their lives. A top website for both sexes then? Definitely!

**4** Identify the topic of paragraphs 2 and 3 in the model answer.

**5** Describe how your favourite website works using words or phrases from the box.

> On this site you can ... /This site offers ...
> Let me explain how ... works.
> You start by ... /The first thing to do is ...
> Then, ... /Next, ... /After that, you ...
> Once you've done that, you ...
> If/When you ... you are then able to ...
> Click on ... if you ... /Clicking on ... enables you to ...
> Just hit the ... when ...
> You can choose to ... or ...
> There's even a ...
> What makes it better than similar sites is that it's (far) more ...

**6** Find words and phrases in the review which mean the same as a–g. There may be more than one answer. Why is each equivalent word or phrase in the model more suitable?

a I had difficulty thinking of an idea
b use your computer mouse to select
c I will now tell you how to use the website
d how much you have to pay
e a lot of men would probably like the wrapping service
f (it's) easier for people to use
g it's not surprising that it is so popular

**7** Make a plan of four paragraphs for a review of a website you have used. Base your plan on the following:

- Introduction
- How the site works
- Why the site is better than other similar sites/extra features of the site
- Conclusion

**8** Using the paragraph plan you prepared in 7, write your answer to the exam task. Use the how to do it box to help you.

**how** to do it

- Read the task carefully.
- Make notes for all the points you must include.
- Make sure the information you give is clear and concise.
- Engage your readers by using an interesting range of vocabulary and structures.

# Review

**1** Rewrite the second sentence in a–c keeping the meaning the same. Use three to six words including the word given.

a No one believed the accused's explanations about the illegal merchandise during the trial.
**RING**
The accused's explanations about the illegal merchandise ............. to anyone during the trial.

b Tom deceived Sally when he married her, as he already had a wife.
**PRETENCES**
Tom married Sally ............. , as he already had a wife.

c Buying poorer quality products at lower prices is not financially sensible.
**FALSE**
It is a ............. poorer quality products at lower prices.

**2** Circle the verb which matches the definitions in a–d.

a plod   limp   trip   = walk slowly with heavy steps
b totter   stagger   creep   = walk in an unsteady way
c hobble   stumble   crawl   = almost fall over
d glance   gaze   peep   = look steadily at

**3** Match one of the words you did not circle in 2 to definitions a–e.

a look quickly then look away
b walk with difficulty when one leg hurts
c move on your hands and knees
d walk with difficulty when both legs hurt
e walk silently and slowly

**4** Circle the correct preposition in each sentence.

a I remember being very self-conscious **with/about/of** my appearance when I was young.
b If you want to succeed in life, you need to be committed **for/with/to** everything you do.
c What's the matter with Terry? He seems to be lost **in/for/to** a world of his own nowadays.
d Despite being understandably apprehensive **for/of/about** her interview, it went off very well.
e The team were excited **with/for/at** the thought of meeting their opponents in the Cup Final.

**5** Complete the comments in sentences 1–6 using a word or phrase with *right* or *left*.

1 A I don't suppose you know what's showing at the cinema this weekend?
B I've no idea but I can find out ............. .

2 A I can't believe Tim hasn't passed his driving test yet.
B It's no surprise to me – he doesn't know his ............. from his ............. !

3 A I'm sorry to hear that you were held responsible for the accident.
B It was extremely unfair. I was definitely in ............. and I intend to make an official complaint.

4 A What makes you think that Richard will never make a decent footballer?
B Well, for a start, he's got two ............. .

5 A I'm starving. I don't suppose there's anything in the fridge to eat?
B Only some ............. from last night's supper, I'm afraid.

6 A How come you're working this Saturday?
B ............. I shouldn't have to work weekends at all, but I'm covering for a colleague.

**6** Use the following link words to complete this text about the popularity of soap operas.

although   after   on the other hand
despite   while   so that   as well as

**1** ............ the fact that soaps come in for a lot of criticism, they remain one of the most popular forms of entertainment, **2** ............ being money-spinners for their producers. **3** ............ , this does not necessarily mean that they are of a consistently high quality. Perhaps it is not quality but suspense that attracts so many ardent viewers. **4** ............ being left on tenterhooks at the end of each episode, fans have no option but to tune in again next time **5** ............ they can learn the characters' fate. In addition, **6** ............ many people sneer at soaps, it is surprising how they enthusiastically participate in conversations based on their characters and storylines. The secret of their success may lie in the fact that fans identify with the characters **7** ............ , at the same time, remaining detached from their trials and tribulations.

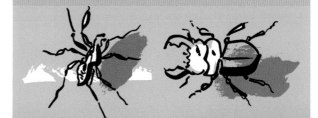

# Traces of the past

## Lead in

**1** Look at the pictures and discuss these questions.

a Which periods of history are represented here?

b What do you know about each one? Think about the following aspects:

- art
- buildings
- medicine
- knowledge of the world
- technology
- writing and learning

c Where do we get our information about these different periods of history?

d What effect did these or other periods of history have on future generations? Use the phrases below to help you.

… led to …
… resulted in …
… was (directly) responsible for …
… had an effect on …
… was the source of …

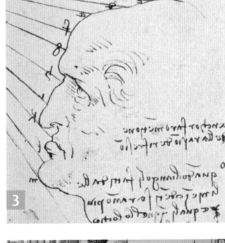

# Reading Part 6 Cross-text multiple matching

**1** Quickly read the book reviews opposite. Which two are the most positive?

**2** Read the texts again. For questions 1–4, choose from the reviews A–D. The reviews may be chosen more than once. The tip box will help you.

Which reviewer, A, B, C or D:

| | |
|---|---|
| has a different view from the others on Bryson's tone and style? | 1 .... |
| shares reviewer D's opinion on the subjective nature of Bryson's book? | 2 .... |
| takes a similar view to A on how well Bryson achieves his aims in this book? | 3 .... |
| has a different view from the others on the factual accuracy of Bryson's writing? | 4 .... |

**3** Discuss the meaning of these phrases from the texts.

a lose something in a sea of detail (l.9)
b steer a middle course (l.10)
c a whirlwind tour (l.14)
d duck a challenge (l.43)
e the devil is in the detail (l.58)
f waste too much ink on (doing) something (l.63)
g write something off (l.70)

**tip**

Use the question to decide 'how' to read, e.g. if the question mentions an opinion or point from one particular text (q.2 and q.4) highlight the relevant section in that text and then look for similar content in the other texts.

# A Short History of Nearly Everything

Four reviewers comment on best-selling author Bill Bryson's book called *A Short History of Nearly Everything*.

**A** Bryson is not a scientist. However, his curiosity led him to ask some good questions, such as: 'How can scientists know how and when the universe started and what it
5 was like when it did?' But could Bryson really write a 'short' history of 'nearly everything'? No way, I thought. The world's too big and it's been around far too long for any such project to work. Either the author would lose us in a sea of detail,
10 or he'd oversimplify. Steering a middle course between these extremes seemed too much to hope for. Yet the more I read, the more I was convinced that Bryson had succeeded in his aim.

**B** Bryson gives us a whirlwind tour of the
15 history of the universe. With a keen instinct for the outlandish aspects of scientific discovery, he keeps the reader entertained. Bryson describes what scientists think happened back in time, but with little explanation of how
20 these events came about. For example, how did the universe originate? The best Bryson can offer is – the fact that the universe did originate shows us that it could originate. He has clearly formed the impression that human
25 beings are the result of an accidental, natural process of evolution, rather than an act of God. This fascinating book opens up science to the ordinary reader. If this makes scientists more accountable to the public, it could help discredit
30 theories whose persistence is due to bias in the minds of scientists. It is unfortunate that Bryson's philosophical views coincide with those of scientists promoting a naturalistic view of origins, otherwise he might have been more
35 critical of evolutionary theories and given space to sceptical scientists.

**C** In this book, Bryson takes us by the hand and leads us on an amazing scientific journey through space and time. Along the way, he uncovers the most
40 amazing facts about our world and the rules that govern it. Explaining the formation of the universe to readers with scant knowledge of particle physics might seem daunting but Bryson is not a man to duck a challenge. A non-scientist himself, he works at making complex
45 areas of science accessible to all. But Bryson's focus is not only what scientists have discovered, but on how and why these discoveries have been made. This leads him to investigate the lives of some true eccentrics – such as the 19th-century naturalist who served
50 spiders and moles to his guests as part of his research. These humorous interludes, along with Bryson's witty interjections, act as a perfect counter to the seriousness of the science he is describing and lift what could be a dry scientific account into a lively, entertaining tale.

**D** The best thing about Bryson's book is that it
55 reveals how little we know about our world and its history. But as usual with such ambitious undertakings, the devil is in the detail. Let me just say that the author does not always present the finer
60 points correctly. What a pity no trained scientist was hired to edit this book – after all, the author interviewed several scientists who would have been suitable. Bryson wastes far too much ink on relating strange facts (like one geologist's ambition to eat
65 an example of every animal in existence!). These anecdotes might enliven the narration, but after a while you get tired of them and start asking yourself what this book is really about. It is all too easy to see which theories appeal to the author and which are
70 written off by him as wacky. I suggest that if you are someone who deals with science, you should be a tad more objective yourself.

# Vocabulary GR p182–183

## Phrasal verbs with *off* and *in*

**1** For each pair of sentences in 1–4, use the same verb, in the correct form, to make a phrasal verb with two different meanings.

1 a Even though we ............ off relatively early, we still arrived extremely late.

 b When ............ off fireworks, stand at arm's length and make sure children are supervised.

2 a After ten minutes trying to solve the puzzle, I ............ in and looked at the solution.

 b The authorities refused to ............ in to the ransom demand.

3 a Never ............ off until tomorrow what you can do today.

 b Although he's really good-looking, I was completely ............ off by his bad reputation.

4 a It's almost impossible for us to ............ in statistics to do with our solar system.

 b His lies were so convincing that even his closest friends were ............ in.

**2** Match meanings a–h with the phrasal verbs as they are used in the eight sentences in 1.

| | | | |
|---|---|---|---|
| a | light | f | make you dislike |
| b | deceive | g | agree to something you do not want |
| c | postpone | | |
| d | understand | h | admit defeat |
| e | begin a journey | | |

**3** Use a dictionary to look up the different meanings of the phrasal verbs in italics in a–d. Then complete the sentences appropriately.

a Our week in the mountains was ruined when ............ *set in*.

b You wear a protective mask for this experiment as the chemicals used *give off* ............ .

c Although I specifically asked the hairdresser to *take off* just a few centimetres ............ .

d Whenever a member of staff leaves the firm, we all *put in* some money ............ .

# Grammar

## Reduced clauses GR p177

**1** Match the reduced clauses in italics in a–f with functions 1–6.

a *Grown in the right conditions*, the plants will flower all summer.

b *Parking his car in a side road*, he strolled towards the town centre.

c A massive earthquake has hit parts of India, *leaving thousands of people homeless*.

d A group of archaeologists *exploring the island* have discovered the skeleton of a new species of dinosaur.

e *Not having a mobile phone*, we were unable to ring our hosts and warn them we would be late.

f *Having finished his medical training*, my brother decided to work in Africa for a charity.

1 emphasising that one thing happened after another had finished
2 replacing a relative clause
3 showing that two actions happened within a short time period of each other
4 expressing a condition
5 expressing a reason
6 expressing a result

**2** Rewrite the information in a–f using reduced clauses.

a The Shard, which was completed in 2012, is the tallest building in the European Union.

b If they are washed with care, woollen sweaters will retain their shape.

c They hoped to confirm the suspect's part in the robbery so the detectives arranged an identity parade.

d The winner crosses the finishing line and he raises his hands in triumph as he does so!

e The explorer will undergo final medical checks and then he will set out on his polar expedition.

f Because he didn't realise how dangerous the snake was, the toddler reached out towards it.

**3** Give the present participles of verbs a–i.

| | | | | | |
|---|---|---|---|---|---|
| a | make | d | offer | g | travel |
| b | build | e | prefer | h | argue |
| c | stop | f | lie | i | occur |

**4** Give the past participle of these irregular verbs.

a bite      h leave
b bring     i meet
c catch     j prove
d drive      k sell
e fight      l set
f fly        m speak
g hide      n wake

**5** Join the two sentences in a–e using the words in brackets and participles.

Example

*I lost my purse. I was travelling to work. (while)*
*I lost my purse while travelling to work.*

a A group of cavers have spent ten hours trapped underground. They have finally been rescued. (after)
b I admit that driving at excessive speeds is dangerous. I don't accept we should have speed cameras everywhere. (while)
c He wasn't a local. He didn't know the area. (not)
d Civilians heard that a peace treaty had been signed. They began celebrating in the streets. (on)
e The judge didn't agree with the defendant's actions. He said he did sympathise with her situation. (although)

**6** Say what is wrong with sentences a–f and suggest how they could be rewritten.

a Roaring ferociously, the girl fled from the lion.
b Two of the terrorists shooting the President have been caught.
c The man inventing the digital camera has won an award.
d Not wanting to spoil the fun, the wedding celebrations went on well into the night.
e Planted with care, novice gardeners will be amazed how easy it is to grow things.
f Passing his driving test, Gary became rather big-headed.

**7** Rewrite the text below, replacing the underlined information with reduced clauses, and making any other necessary changes.

After he had spent three days trapped on an ice floe, explorer Ben Miller was finally rescued last night. Because he wanted to become the first man to walk solo from Canada to the North Pole, he had set out last April, alone and unaided. He had no way of transporting possessions so he took very little with him apart from camping equipment, a mobile phone and a shovel. He made good progress at first but he then experienced a number of setbacks. The longest day of the year was approaching, which meant that the temperature was starting to rise. The ice gradually started to melt around him with the result that he was prevented from going forward or back. Ben, who was now feeling desperate, searched around him. Because he didn't have any advanced technical equipment, he had to rely on common sense. He took out his shovel and he dug a runway in the ice. He then took a photo of the runway and sent it to a rescue team via his mobile phone. The pilot succeeded in landing on the narrow strip of ice, with the result that he saved Ben from almost certain death.

# Listening Part 2 Sentence completion

1 Read the exam task in 2 and think of words or phrases with similar meanings to the underlined words.

2 🎧 Listen to a local historian talking about shipwrecks in a place in south-west England called The Lizard and complete sentences 1–8. The tip box will help you.

The Lizard is an <u>attractive</u> place for divers <u>due to</u> the many shipwrecks on the 1 .................... .

Divers may <u>come across</u> 2 ................... in the treasure.

*HMS Anson* <u>left</u> the port of Falmouth on 24th December, 3 ................... .

The Captain had to <u>look for protection</u> from a full 4 ................... .

Sailors on the *Anson* thought the land they could see <u>in front of them</u> was the 5 ................... into Falmouth.

The *Anson*'s <u>damaged</u> mast provided a type of 6 ................... between the boat and the beach.

<u>Despite</u> being so close to 7 ................... , many of the <u>men on board</u> were lost.

Divers should only visit the wreck when the 8 ................... are <u>suitable</u>.

> **tip**
> Remember that answers are no longer than three words in the exam.

# HMS ANSON

# Speaking Part 2

1 Look at the sets of photos opposite and discuss what you might be asked to talk about in the exam.

2 Match these phrases with the photos.

a traditional crafts or skills
b personal reminders of the past
c an archaeological dig/excavation
d period costume
e documentary evidence
f early civilisations
g film footage
h medieval manuscripts
i battle re-enactment

3 How might these factors influence your choice of photos?

a knowledge of the topic
b interest in the topic
c ability to interpret the context
d ability to think quickly of something to say about the photo

4 Bearing in mind your conclusions in 3, in pairs, each choose two photos from either set, A or B. Then allow each person one minute to do this exam task.

> • What can these things teach us about the past?
> • How successfully might they bring the past to life?

5 Now, in turns, comment on your partner's set of photographs. Allow each person 30 seconds to answer the question below.

> • Which of these ways of learning about the past do you think gives the most accurate information?

> **tip**
> When commenting on your partner's photographs you can choose any of the three photos to talk about. However, selecting the photo your partner did not choose may give you the opportunity to say something different.

Set A

Set B

# Use of English Part 3 Word formation

**1** Do you think it's worth studying history at school? Why/Why not?

**2** Read the text below quickly, ignoring the gaps, to find out who is being described and why he is described as 'The Father of History'.

**3** Read the text again carefully and choose the correct answer from each pair below for gaps 1–4. The tip box will help you.

1 passionately/passionate
2 extendable/extensively
3 skilful/unskilled
4 unforgettable/forgetful

**4** Complete the rest of the text with words formed from 5–8 below.

**tip**

Check your answer is grammatically correct <u>and</u> has the correct sense.

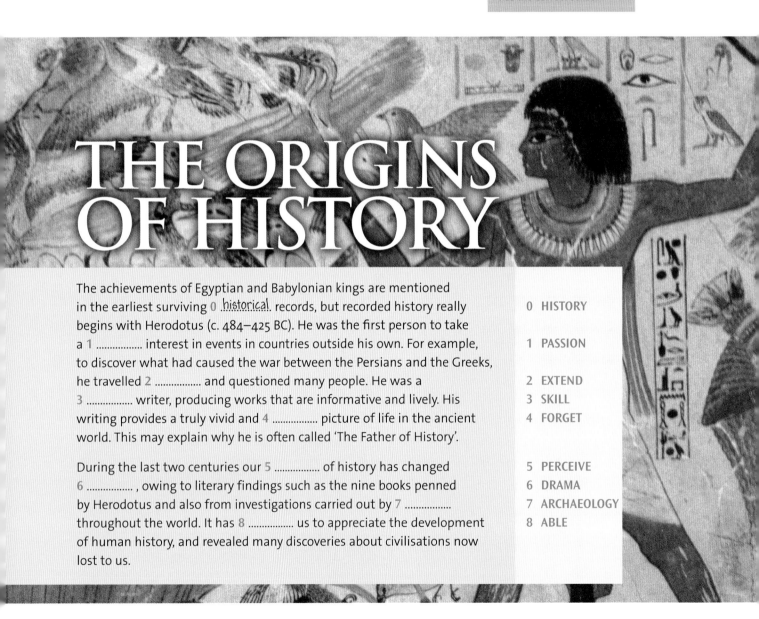

# THE ORIGINS OF HISTORY

The achievements of Egyptian and Babylonian kings are mentioned in the earliest surviving **0** <u>historical</u> records, but recorded history really begins with Herodotus (c. 484–425 BC). He was the first person to take a **1** ................ interest in events in countries outside his own. For example, to discover what had caused the war between the Persians and the Greeks, he travelled **2** ................ and questioned many people. He was a **3** ................ writer, producing works that are informative and lively. His writing provides a truly vivid and **4** ................ picture of life in the ancient world. This may explain why he is often called 'The Father of History'.

During the last two centuries our **5** ................ of history has changed **6** ................ , owing to literary findings such as the nine books penned by Herodotus and also from investigations carried out by **7** ................ throughout the world. It has **8** ................ us to appreciate the development of human history, and revealed many discoveries about civilisations now lost to us.

| | |
|---|---|
| **0** | HISTORY |
| **1** | PASSION |
| **2** | EXTEND |
| **3** | SKILL |
| **4** | FORGET |
| **5** | PERCEIVE |
| **6** | DRAMA |
| **7** | ARCHAEOLOGY |
| **8** | ABLE |

# Vocabulary Word formation (2)

**1** Make nouns from adjectives a–h using these suffixes. More than one answer is possible.

> -ion   -ence   -acy   -ance
> -ly   -ility   -ness

a evident
b adaptable
c significant
d ambitious
e aware
f accurate
g democratic
h independent

**2** Choose the correct prefix to make adjectives a–k negative in meaning. Use a dictionary to check your answers.

> dis-   im-   in-
> il-   ir-   un-

a practical
b decisive
c capable
d relevant
e suitable
f logical
g moral
h regular
i legal
j agreeable
k honest

**3** Use your answers from 2 to complete the rules below.

We generally use:

- ......... before the letters *p* and *m*.
- ......... before the letter *l*.
- ......... before the letter *r*.

**4** Look at the prefix *un* in a dictionary to find examples of adjectives that do not follow these rules.

**5** Match the prefixes with their meanings a–g.

> co-   inter-   over-   mis-
> trans-   un-   under-

a across, beyond
b the opposite of
c together with
d bad or wrong
e between
f too much
g not enough

**6** Complete the words in a–g with prefixes from 5. Then use a dictionary to find two more words with these prefixes.

a The .........atlantic flight takes seven hours.
b This fish is .........cooked. I'll just pop it back in the oven for a couple of minutes.
c I'm afraid that you have .........understood what I was trying to say.
d Unfortunately, we lost the final of the .........departmental football tournament.
e Could you give me a hand? I can't .........lock the door to the safe.
f This job is easy. I think you've .........stated the problems involved.
g It's now known that humans never .........existed with dinosaurs.

# Writing Part 2 A proposal WG p164

**1** **Look at the pictures and answer questions a–d.**

a Which country's history is shown in these pictures?

b What do you know about these events?

c What else do you know about the country's history?

d Which two periods in *your* country's history do you think people find most interesting? Why?

**2** **Read the exam task below and highlight the key words you need to keep in mind while writing your proposal.**

> You are chair of your local history society and have received this memo from a government representative.
>
> We have been invited to make a presentation on the history of our country to groups of older teenagers who are here on a cultural exchange. Please write me a proposal suggesting which two periods in our history we should focus on, and how we can best display them.
>
> Write your **proposal** in **220–260** words in an appropriate style.

**3** **Decide which of the phrases a–j are suitable for the proposal, and say what is wrong with those you reject.**

a I am writing this letter to …

b The aim/purpose of this proposal is to …

c I'd advise you to …

d I propose that we … because …

e How about we … ?

f You must …

g I suggest we … . This would mean we could …

h I think we should … because this would allow us to …

i Let's just recap then.

j In conclusion/To sum up, I believe we should …

**4** **Read the model proposal opposite and answer the questions below. Justify your answers with examples from the text.**

a Has the writer used an appropriate register?

b Is the text well organised? Can you see any topic sentences?

c Could the format be improved? If so, how?

d Is the writer's range of vocabulary, including set phrases, sufficiently complex?

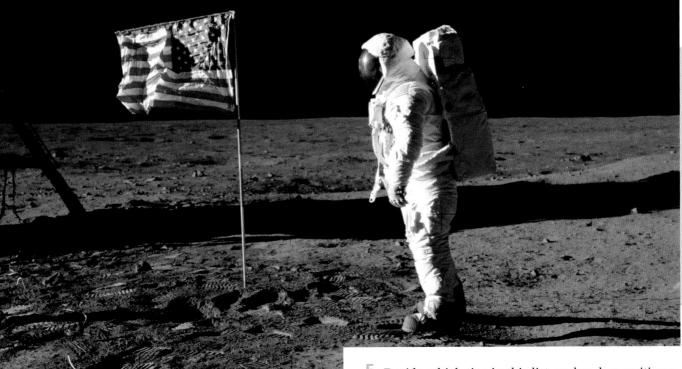

**Proposal for World History Day**

The aim of this proposal is to suggest which periods or events from our country's history would interest and excite our young audience and how we should present them.

In order to illustrate how exciting our history is, I believe we need to make our display dramatic and colourful. For that reason, I suggest that one of the periods we focus on should be early America, when the first settlers arrived and had contact with native Americans. Our people could dress in the costumes of the day and re-enact a scene from that period. Having a representative from the native American community would be ideal, if that could be arranged.

We need to inform our young audience about our country's recent history too, so I propose that our second display focus on the 20th century. Visitors would be fascinated to know more about the work involved in putting men on the moon, and about our plans to travel to Mars. We could recreate a model of part of the spacecraft our astronauts travelled in, show the young people the spacesuits the astronauts wore, and perhaps even arrange an on-the-spot interview with someone involved in that event.

This is an exciting opportunity to paint a vivid picture of the fascinating events that formed our country and helped to make it great. We need to make our history come alive for our visitors. I hope you will find that the suggestions made in my proposal provide an effective way to accomplish this aim.

5 Decide which tips in this list apply when writing a proposal.

a Be persuasive and 'sell' your ideas.
b Be clear and precise.
c Organise your text into sections or paragraphs.
d Always use section headings.
e Give reasons for your suggestions.
f You do not need to include an introduction or conclusion.

6 Read the exam task in 2 again. Then write your own proposal, using ideas you discussed in exercise 1d and the plan below. The how to do it box will help you.

**Plan:**

Introduction – State the reason for the proposal and summarise what you propose. Make it sound exciting!

Body – Explain what you are proposing and why it will be effective. (You will need two paragraphs for this.)

Conclusion – Briefly summarise the main point again, and recommend your proposal to the reader.

**how to do it**

■ Read the task, highlight points you must include and then make a quick plan.

■ Check who will read the proposal and use the correct register.

■ Use the correct format; most proposals will be divided into sections, with headings.

■ Make your proposal interesting and persuade your reader to do what you want!

# Review

## 1
Complete sentences a–e with the correct prepositions.

a The Industrial Revolution resulted .......... dramatic changes to the structure of society.

b It is essential for journalists to check the source .......... all the information they receive.

c Overeating can lead .......... health problems in later life.

d Within days of taking the antibiotics, there was a dramatic effect .......... her condition.

e The authorities are keen to discover who was responsible .......... the destruction of the ancient monument.

## 2
Complete sentences a–h with phrasal verbs with *in* or *off* in the correct form.

a There have been a number of cases of bogus doctors .......... in staff and patients and performing medical examinations.

b None of the lights are working. Has someone .......... off the electricity?

c At times we felt like .......... in but we carried on and managed to achieve our goal.

d This year's festival will end with a display of fireworks to be .......... off at midnight.

e The training centre isn't difficult to find – .......... off the road at the lights and follow the signs.

f Please don't be .......... off by Bella's rather distant manner. She's very friendly once you get to know her.

g What time will we have to .......... off to arrive in time for the ceremony?

h It looks as if we shall have to .......... off our decision to relocate until we have found more suitable premises.

## 3
Find adjective forms of a–f which match definitions 1–6.

**Example**

*a4 attractive*

| | | |
|---|---|---|
| a~~attract~~ | 1 | corresponding |
| b signify | 2 | sensational |
| c compare | 3 | widespread |
| d extend | 4 | ~~pleasant to look at~~ |
| e perceive | 5 | important |
| f drama | 6 | observant |

## 4
For a–i, add a suitable negative prefix to make adjectives with the opposite meaning.

a relevant    d moral    g suitable
b legal    e capable    h logical
c honest    f decisive    i patient

## 5
For a–e, use the correct word in brackets in its noun form to complete the sentence.

a There was insufficient (accurate/evident) to convict the accused of the crime.

b Our tennis coach says we must improve the (adaptable/accurate) of our strokes.

c (Ambitious/Significant) is a quality politicians must have to achieve success.

d Good drivers have an acute (aware/significant) of impending hazards.

e The newly formed country gained its (independent/ambitious) only last year.

## 6
Replace the words in brackets with a suitable prefix.

a Could you (an opposite action) ..........fasten this knot in my shoelace?

b (with) .......operation between several countries meant that emergency aid arrived quickly.

c The (across) ..........continental express is a luxurious way to travel.

d If there's one thing I can't stand it's (too much) ..........cooked vegetables.

e Police have been (wrongly) ..........informed about the whereabouts of the suspect.

f London's Heathrow is one of the world's busiest (between) ..........national airports.

g I think we have (too little) ..........estimated the strength of the opposition.

## 7
Complete this review using the words in brackets in the correct form.

A free open-air concert on an international level, 'Live 8' was an **1** (inspire) .......... event. Its aim was to help counteract the **2** (devastate) .......... and **3** (catastrophe) .......... effects of world poverty, and to make a **4** (signify) .......... impact on its eradication. Some critics raised doubts about whether financial aid is actually **5** (benefit) .......... in the drive to stamp out poverty, claiming that it can often have **6** (foresee) .......... consequences. This made little difference to the millions who tuned in to watch the concert and to pledge their money.

# The big issues

## Lead in

**1** Discuss why the issues below should concern us in the 21st century. Which are the three most burning issues? Why?

- privacy
- crime and terrorism
- the Internet
- globalisation
- warfare
- the environment
- an ageing society

**2** For each group (A, B and C), decide which word is missing from the three sentences, then write it as a heading.

**A** ..............................

1 'Governments should give as much foreign .......... as possible to poorer countries.'

2 'In certain circumstances, emergency .......... in the form of money should be sent immediately.'

3 'The most successful long-term .......... programmes encourage self-help.'

**B** ..............................

1 'A lot of people only appreciate school after they leave full-time .......... .'

2 'State .......... should be more academically based.'

3 'A practical .......... makes it easier to change jobs later in life.'

**C** ..............................

1 'Few people could have predicted the huge impact of information .......... .'

2 'No matter how advanced .......... becomes, machines will never be able to think like humans.'

3 'It's a waste of time for humans to do tasks that modern .......... can do.'

**3** 🎧 Listen to three people talking about the issues in 2. Check your answers for A–C and tick the statement for the issues in each one that best reflects the speaker's point of view.

**4** Do you share any of the views in 2? Why/Why not?

# Reading  Part 5  Multiple choice

**1** What films or books do you know that feature robots? What relationship do these robots have with humans?

**2** Match words a–e from the text opposite with meanings 1–5.

   a gadget             d automation
   b artificial intelligence    e robotics
   c malfunction

   1 the science of designing and operating robots
   2 a small mechanical or electronic device
   3 the use of computers for human functions such as learning and making decisions
   4 the use of machines, instead of people, to do work
   5 a fault in the way something works

**3** Read the text and discuss questions a–e.

> **tip**
> Before reading the options, see if you can answer the questions or complete the statements in your own words.

   a In paragraph 1, what does the robotic engineer Daniel Wilson conclude is the real truth about robots?
   b How do the developers of Robot Land differ in their aims from other theme-park experts?
   c How did the idea of robots as 'bad guys' begin?
   d Why do reports of robot 'attacks' annoy the writer of this article?
   e What do many experts think about the dangers posed by nanotechnology?

**4** Read the text again and choose the best option (A, B, C or D) to complete 1–6.

   1 In the first paragraph, Daniel Wilson
      A exaggerates the dangers of robots.
      B states that we are menaced by robots.
      C doubts the threat presented by robots.
      D claims we are too dependent on robots.

   2 The developers of Robot Land hope that their theme park will
      A have more scary robots than similar destinations.
      B change people's attitude towards robots.
      C encourage more people to study robots.
      D make people aware of the dangers of using robots.

**3** It seems that theme-park experts
   A are concerned about a loss of control if people depend on robots.
   B have more confidence in ride operators than in computers.
   C believe conventional roller coasters are the safest.
   D think using artificial intelligence will be good for business.

**4** According to the text, people have come to think of robots as evil because
   A their fictional representations were originally depicted this way.
   B the designers of the first robots spread this idea.
   C movie directors continue to give this impression.
   D reality shows they are the same as in the movies.

**5** The writer believes that reports such as those of a robot attack in Sweden
   A are deliberately untruthful.
   B serve as a serious warning.
   C distort the real problem.
   D are intended as a joke.

**6** According to the text, what are experts afraid of when considering nanotechnology?
   A Robots could use it inappropriately.
   B It could make robots harder to control.
   C The rate of terrorism might be increased as a result of it.
   D It could be more dangerous than robots.

**5** Discuss these questions.

   a What sort of jobs do you think we should use robots for? Think about:
      • safety
      • health
      • human limitations

   b Are there any jobs you think we should not use robots for? Why?

# mean machines?

**If** popular culture has taught us anything, it is that some day mankind must face and destroy the growing robot menace.' Author and robotic engineer Daniel H. Wilson's description of *How to Survive a Robot Uprising* seems like it is straight out of a robot disaster movie. 'The problem with gadgets or tools – which is what robots are – is that we become dependent on them,' says Wilson. 'That's scary, so we contemplate the disaster scenarios that could come from being over-dependent on them. It's true – our tools could fail some day – but it doesn't mean they're malevolent or immoral.'

While he writes about it, Wilson does not really believe the end of the world is coming. And developers are trying to turn the tide of robotic prejudice with a project in South Korea called Robot Land – a theme park and research institute not only using robots for ride technology, but as waiters and ticket inspectors too. Its Chief Executive Officer hopes the rides act as a Trojan horse for greater understanding about robot technology. But theme-park experts see the robots themselves as a source of the horror that thrill-seekers are looking for. 'If you take a normal industrial robotic arm – it can provide so many more movements and sensations than conventional roller coasters,' says thrill engineer Brendan Walker. 'Then you start thinking about controlling our experience through artificial intelligence … Maybe I'm going to trust a ride operator to give me a good time, but can I trust a computer? There is this idea of horror that is creeping onto rides – darker themes of loss and power and control.'

Theme parks can be scary places when robots get involved. The classic film *Westworld* depicts a fictional amusement park where, after a safety malfunction, the robots go on a killing spree. Yet in reality, statistics show that as technology improves there is a trend towards increased safety in these places. Similarly, automated public transport systems are believed to be more reliable than those in human control, and robot-assisted surgery is more precise and results in fewer complications. And while automation as an idea is often worrying, experts think the reality is nothing like as dramatic.

But where does the idea of robots being evil come from? 'Robots were pop culture icons before they even existed,' says Wilson. 'They were space creatures and monsters. When robots really started existing, they already had this whole image set up not based on reality. It would be like if someone found a living mummy and he was actually a really nice guy but we'd only ever seen evil mummies in fiction. That's exactly what happened – a movie monster became real.'

When announcing funding for a robotics initiative, the President of the United States continued this type of rhetoric. 'One of my responsibilities as commander-in-chief is to keep an eye on robots,' he said. 'And I'm pleased to report that the robots you manufacture here seem peaceful – at least for now.' But despite the president's joke, some of the media already believe that the fight has started. Recent reports talked of a robot 'attack' on a worker in a factory in Sweden. Even if these references to an attack rather than a malfunction are meant in jest, this – according to some – only makes the problem worse. 'We're so enamoured with the robot-attack storyline that it can skew the way real robot-safety issues are discussed,' says one journalist. But with robots becoming increasingly advanced, is there going to come a time when an error could become a malicious attack?

'Robots are just a bunch of metal and silicon,' says one professor. 'They have no agenda. If you are scared, then you are scared of the people building them.' So what do engineers think we should be afraid of? Nanotechnology is the science of changing and developing new materials on a molecular and atomic level. The Centre for Responsible Nanotechnology suggests that with these new developments comes 'severe dangers' if they are used inappropriately. Its theory goes that 'the small size, portability and rapid potential of nano-built weaponry will make it difficult to control and hard to keep out of the hands of terrorists.' And this is a view that is shared by at least one artificial intelligence expert. 'I'm more afraid of things that can be manipulated that I cannot see,' he says. 'With robots … if it malfunctions, you can unplug it and shut it down. If you have billions of nano-particles, there is no way you can do the same thing.'

# Vocabulary

## Big issues

**1** Discuss the answers to questions a–g.

a If a city is *overpopulated*, is it too big or are there too many people living there?

b What is the difference between a *famine* and a *drought*?

c What is the difference between a *natural resource* and a *financial resource*?

d Which one can erupt: a *tornado* or a *volcano*?

e Can soil erosion cause a *flood* or a *landslide*?

f Which is more serious: an *earth tremor* or an *earthquake*?

g Are epidemics caused by *contagious* or *controversial* diseases?

**2** Match the words from each pair in 1–5 with definition a or b. Use a dictionary to check your answers.

1 vital/trivial
  a necessary or essential
  b not important or serious

2 controversial/critical
  a serious, uncertain and possibly dangerous
  b causing discussion and disagreement

3 momentous/momentary
  a lasting for a very short time
  b very important or serious

4 principal/principle
  a most important; main
  b moral rule or strong belief

5 antisocial/unsocial
  a harmful or annoying to others
  b outside normal working hours

# Grammar

## Conditionals GR p178–180

**1** Match sentences a–d with descriptions 1–4.

a If a virus attacks a computer, it prevents it from working properly. (zero conditional)

b If their best side plays, Manchester United will probably come out on top. (first conditional)

c If I had enough money, I would buy a new digital camera. (second conditional)

d If you had told me that you needed some advice, I would have helped out. (third conditional)

1 a hypothetical statement about the past
2 a condition which is improbable/impossible in the present
3 a statement of general fact
4 a condition that is possible/probable in the future

**2** Underline the correct verb forms in a–f.

a *I'll give up/I'd give up* my job and go backpacking round the world if *I'd have/I had* a bit more courage.

b Nobody *would find/would have found* the climbers if they *hadn't managed/didn't manage* to attract the mountain rescue team.

c If you *stayed out/stay out* all night without telling your mum, she *probably kills/will probably kill* you.

d If *I realised/I'd realised* the first prize in the raffle was a sports car, I *would have bought/would buy* a lot more tickets!

e If *you leave/you'll leave* metal objects in the rain, they generally *rust/will rust*.

f She *wouldn't crash/wouldn't have crashed* the car if a dog *hadn't run out/wouldn't have run out* in front of her car.

**3** Explain the differences in meaning or function between these pairs of sentences.

1a If *you're finding* it difficult to do your homework, I'll give you a hand.
 b If you *find* it difficult to do your homework, I'll give you a hand.

2a Those swimmers *could have drowned* if passers-by hadn't raised the alarm.
 b Those swimmers *would have drowned* if passers-by hadn't raised the alarm.

3a Please let me know if *you need* any advice.

b Please let me know if *you should need* any advice.

4a If *you stayed* in this country a bit longer, we could spend more time together.

b If you *were staying* in this country a bit longer, we could spend more time together.

5a If we *offered* you the position, would you accept?

b If we *were to offer* you the position, would you accept?

**4** Complete a–f by putting the verbs in brackets into the correct form.

a If the bridegroom's friends .......... (not/tie) him to a lamp post on his stag night, he .......... (not/end up) in a police station.

b If you .......... (look) for something to do, .......... (go) and dig the garden!

c As a rule, coloured clothes .......... (fade) if you .......... (leave) them in the sun for too long.

d If you .......... (want) to get rid of your old football kit, .......... (try) selling it on the Internet.

e We .......... (arrive) sooner if the workmen .......... (not/dig) up the road on our way here.

f .......... (be) the manager to discover what has been going on in the office, he .......... (be) horrified.

**5** Complete sentences a–f with your own ideas.

a If I could spend a romantic evening with anyone I chose, …

b I will be really disappointed if …

c If I could change one thing about my life, …

d It would have been unbelievable if …

e I would feel absolutely ecstatic if …

f If I could change places for one day with anyone in the world, …

**6** Underline the words used instead of *if* in these conditional sentences, then correct any mistakes you find.

a They would have ended up divorced unless the intervention of their friends.

b I'll marry you provided you don't expect me to get on with your mother!

c As long as you won the lottery, how would you spend the money?

d Jim will be allowed out of prison supposing he reports to the police station twice a week.

e Tonight's open-air concert will be cancelled provided the weather improves.

f I'll be raring to go tomorrow as long as I get a good night's sleep tonight.

g There's no hope of our team winning the League unless we start to play better.

**7** Complete gaps 1–12 in the paragraph below, using the verbs in brackets in the correct tense.

I was kicked out of school at the age of 16 because I was bone idle. If anyone .......... (1 tell) me then that I would end up making a living as a scriptwriter, I .......... (2 never/believe) them. I admit that writing is one of the few things I've ever been good at. At school, if one of my mates .......... (3 have) trouble writing up a project, I .......... (4 do) it for them – provided they .......... (5 pay) me enough, of course! But write for a living? That was never on the cards. After I left school, I drifted in and out of various jobs. I wanted to travel the world but I knew I .......... (6 not/get) very far unless I .......... (7 have) a few dollars under my belt. So how to earn it? A friend of mine came up with a brainwave. Why not try writing a TV screenplay? Supposing it .......... (8 be) good enough, it .......... (9 may/earn) me enough money to travel the world. I owe that friend a lot. If he .......... (10 not/urge) me on, I .......... (11 never/get) started as a writer. And instead of having homes in Paris, Brisbane and Los Angeles, I .......... (12 still/work) in a dead-end job in my hometown.

# Listening Part 3 Multiple choice

**1** Look at the advertisement below and discuss these questions.

a  Which countries might volunteers be needed in?
b  What resources might be lacking in places like these?
c  What kind of professional skills would be useful in developing countries?
d  Why would jobs like these be rewarding?

## Volunteer jobs

Each year, hundreds of people start rewarding jobs as volunteers in developing countries. These countries need you to:

- use your professional skills to train and advise colleagues.

- live and work within the local community.

- work creatively and adapt to new surroundings – often with few resources.

**2** 🎧 Listen twice to a radio interview with Tom Davies, who spent a year as a volunteer in Nepal, and choose the best answers for questions 1–6.

**tip**

Make sure <u>all</u> the information in the option you choose is correct, not just some of it.

1  Why did Tom go to live and work abroad?
   A  He was bored with his routine.
   B  He wanted to do something useful.
   C  He saw an advertisement in a newspaper he had bought.
   D  He wanted to take advantage of every opportunity in life.

2  How did he regard his experience abroad?
   A  He was worried about being away from home.
   B  He was apprehensive about what lay in store.
   C  He thought the time would pass all too quickly.
   D  He knew he would have very little time to appreciate his surroundings.

3  What does Tom say was the most important thing offered by the organisation?
   A  enough money to make ends meet
   B  paid travel and accommodation
   C  the opportunity to meet fellow volunteers
   D  help to readjust on his return home

4  What does Tom say about the snow leopards?
   A  Some hunting of the animals is allowed.
   B  Larger numbers breed away from inhabited areas.
   C  They are regarded as the most important animals in the Himalayas.
   D  They have become more domesticated.

5  How has the programme Tom and his colleague devised helped?
   A  Farmers can be compensated for lost animals.
   B  The government runs an insurance scheme for farmers.
   C  Farmers have the funds needed to buy more land.
   D  Local groups have formed to protect the snow leopard.

6  What does Tom say he cannot do at the moment?
   A  Give an example of a profitable local scheme.
   B  Prove that fewer snow leopards have been killed by hunters.
   C  Show that the number of snow leopards has increased.
   D  Promise that profits from his scheme will go back into the community.

**3** Would you be interested in doing voluntary work abroad? If so, where and doing what? If not, why not?

# Speaking Parts 3 and 4

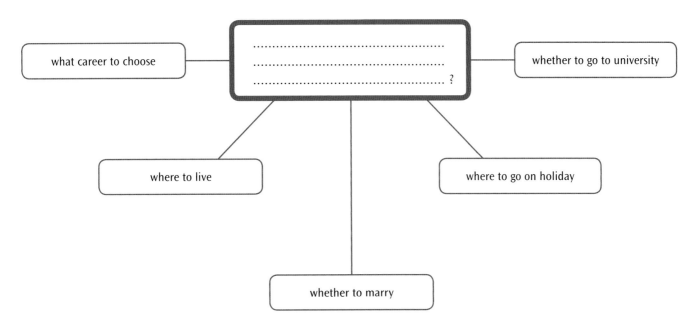

what career to choose

whether to go to university

............................................
............................................
.............................................. ?

where to live

where to go on holiday

whether to marry

**1** Look at the Part 3 task above. What initial question do you think the examiner might ask?

**2** Now listen to the examiner's question and write it in the centre of the Part 3 task. How different was it from the question you thought of?

**3** In pairs, do the Part 3 task. After two minutes, stop and compare your comments and ideas with those of another pair.

**how** to do it

Try to avoid dominating the conversation; take turns to speak with your partner.

If your partner gives you very few opportunities to speak, interrupt politely by saying, *I'm sorry to interrupt, but … .*

**4** Now listen to the instructions for the second part of the Part 3 task. What decision do you have to make?

**5** In pairs, do the task in 4. Allow yourselves one minute. Then compare your answers with the rest of the class.

**6** Read the Part 4 questions a–c below. Then listen to six students' answers and decide which of the questions they are answering. How appropriate are their answers?

a   What decisions in life do you consider the most difficult to make?
b   Some people believe that a lot of important decisions are out of our hands. What do you think?
c   What sorts of decisions in life are influenced by money?

Student 1: ..........    Student 4: ..........
Student 2: ..........    Student 5: ..........
Student 3: ..........    Student 6: ..........

**7** Discuss your own thoughts on the questions in 6. These words and phrases might help you.

| | |
|---|---|
| at stake | short term |
| in the long run | out of the blue |
| on the spur of the moment | out of our control |

On the whole I feel (that) …
It's generally the case (that) …
I should think (that) the hardest/most challenging thing is …
Would you agree with me on that?

# Use of English Part 1 Multiple-choice cloze

**1** How important in life are the four things below? Is there anything else that is more important?

- helping others
- enjoying yourself
- doing something to be remembered for
- passing on your genes by having children

**2** Read the text below quickly. Which word best describes the writer's tone?

a humorous          b philosophical          c pessimistic

**3** Read the text again and the tip box and decide which word (A, B, C or D) best fits each space 1–8.

> **Look for:**
> - slight differences in meaning between A–D
> - words that look similar but have different meanings
> - fixed phrases and expressions
> - dependent prepositions.

It is often **0** ....*C*.... that a look at our origins will **1** ............ us to the meaning of life. This certainly did not work for Dr Frankenstein's creation. Desperate to know his origins, he discovered the awful truth. Yet what he found did not **2** ............ life's meaning, it just upset him. Perhaps, instead of looking backwards, we should look forwards. What future goal would **3** ............ this life worth living? The problem with everything being a means to an end, or working towards goals, was identified by the philosopher Aristotle. His **4** ............ was that we do most things for the sake of something else, but unless at least one action is done for its own sake, there is no **5** ............ in doing any of them. What gives people's lives value might be **6** ............ the suffering of others or helping one's children. But life is uncertain and we are often thrown off **7** ............ . The basic answer is probably that there are more **8** ............ to live than die, and they are found in the living of life itself.

| 0 | A | granted | B | grasped | C | assumed | D | assigned |
|---|---|---------|---|---------|---|---------|---|----------|
| 1 | A | influence | B | persuade | C | show | D | lead |
| 2 | A | relate | B | exhibit | C | reveal | D | tell |
| 3 | A | make | B | judge | C | value | D | rule |
| 4 | A | argument | B | discussion | C | reason | D | debate |
| 5 | A | aspect | B | point | C | design | D | matter |
| 6 | A | relaxing | B | releasing | C | relieving | D | relenting |
| 7 | A | route | B | plan | C | way | D | course |
| 8 | A | purposes | B | excuses | C | ideas | D | reasons |

**4** Choose the best word to complete sentences 1–5. Try to give reasons for your choices.

1 There are many things which make life ..... living.
   A valuable          B worth          C precious          D esteemed

2 The idea that working towards goals was problematic apparently ..... with Aristotle.
   A unearthed          B devised          C originated          D revealed

3 I'm afraid we will never agree on this ..... .
   A debate          B matter          C way          D argument

4 There must be things in life which are valuable in their own ..... .
   A kind          B right          C reason          D design

5 Not everything can be a ..... to an end.
   A way          B means          C road          D path

# Vocabulary

## Expressions with *end*

**1** Use 1–8 to complete the expressions with *end* in a–h.

| 1 | in | 4 | up | 7 | meet |
|---|---|---|---|---|---|
| 2 | sight | 5 | means | 8 | at |
| 3 | loose | 6 | on | | |

a  I'm at a .......... end this week. Do you fancy doing something?

b  I've been overwhelmed with work for weeks and there's no end in .......... .

c  Helping my brother move house was just a .......... to an end; I want him to do an even bigger favour for me!

d  I'm struggling to make ends .......... what with three children to feed and all the bills to pay.

e  I got on the wrong train last night and ended .......... in the middle of nowhere!

f  The best thrillers have an unexpected twist right .......... the end.

g  My mum wasn't keen on lending me her car, but .......... the end she gave in.

h  We can make more space in the classroom by putting the tables .......... end and leaning them against the wall.

**2** Use a dictionary to check any unknown expressions in 1. Which word in the dictionary did you find expressions a–c under?

> **tip**
>
> Expressions like those in 1 can appear in dictionaries under the noun or the verb. Read the entry carefully to find them.

**3** Match the expressions with *end* in 1 with meanings a–h.

a  finally

b  have nothing particular to do

c  things are unlikely to change

d  eventually arrived

e  as something finishes

f  upright

g  manage financially

h  something done to achieve something else

# Writing Part 2 An informal letter or email WG p156

**1** Given the choice, do you think it's worth going into further education and doing without a salary for a few years? Talk about the pros and cons, using the ideas given below.

- career choices
- finances
- independence
- broadening your horizon
- responsibilities
- free time

- satisfaction
- promotion
- commitment
- pressure
- lifestyle

**2** Read the exam task opposite and the model email below it, and answer these questions.

a Has the writer covered all the aspects required in the exam task?

b Has the writer organised her email well? Explain your answer.

c Does the writer vary the way she starts sentences? For example, does she always start with a main clause? Give examples.

d Does the writer use a good range of linking words and phrases? Highlight examples, including sequencing words.

e Is the tone of the email appropriate for the subject matter and the age of the recipient? Explain why/why not.

f Has the writer begun and ended the email in an appropriate way? What alternatives could she have used?

This is part of an email you have received from Tom, who was a member of a youth group you led two years ago. Write back to Tom outlining the advantages of further education, comparing this with the option of going straight into work, and advising Tom on what you think is the best choice.

From: Tom Reeves

Subject: Future plans

I'll be nineteen this summer, so I have to decide whether to go straight into work or to opt for higher education. I haven't decided what I want to do as a career yet. At the moment, earning a salary seems the most attractive choice; if I were to continue studying, I don't know how I'd finance it! I'd really appreciate your advice.

---

Dear Tom

It was great to hear from you after all this time and incredible to think you are now nineteen! Leaving school is a really major event; the decisions you make now can determine the rest of your life so it's important you take time to consider your options.

The first choice you mention, going on to further education, would bring you huge benefits; let me explain why. In the first place, the world of work is very competitive these days and employers are increasingly looking for staff with the highest possible qualifications. If you want to reach the top of the ladder in your chosen career, going to college or university is therefore a must. Secondly, further education would help you personally by broadening your horizons and making you aware of the choices you have in life.

Getting a job straight from school has advantages too, of course. Not everybody is academic. Besides, many employers provide training on the job and finance it as well. This could make it a more attractive option if paying for further education is a problem. However, you will probably not end up with as many choices regarding work in the future if this is what you decide.

So there you have it, Tom. I think it's pretty clear from what I've said that I'd recommend going on to further education. You're a bright guy and you'd do well at university. The choice is yours, of course, so good luck whatever you decide.

Very best wishes

Paula

**3** Find words or phrases in the model email with a similar meaning to a–j.

a   difficult to believe
b   a very big occasion
c   what you decide now will affect you from now on
d   think about your choices
e   would do you a lot of good
f   people are fighting for the best jobs
g   get promoted up the chain in your job
h   essential
i   give you training while you work
j   that's the situation

**4** Read the task below, weigh up points for and against the two options, and discuss which you would recommend and why.

> This is part of an email you have received from Ella, who was in a youth group you led two years ago, and is now going to university. Write back to Ella outlining the advantages of living at home while studying, comparing this with the option of moving away and sharing a flat. Advise Ella on what you think is the best choice.
>
> > I'm eighteen now and I've started applying for university. But first I have to decide whether to apply to somewhere nearby so I can keep living at home, or to opt for a university in a different town, which would mean moving away from home and possibly sharing a flat. I just don't know which would be best. What would you recommend?

**5** Note down your ideas and make a paragraph plan for your email. You will generally need to write about four paragraphs for an email or letter. Make sure you include ideas for a fully developed introduction and conclusion.

**Plan**

Paragraph 1:
...........................................................................
...........................................................................

Paragraph 2:
...........................................................................
...........................................................................

Paragraph 3:
...........................................................................
...........................................................................

Paragraph 4:
...........................................................................
...........................................................................

**6** Write your **email** in **220–260** words in an appropriate style.

tip

Think carefully about how you phrase ideas. You need to demonstrate that you can use quite complex language at this level to get good marks.

# Review

**1** Write the missing words in sentences a–f. The first letters are given.

a Heavy rain caused a l........... after many trees on the hillside had been felled.

b Coal is a n........... r........... which is often uneconomical to mine nowadays.

c A severe f........... in the south of the country left thousands starving.

d During the violent storm, a t........... was reported to have caused extensive damage to property in the city centre.

e A c........... d........... like tuberculosis can be life-threatening.

f The city has become o........... because of all the new housing estates which have sprung up over the last few years.

**2** Circle the correct word in italics to complete sentences a–f.

a Your suggestion will provide only a short-*haul/term/stay* solution to our traffic problems.

b An all-round education always pays off in the long *run/way/time*.

c We must act on global warming now – the future of our planet is at *stake/hand/large*.

d Ted didn't plan his decision – he resigned on the *point/head/spur* of the moment.

e The announcement that the company was to be sold shocked everyone as it came completely out of the *question/blue/ordinary*.

f I regret that we can't help with your query. The matter is now out of our *reach/touch/control*.

**3** Decide which of these adjectives best collocate with the nouns in italics in a–g.

| principal | trivial | controversial |
| momentary | momentous | antisocial |
| unsocial | | |

a The accident is thought to have been caused by a *lack* of concentration on the part of the driver.

b There is no doubt that 'not guilty' was a *verdict* – there was widespread disbelief that the accused was found innocent.

c A board of directors meeting is not the occasion to discuss such a *matter*. Details such as this can be dealt with at a much lower level.

d Ted made a *decision* when he resigned from his city law firm and relocated to a remote island.

e His new job is interesting but it will entail working *hours* and some night shifts.

f One of the *causes* of the declining bird population is the destruction of their natural habitat, but there are many other factors.

g The penalty for *behaviour* such as vandalism can be a short spell in prison.

**4** Replace the words in italics with a suitable expression with *end*. The words in brackets will help you.

a If you find yourself *with nothing particular to do* (loose) this weekend, why not visit our new department store?

b Property prices have been rising for months and *things are unlikely to change* (sight).

c It's difficult to *manage financially* (meet) when you're out of work.

d We were enjoying the film, but *as it finished* (at), there was a power cut and we never found out what happened!

e Paul didn't enjoy his job – it was *something he did to achieve something else* (means).

f After driving for two hours, we *eventually arrived* (up) right back where we'd started from.

g Jack took his maths exam four times but *finally* (in) he passed it.

h If you put the desk *upright* (on), it will go through the door.

**5** Complete gaps 1–6 in the paragraph below, which gives advice about finding a job.

There are lots of factors to **1** .............. if you're young and looking for your first job. Before you **2** .............. up your mind about what career path to take, get as much advice as possible, and be advised **3** .............. rushing into a decision without careful research and consideration. Bear in **4** .............. that you could be making a choice that will affect you for several years to come. **5** .............. up the pros and cons of different jobs, how much they pay, where they are located, promotion prospects and so on. At the end of the day, remember that it's up **6** .............. you to choose your own path.

# It's a crime

## Lead in

**1** Read the information below about crime in the UK and explain the meaning of these words.

arson                  burglary
criminal damage        domestic violence
counterfeit            mugging
robbery                fraud

**2** Discuss these questions.
a  Are you surprised by any of the statistics? Say which and explain why.
b  Why might the number of some crimes appear to have fallen whilst others have risen?
c  How do you think crime statistics in your country might compare with these?

### Crime in England and Wales

England and Wales have a combined population of around 57 million.

In 2013, the total number of crimes in England and Wales was around 8.6 million.

Total crime numbers peaked in 1995, and have since fallen by more than 50%.

In 2013, there were 55 recorded offences per 1,000 of the population.

### Fraud

In 2013, 4.6% of plastic card holders had been victims of fraud during the previous year.

Financial fraud losses on UK cards totalled £388 million in 2012, which represents a 14% increase compared with 2011. This rise has come from an increase in the use of counterfeit cards and the fraudulent use of card details – not through the misuse of stolen cards.

### Violent crime

In 2013, the total number of violent offences in England and Wales was 1.9 million. These included:

552 incidents of murder.

312,000 incidents of violence with injury.

288,000 incidents of violence without injury.

### Criminal damage

In 2013, the number of incidents of criminal damage in England and Wales was 230,000. 19,000 of these were incidents of arson.

In 2013, around five in 100 households experienced some type of criminal damage.

After a peak in 1993 of 3.5 million incidents, criminal damage continues to fall every year.

### Robbery

In 2013, the number of robbery offences in England and Wales was 62,000.

In that year, five in every 100 households were a victim of vehicle theft, while two in every 100 households were a victim of burglary.

# Reading

## Part 8  Multiple matching

**1**  Do you enjoy crime stories in books or films? What would you say are the elements of a good crime story?

**2**  Read the text opposite and suggest a heading or brief summary for each section to show you understand the development of the text. Compare your ideas with a partner's.

**3**  Read the text again and say in which section of the text (a–e) 1–10 are mentioned. The how to do it box will help you.

### how to do it

Read the text for general meaning.

Highlight key words in the questions.

Read the text again, looking for the key words from the questions expressed in a different way.

Underline relevant sentences, write the question number next to them, and tick off the question; this reduces what you need to read each time.

Do the same with each section, leaving the most difficult questions until last.

| | |
|---|---|
| the importance of understanding how a character thinks | 1 … |
| the necessity of writing a convincing plot | 2 … 3 … |
| the character's belief that he will go unpunished | 4 … |
| using human emotions as a basis for a story | 5 … |
| the risk of basing characters on reality | 6 … |
| why killing makes a good story | 7 … |
| not underestimating the difficulty of writing a crime novel | 8 … |
| a crucial question to ask about your main character | 9 … |
| the different ways that readers will see a novel | 10 … |

**4**  Complete these phrases with an appropriate preposition and check your answers in the text.

  a  to be misled … doing something (section a)
  b  to enthuse … something or someone (section a)
  c  to be based … something (section c)
  d  to be … pressure (section c)
  e  to be capable … doing something (section d)
  f  to be burdened … guilt (section d)
  g  to blame somebody … something (section d)
  h  to come … to scratch (section e)

**5**  Do you have a favourite fictional criminal and/or detective? What makes them so appealing?

### a

Why do so many of us enjoy reading crime fiction? The predictable answers are that the books are exciting and easy to read. But if you don't read the genre
5 or don't admire it, then you will find it very hard to write. Don't be misled into imagining that a detective story is a simple matter because there are rules to follow. The best way of learning
10 about any kind of writing is to read good examples of it. Obviously, your verdicts will be subjective. While you are muttering about situations not being fully explained, another reader
15 may be enthusing about the subtlety of the novel. But you will be learning what can be achieved within the genre.

### b

Criminals make good characters for fiction because they are active, not
20 passive. They are not the stupidest people, either. To commit a crime they have shown initiative and intelligence in the planning and audacity in carrying it through. Their moral failing
25 is in wanting to do it; their folly is in believing they can get away with it. It is acceptable to take actual people as the basis for fiction but they must be distinctly altered. You wouldn't want to
30 libel anyone by having him appear only transparently disguised as a murderer. Besides, the fewer fetters on your creative powers the better. Even when you set out thinking you are going
35 to use a real person, you will rapidly dr from him as you dream up ways

# Writing crime fiction

*Do you enjoy a good thriller or detective novel? Have you ever thought about writing one? Lesley Grant-Adamson has some advice for aspiring writers.*

to enhance the character. It may help the plot if the vet changes career and becomes a doctor or you might prefer him to live in a haunted mansion on the moor. By the time you have finished, you will hardly recognise the vet, and more to the point, neither will he.

## c

All novels are based on conflict. In crime fiction the difficulty or challenge will be caused by, or result in, a crime. That crime is almost invariably murder because it's the extreme, the one for which there is no expiation for the wrongdoer. To achieve a believable story, the method must be suited to the character who murders. Common methods of dispatching victims include shooting, stabbing, hitting with a blunt instrument, poisoning or drowning. A habitual criminal might reasonably produce a gun, but an elderly housewife is more likely to brandish a heavy pan. At least one of your characters must be under pressure, and it will increase during the spinning of the yarn. Trouble in relationships, and the excesses that can result when someone becomes stubborn, jealous, obsessive or vengeful, is a bountiful source of story ideas.

## d

For some writers, the idea for a whole book begins with the appearance in their mind of an insistent character. Whether he came to you as a gift out of nowhere or as the result of a real effort to create

him, you should pose some searching questions about him. They boil down to this: is he strong enough? That doesn't mean he has to be physically 75 or mentally robust, merely that he must be capable of interesting the reader for the length of the book. A good character always has an internal conflict. He might be burdened with 80 guilt, say, or struggling to overcome a personal failing. Whatever it is, the problem colours his view of life. If your character does not interest you very much, you can be certain 85 he will not interest anyone else. Get inside your character's head. Find out whether he enjoys his own company or is lonely. Check what he thinks about his parents, his siblings, his 90 colleagues. Maybe he blames them for his problems?

## e

If a story comes to you very easily, be wary. First ideas should always be challenged. If they are good, scrutiny 95 won't damage them. When they don't come up to scratch, you will save yourself much disappointment by dropping them. Although a reader knows it's 'only fiction', he'll cringe 100 when your hero is thumped and sigh when your heroine is sad. But he is no fool. He knows when you are telling the truth about human beings. When you are not, he may become 105 impatient and close the book.

# Vocabulary

## Crime and punishment

**1** Discuss the difference between:

a murder and manslaughter
b mugging and smuggling
c bribery and blackmail
d burglary and robbery
e arson and assault
f fraud and forgery

**2** Complete the table with the missing words.

| | verb | person | act |
|---|---|---|---|
| a | mug | ............ | ............ |
| b | rob | ............ | ............ |
| c | ............ | burglar | ............ |
| d | ............ | ............ | murder |
| e | steal | thief | ............ |

**3** Look up *murder* and *mug* in a dictionary. How many other sayings and meanings can you find in their entries?

**4** Complete this paragraph about the British legal system with the missing prepositions.

with    of    on    for    against    into    to

If you are arrested **1** .......... committing a crime, the police must caution you immediately. You will be taken to a police station and interviewed, and may then be charged **2** .......... a criminal offence and taken **3** .......... custody. For a serious crime, you will appear in court as a defendant and be tried by a jury. If you are found guilty **4** .......... the crime, you can appeal **5** .......... the verdict. You may be sentenced **6** .......... a number of years in prison, but could be released **7** .......... parole for good behaviour.

**5** Is the legal system in your country similar to the description in 4?

# Grammar

## Passives  GR p170–171

**1** Underline the passive verbs in a–g.

a Viewers were appalled to hear that the reality TV show is to be axed. Two soap operas are also said to be under threat.
b The idea that Mars could one day be colonised by human beings is no longer fiction.
c Local residents, annoyed about the siting of wind turbines near their village, complained that their views were not being taken into account.
d Environmental issues are the focus for discussion at the conference to be hosted by the United Nations.
e Although experts are convinced that robots can be made to think for themselves, their efforts have met with little success so far.
f If governments want to clean up the planet, they must act now, and more funding for research will have to be made available.
g All adults eligible to vote are required to complete and return the enclosed form.

**2** Complete rules a–c for forming the passive.

a We form the passive with the verb .......... in an appropriate tense + the .......... participle of the main verb.
b The object of an active verb becomes the .......... of the passive verb.
c If the name of the agent needs to be mentioned, we put the word ' .......... ' in front of it.

**3** Match these uses of the passive (a–c) with sentences from 1.

a when the agent is unknown, unimportant, or obvious, or is deliberately not mentioned
b to make reports and official documents more impersonal, and to show that the actions are more important than the agent
c to avoid the overuse of personal pronouns or vague words, e.g. *people, they*

**4** Make this newspaper report more formal by putting the italicised sections into the passive.

*They have recently discovered a 2,000-year-old shoe* in Britain in a disused well, on an area due to be quarried. The 30-cm piece of leather is still flexible because *something has kept it damp* and away from air for thousands of years. Experts are excited about the find but warn that *they need to do a lot more work* before *they know everything* about it. *They have never found anything like this* before. *They have found similar shoes* in bog sites in Ireland and on the continent, but these are undateable. *Someone may have placed it* into the well as part of a ritual, or *someone could have simply lost it.* In the distant past, *people often buried shoes* in the foundations of new buildings as good-luck charms.

**5** Write the passive equivalents of these sentences.

a  In a crackdown on antisocial behaviour, police are making teenagers remove neighbourhood grafitti.
b  They heard the politician say under his breath that 'all journalists were troublemakers'.
c  They wouldn't let anyone into the building until firefighters said it was safe to do so.
d  On the CCTV footage, we clearly saw money change hands in return for a small package.

**6** Complete sentences a–d with your own ideas.

a  I would feel ashamed of myself if I was ever heard …
b  As part of the act, the magician was seen …
c  In many countries, until you are 18 you are not allowed …
d  One thing many kids hate about school is being made …

**7** Give advice for the situations in a–e, using *have/ get something done.* Try to vary the ways of giving advice.

Example

*I've been having splitting headaches recently and can't read things clearly.*

*You should get your eyes tested./Why don't you get your eyes tested?*

a  Water has been coming in through your parents' bedroom ceiling.
b  I bought a pair of trousers but they're too long for me.
c  Your pet dog has lost his appetite recently.
d  I want to sell my house but it's looking a bit shabby.
e  Your sister's car has been making strange noises.

**8** A reporter has gathered rumours and facts from sources who don't wish to be named in print. Rewrite the information more formally for his newspaper, using the reporting verb in brackets and beginning with the words in italics.

Example

'I hear *the Prime Minister* is really angry with his Foreign Minister.' (report)

*The Prime Minister is reported to be furious with his Foreign Minister.*

a  'Don't quote me on this, but I've heard that *a UFO* has crashed in Texas.' (rumour)
b  'I've been told that *Robbie Williams* is going to do another world tour.' (say)
c  'They reckon that *scientists* have found a new planet.' (believe)
d  'Apparently *factory bosses* are planning to make 200 employees redundant.' (think)
e  'Everyone imagines that *the event* was cancelled because of the singer's poor health.' (assume)

# Listening Part 1 Multiple choice

1 Do you know any stories of daring robberies, real or fictional?

2 🎧 Read questions 1–6 below before you listen to the three different extracts. Then listen and choose the best answer (A, B or C) for each question. The tip box will help you.

**tip**

Use the question to decide 'how' to listen, e.g. listen for specific information (q.4) or infer an opinion (q.6).

**Extract one**
You hear part of a radio programme concerning an attempted robbery.

1 What was the thieves' plan?
   A to carry out a raid on a local bank
   B to make off with a collection of priceless objects
   C to steal money from a national monument

2 The outcome of the attempted robbery was that the thieves
   A were tricked into stealing the wrong things.
   B were unable to break into their intended target.
   C were caught in a trap.

**Extract two**
You hear a woman and a police officer talking about credit card fraud.

3 The woman was surprised because
   A someone had obtained her credit card details without her knowledge.
   B a hotel receptionist had refused to accept her credit card.
   C her credit card company had contacted her about some transactions.

4 What information does the police officer give?
   A It's difficult to use a credit card without knowing a PIN number.
   B Credit card companies accept the risk that fraud will occur.
   C The woman will be liable for any bills.

**Extract three**
You hear two people on a current affairs programme talking about crime and punishment.

5 The two speakers agree about
   A the support that even violent criminals deserve.
   B the need to ensure that prisoners do not reoffend.
   C the problem of preventing prisoners escaping.

6 What is the man's opinion of punishment for offenders?
   A Punishment can be turned into something that benefits society.
   B Community service is suitable for non-violent and violent criminals.
   C Offenders should be consulted about their punishment.

# Speaking Part 2

1 Look at the photos opposite and discuss what topics you may be asked to talk about in the exam.

2 Think of a topic heading for each group of words A–C. Which photo does each phrase in A and B refer to? Which photos might the phrases in C match?

A ....................
   a controlled parking zone
   a factory environment
   a building site
   an airport check-in queue
   a library
   a train carriage

B ....................
   to prevent interruptions
   to prevent damage to property
   to avoid accidental fires
   to prevent accident or injury
   to avoid congestion
   to protect passengers and crew

C ....................
   having to pay a fine
   being given a verbal warning
   having your property removed
   being sacked
   being asked to leave the premises
   receiving a warning letter

3 🎧 Listen to the Part 2 task and write the two questions in the box above the photos. Now, in pairs, choose two photos from each set and in turn, do the task.

4 Now look at each other's photos again and briefly say in which situation you think the rules and regulations are the most important.

**tip**

Try to give reasons for your opinions.

- ......................................................................................... ?
- ......................................................................................... ?

**tip**

Use the prompts above the photos as a reminder to answer the complete task.

## Set A

## Set B

# Use of English

## Part 2  Open cloze

**1** What means of identification are commonly used nowadays? In your opinion do they restrict or protect our personal freedom?

**2** Read the text opposite, ignoring the gaps, and find examples of how our privacy may be at risk.

**3** Read Part 1 again and choose the best options below for gaps 1–4 in the text, then write in the missing words in 5–8.

Example

*0  out/up*

1 while/as
2 there/it
3 like/as
4 into/inside

**tip**

The missing answers in 5–8 include:

- one adverb
- three prepositions

**4** Now read Part 2 of the text and complete gaps 9–16 with an appropriate word.

**5** Do you agree with this statement? Why/Why not?

'If you aren't doing anything wrong, there's no reason to object to being checked up on.'

# AN INVASION OF
# PRIVACY?

### Part 1

You are at work. A message from the police pops 0 ...up.... on your computer screen. 'Your car has been recorded by a roadside camera 1 .......... having exceeded the speed limit at 8.31 a.m. today. The camera images were checked with the national facial recognition system and 2 .......... has been confirmed that you were the driver.' It sounds far-fetched but technology 3 .......... this is already in place. This increasing intrusion 4 .......... our private lives will force us to consider the balance between personal freedom and the power of the state.

But surely we do still have some personal privacy? Apparently very little. You might not want your bank account to be public knowledge, but if you look at the number of different people, 5 .......... the police to credit card companies, who have the right to look at your financial details 6 .......... your knowledge, you soon realise that privacy no longer exists. Unfortunately, there are 7 .......... easy answers to how much privacy we should be entitled 8 .......... nowadays.

### Part 2

There are some people 9 .......... believe that the rules and regulations 10 .......... have protected people's privacy up to now will go 11 .......... doing so. 12 .......... , however, take a much 13 .......... pessimistic view. They believe that the freedom of the individual is already in danger of 14 .......... seriously weakened. But 15 .......... people are to accept even more invasions of their personal privacy, they will need to believe that these really are for their benefit and 16 .......... for some other sinister purpose.

# Vocabulary

## Phrasal verbs with *out* and *over* GR p182–183

**1** Identify the object of the phrasal verbs in a–e if there is one. Then complete the sentences to illustrate the meaning of the phrasal verbs.

a The last album that my favourite band brought out …

b I can't get over the fact that I came top in my exams. It must …

c Hearing a strange noise from the engine, the driver pulled over to …

d Take a look at these figures. Can we go over them once more because …

e As soon as the lights were put out …

**2** Complete sentences a–f using phrasal verbs with *out* in the correct form.

a Our TV has been faulty for weeks, and it finally ……… out at the weekend. Now we'll have to pay for a new one.

b We should have ……… out on our trip much earlier but we overslept.

c Guests are requested to ……… out of the hotel by midday at the latest.

d I'm desperate for a cup of coffee. I'm not sure that I can ……… out for much longer!

e Signs on the door show you where to ……… out of the building in an emergency.

f It seemed like such a ridiculous plan that I'm absolutely amazed it ……… out.

**3** The phrasal verbs in 2 change their meaning when used with or without an object. Use a dictionary to match each one with their two possible meanings in a–j below.

Example

*set out – start a journey, arrange/display*

a calculate
b manage to wait
c leave a hotel
d extend (e.g. your hand)
e succeed
f stop working
g escape
h take from somewhere
i distribute
j investigate

**4** Complete sentences a–c in an appropriate way.

a All of a sudden there was a ghostly noise from the cellar so I got out … .

b If you're staying at that hotel, you should check out … .

c At the recent film premiere, some of the fans held out … .

# Writing Part 1 An essay WG p154

**1** What types of court cases have been in the media recently? Did the culprits get an appropriate sentence, in your opinion? Do you think the sentence would prevent them from offending again? Explain your answers.

**2** Read the exam task and input text below and say which two strategies you would choose and why. Then explain which you think is more important. Give reasons.

You have just attended a debate on the subject 'Crime and Punishment'. The discussion focused on effective ways in which governments could cut the reoffending rate and therefore reduce the numbers of people in prison. You have made the notes below.

Ways in which governments could cut the reoffending rate:

- a better probation service
- tougher sentences
- better vocational training

Some opinions expressed in the debate:

'If there were more probation officers to monitor ex-prisoners and check they were OK, these people might resist returning to crime.'

'Criminals might think twice if prisons and prison sentences were tougher.'

'Give criminals job training and they wouldn't need to steal when they get out of prison.'

Write an essay discussing **two** of the strategies in your notes. You should **explain which strategy you think would be more effective, giving reasons** in support of your answer.

You may, if you wish, make use of the opinions expressed in the discussion, but you should use your own words as far as possible.

Write your **essay** in **220–260** words in an appropriate style.

Reforming criminal behaviour

.............

It is a fact that one of the biggest problems criminals face when they leave jail is finding employment. Many lack educational skills, meaning they are virtually excluded from the job market. Without a wage, they resort to crimes such as robbery and end up back in jail. If they were given the skills needed to find a job, this problem would be solved. Additionally, it would give prisoners a worthwhile goal to pursue during their prison term.

While job training is the most important step for governments to take, they should also consider improving the probation service. There are many pitfalls facing ex-prisoners and they need advice and support to avoid them. A good probation officer can provide counselling to those with personal issues such as anger management or drug addiction. Conquering such things, as I'm sure most people would agree, is important if a prisoner is to stay out of trouble and hold down a job.

To sum up, a good probation system would help the problem of reoffending but would have less impact than improved job training. Implement both, and the benefits to the prison system would be very significant.

a   The best way to discourage criminals is to give them vocational training so they do not need to commit crimes to get money. The second step should be to give them a good probation officer. In my opinion, these are the only ways to address this serious problem.

b   Nearly 50% of crimes are committed by offenders who have already been in prison at least once. What's more, many reoffend within the space of 12 months. The cost to taxpayers is serious, but the cost to victims is even worse. So what should the government do to improve the situation?

c   Everybody knows criminals get away with murder these days. Prisons just aren't tough enough, in my opinion. Forget vocational training. I mean, deep down we all know that's a total waste of time, don't we? Probation isn't much better as an idea. If that worked, we wouldn't have the sort of reoffending rates we have now, that's obvious.

**3** Read an extract from the essay one student wrote opposite. Then decide which paragraph from a–c below would make the best introduction and why.

tip

In a good introduction to an essay, a writer makes a general assertion and then provides evidence to back it up.

**4** Look at the highlighted words in the main body of the essay and say what they refer to. What is their function?

**5** Find one more example in the model essay for each category of phrases below.

**Comparing and contrasting**
Although X is the top priority because … , it is also important to …
As we have seen, X is the most important because … . Nevertheless, …
.........................

**Stating facts**
It goes without saying that …
As should now be clear …
.........................

**Adding points**
In addition, …
Furthermore, …
.........................

**Being persuasive**
Surely nobody can deny that …
Clearly/Obviously, …
.........................

**6** Now write your own answer to the essay task in 2. First, make a plan. Ensure each paragraph in the main body of your essay gives both reasons and explanations, and is introduced by a topic sentence.

# Review

**1** Join sentence halves a–h with 1–8 using a suitable preposition.

a Richard is a quiet man and certainly not capable
b Many young readers enthuse
c Not all murderers are burdened
d My religious beliefs are based
e My poor husband feels
f I was misled
g I'm afraid the children were to blame
h I hope the essays I write come

1 the guilt of their crime.
2 the *Harry Potter* series.
3 any kind of violent behaviour.
4 eating all the ice cream in the freezer.
5 pressure to work long hours.
6 my experiences as a child.
7 to scratch this term.
8 thinking that my valuables were secure.

**2** Divide a–m into three groups of crimes connected with:

1 violence
2 obtaining money, goods or other advantage
3 damage to property

| | | | |
|---|---|---|---|
| a | arson | f | fraud | j | assault |
| b | robbery | g | burglary | k | blackmail |
| c | murder | h | forgery | l | mugging |
| d | bribery | i | smuggling | m | theft |
| e | manslaughter | | | |

**3** Match sentence halves a–g with 1–7.

a A convicted criminal can appeal
b You must be read your rights if you are arrested
c If you are a suspect, the police may take you
d With enough evidence, you may be charged
e A prisoner released on the promise of good behaviour is
f If you're found guilty
g For serious offences you may be sentenced

1 into custody.
2 to several years in prison.
3 against their sentence.
4 of some offences you may get a suspended sentence.
5 for committing a crime.
6 on parole.
7 with an offence.

**4** Replace the words in italics with phrasal verbs with *out* or *over*.

a When he got a burst tyre, Bob *drove* onto the hard shoulder of the motorway.
b After so many problems, we were delighted when our plans *were successful*.
c We *left the house* so late that we got caught in the rush hour.
d After working round the clock, the newspaper staff managed to *produce* the special edition.
e If you can *manage to wait* another ten minutes, we'll stop at the next service station.
f Don't forget to *switch off* the lights.
g The paintings in the exhibition were *arranged* in a circle round the room.
h Do you think Jason will ever *recover from* the shock of not being chosen to play in the match?
i The Prime Minister *extended* her hand to each member of the winning team.
j It's advisable to *investigate* all the facilities before deciding to join a gym.
k Didn't you get the fact sheet that I *distributed*?
l By deducting the bottom figure from the top one, we can *calculate* how much money we've got.

**5** Rewrite this extract from an essay in a more formal style.

One of the biggest reasons why these criminals go out and do criminal things is because the law is too soft. As long as they don't go out and murder anyone or rob a bank they can be pretty sure they'll get off with a useless little warning or something like that. Even for a really big crime, they'll probably only get put away for a short time and if they don't mess around in prison they'll be allowed to come out in no time. No wonder we've got so much crime!

# Buying and selling

## Lead in

**1** What ways of buying and selling are shown in the photos?

- from a catalogue
- online
- in a market
- second-hand
- through an agent
- at an auction
- charity shop

**2** Answer these questions about the ways of buying and selling in 1.

a What kinds of things can be bought and sold?
b What do you already buy or sell in these ways?
c What ways would you not use to buy or sell?

**3** Discuss your monthly spending habits and put these in order of how much money you spend on each.

- cinema
- clothes
- accommodation
- books/magazines
- music
- eating out

**4** Discuss these questions.

a What else do you spend your money on?
b Do you think you spend too much on anything?
c Have you ever bought anything just because of an advert? What was it and how did the advert persuade you to buy it?

# Reading Part 7 Gapped text

**1** Quickly read the text below to find out how eBay was started, and what item the writer bought.

**2** Discuss the meaning of these phrases from the text.

   a  media coverage (l.5)
   b  a global giant (1.19)
   c  successful entrepreneurs (1.28)
   d  make a healthy living (1.40)
   e  a low cost base (1.68)

**3** Read the text again, then match paragraphs A–G with gaps 1–6. There is one extra paragraph.

**4** Have you or has anyone you know bought or sold something on eBay? What was it? Is there anything you'd like to buy or sell on eBay?

**the appea**

The history of the Internet is littered with tales of businesses that have flopped. With eBay it is different. The online auction house is a staggering success story. Yet it was the grapevine that ensured its success rather than advertising or
5 media coverage.

**1**

The stories that have got eBay talked about reinforce the message that when it comes to picking up a bargain, or making a few quid out of something you thought was worthy only of the dustbin, the rich and famous are no
10 different from the rest of us. Singer Robbie Williams' bed sold for £15,400 and millionairess Jemima Khan used the site to acquire a second-hand designer dress.

**2**

It's the private individual, rich and famous or not, who really gives the site its character. eBay operates a system whereby
15 buyers and sellers rate each other's honesty and efficiency. If your rating falls much below 100 per cent then people simply won't deal with you.

**3**

With such a range and speed of sales it is hardly surprising that the business is a global giant. It was the brainchild of
20 Pierre Omidyar. He emigrated to the US when he was six, got a degree in computer sciences and moved to California, where eBay was born.

**4**

A revelatory moment soon followed. Omidyar owned a broken laser pointer and he decided to try and sell it on the
25 site he had set up. To his amazement, a buyer came forward. He paid $14. If a broken laser pointer could sell, what couldn't? Seeking to answer that question turned Omidyar into one of today's most successful entrepreneurs.

**5**

More typical, perhaps, are users such as Victoria Egan, a
30 housewife who estimates that she makes £100 a month dealing on eBay. 'I started eBaying after we had our first child,' she says. 'To begin with, I sold a few things just to free up space at home. It's also an environmental thing. It's about recycling things.'

**6**

35 A friendly exchange of emails with the seller ensued. Now I plan to start selling, but I need a digital camera to post photographs of my items on the website. Now, where's the best place to buy a digital camera … ?

**A** He is not alone in seeing the money-making possibilities that eBay offers. There are those who claim to make a healthy living just by selling on the site. In particular, women at home with young children. Julie King earns £70,000 a year buying shoes and bags wholesale and selling them on. Her 'Killer Heels' company has now taken off beyond her wildest dreams.

**B** This personal evaluation clearly works. Other online auction houses have tried to get in on the act, but eBay's statistics dwarf them. At any given time, millions of items are up for sale, of every kind and in any condition imaginable. Objects as small as buttons and earrings to as large as cars and yachts change hands for prices ranging from less than £1 to hundreds of millions of pounds.

**C** As one inveterate observer of social trends put it: 'I hadn't seen it on the telly and wasn't aware of having seen it advertised. I only knew about it through friends when I first started using it.'

**D** The inspiration behind the project came not from the company's founder but from his wife. She was an avid collector of sweet dispensers, commenting to her husband that it would be great if she were able to collect them via the Internet and interact with other collectors. As an early Internet enthusiast, he realised that people needed a central location to buy and sell unique items.

**E** The beauty of the idea lay – of course – in its simplicity. 'It is in a complete class of its own,' says King. 'We have a very low cost base and unlike other online retailers we have no product of our own, so we have no storage. It's a virtuous circle. The more users come, the more follow.'

**F** The experiences related by these women were intriguing and so, in the interests of research, I registered on eBay. I was quickly hooked. I began scrolling through a category of interest to me – cycling memorabilia – and soon spotted a vintage Soviet Union cycling jersey. There was a day and a half to go until the conclusion of the sale and I started bidding. When I got the news that I had won the auction, I was elated. The jersey cost me £36.01, not an absolute bargain but a price I was very happy to pay for something I could never have found elsewhere.

**G** You probably wouldn't find any of those people standing next to you at a car-boot sale on a Sunday morning, but in the virtual auction house, social barriers disappear.

# Vocabulary

## Expressions with *business*, and words connected with shopping

**1** Complete expressions a–e with the correct preposition below, then discuss what each of the expressions means.

> out        of        in        to        on

a   I just need a few tools to fix the car, then we're .......... *business*.
b   I don't think you should interfere. It's *none* .......... *your business* really.
c   I'm afraid the Managing Director is away .......... *business* until the end of the week.
d   Our local shop *went* .......... *of business* when a new out-of-town superstore opened.
e   Right. Let's get *down* .......... *business* and start making some decisions.

**2** Read the definitions for the expressions in italics in a–h to see if they are correct. If not, use a dictionary to give the correct definition.

a   The star was arrested for *shoplifting* designer clothes. (stealing goods from a shop)
b   In some countries, you are expected to *haggle over* the price of goods. (pay the full price)
c   I'm going on a *shopping spree* at the weekend because Friday is payday! (buy one or two necessary things)
d   My sister loves to *go window-shopping* when she's on holiday. (looking at goods in a shop without intending to buy anything)
e   Sometimes it's a good idea to *shop around* before buying anything. (compare the price or quality of goods offered in different shops)
f   It's advisable to keep the *receipt* when you buy something. (piece of paper that shows that goods have been paid for)
g   I absolutely love shopping. I admit I'm a real *shopaholic*! (someone who likes to go shopping now and again)
h   Have you seen Tom's new car? It was so expensive he had to buy it *on credit*. (an arrangement to pay later for something you buy)

# Grammar

## Mixed conditionals and wishes  GR p179–180

**1** Form mixed conditional sentences by putting the verbs in brackets into the correct tense.

a   Our firm .......... (not/be) in debt today if we .......... (listen) to our accountant's past warnings.
b   If our parents .......... (not/lend) us the money, we .......... (not/live) in our own flat now.
c   I .......... (be) a lot better off this year if my last tax bill .......... (not/be) so high.
d   If he .......... (not have to) leave early tomorrow he .......... (come) out tonight.
e   He .......... (not misread) that last road sign if his eyesight .......... (not be) so poor these days.
f   If you .......... (not/listen) just now, you .......... (have) trouble using the equipment later.

**2** Add conditional clauses as shown in brackets to form mixed conditional sentences in a–e.

a   We wouldn't know as much about the universe as we do now if … (3rd conditional)
b   If email hadn't been invented … (2nd conditional)
c   If we haven't discovered intelligent life on other planets by now … (1st conditional)
d   I'd be a lot better off today if … (3rd conditional)
e   Venice wouldn't have become such a popular tourist destination if … (2nd conditional)

**3** Correct the mistakes with verbs in four of these sentences.

a   I wish I had a bit more money. I hate having to borrow from my parents.
b   My sister wishes her boyfriend will propose. She's crazy about him.
c   Don't you wish English grammar would be a bit easier to understand?
d   Is there anything in your life you wish you had done differently?
e   I wish I would afford to buy a car.
f   I wish the rain stopped.

**4** Complete the rules below and find an example for each point from 3.

a *wish/If only* + past simple is used for situations in the present which we would like to be different but which can't change.

b *wish/If only* + .............. is used for situations that could change in the future, and for criticising current situations.

c When the subject of both verbs is the same we use .............. instead of *would*.

d *wish/If only* + .............. is used for regrets about the past.

**5** Talk about your wishes about the past, present and future, giving reasons.

Examples

*I wish I hadn't stayed out so late last night. If I'd gone to bed a bit earlier, I wouldn't feel so tired this morning.*

*I wish I had a good voice. If I were a better singer, I could be in a band.*

**6** Complete the gaps in a–k in an appropriate way.

a If only I .......... go out tonight. The football Cup Final is on TV.

b I do wish you .......... more carefully. I've said the same thing three times already.

c I bet your friend wishes he .......... that girl his phone number. She just won't leave him alone!

d If only someone .......... me not to buy that mobile phone. It's been nothing but trouble since the day I bought it!

e I wish the sun .......... ! Then we could go to the park and play tennis.

f If only 3D TVs .......... so expensive. There's no way I can afford one.

g Like most of the other students, I wish we .......... exams at the end of this course.

h If only you .......... nearer! Then I could see you every single day.

i Sue really wishes she .......... go on the trip but she has too much work to do here.

j I wish I .......... all those prawns. They've given me stomach ache.

k I wish something exciting .......... to me in the next few days.

**7** Complete the text by putting the verbs in brackets into the correct tense.

As a child, Sue Matthews used to watch the birds in the sky and wish that she .......... (**1** be able to) fly like they did. 'If only I .......... (**2** have) wings,' she would sigh, 'then my life .......... (**3** be) perfect.' By the time Sue was 18, her childhood dream was long forgotten. She hated her job and wished she .......... (**4** stay) on at school. 'If only something .......... (**5** happen) to change my life,' she moaned to her friends. 'If things .......... (**6** continue) like this, I think I .......... (**7** go) crazy!' What happened next was a pure stroke of luck. Sue wasn't a keen reader and if she .......... (**8** not/be) forced to sit in the doctor's waiting room for an hour, she .......... (**9** may/never/pick) up the local paper and noticed the ad that was to change her life. A group of enthusiasts planned to set up a skydiving school at the tiny airport outside town and were looking for new members. If enough people .......... (**10** apply), the ad said, classes .......... (**11** start) in a fortnight's time. Fortunately, Sue was not the only person to rush to the phone that day and the skydiving school was soon in business. And as she stepped out of the plane for her first free fall and saw the rolling green hills below her, Sue knew that her childhood dream really had come true.

# Listening  Part 3  Multiple choice

**1** **Look at the two pictures and answer the questions.**

a  What do you think the pictures below are advertising?

b  How successful do you think they are in advertising the products?

c  What for you makes an advert good or bad? Do you have any favourites?

**2** 🎧 **Listen twice to an interview with Paula Stuart, the managing director of an advertising agency, and choose the correct answer for 1–6. The** how to do it **box will help you.**

## how to do it

- Read the task and questions for general meaning.
- Remember that the questions follow the order of the listening text.
- Mark your answers but check them on the second listening.
- Check that the option you choose answers the question accurately.

1  Paula feels drawn to the world of advertising because she is

  A  a hard-hitting business person.
  B  a creative person.
  C  a talkative person.
  D  a persuasive person.

2  What comment does Paula make about her career in advertising?

  A  It's been a long and difficult struggle.
  B  She has succeeded despite the setbacks.
  C  There have been more bad times than good ones.
  D  She quickly got to the top of her profession.

3  What does she feel are the differences between working in advertising and working in other industries?

  A  You can make your reputation overnight.
  B  You can build on past successes.
  C  Success depends exclusively on future achievements.
  D  One inventive idea will guarantee your profitability.

4  Paula says that if you look back on past advertising campaigns, you find that

  A  a campaign which lasts too long can be a disaster.
  B  brand names benefit from high-profile campaigns.
  C  people never forget a successful campaign.
  D  a rejected campaign can be reinvented later.

5  What does she consider to be the secret of continuing success?

  A  constantly searching for innovation
  B  building up a reliable network of contacts
  C  concentrating not on the past or future but on the present
  D  having the courage to carry on with what you are doing

6  Paula sums up the advertising industry as being one in which

  A  long-established brands are beginning to reassert themselves.
  B  newcomers are finding it difficult to make a living.
  C  the number of employees is constantly shrinking.
  D  the average age of employees is younger than it used to be.

**3** Do you agree that all adverts should be 'legal, decent, honest and truthful'? In what ways might they not be?

# Speaking Parts 3 and 4

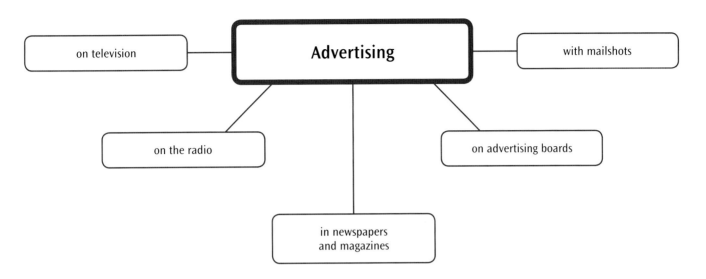

**1** Look at the Part 3 exam task above. Discuss which of the different means of advertising:

- would reach the widest audience.
- would be the most/least expensive.
- might irritate people most.
- would have the most impact.

**2** 🎧 Listen to four pairs of students discussing how effective the means of advertising in 1 would be. In which conversation (1–4) does someone

a explain an opinion? ....
b not expand on their response? ....
c disagree impolitely? ....
d agree with what their partner says? ....
e ask their partner for help? ....
f paraphrase unknown vocabulary? ....

**3** In pairs, look at the prompts in 1 again and discuss the following question. Allow yourselves two minutes, then compare your ideas with those of another pair of students.

> - How successful might these means of advertising be?

 **tip**
If you need a little time to think, don't remain silent. Use fillers such as, *Well, ... , Let me see ...* or *I'm not sure what I think about that.*

**4** With a different partner, discuss the following question. Give yourselves one minute to reach a decision.

> - Which means of advertising in 1 would be the best way of advertising the goods or services of a small company which is just starting up?

**5** Now, in pairs, discuss these Part 4 questions. Try to think of two different things to say in reply to each one, for example:

- what your personal reactions are.
- why other people might disagree with you.

a What kinds of things do you think should not be advertised?
b Some people say there is too much advertising nowadays. What's your view?
c What changes have there been over the years in the way products are advertised?
d Which do you think is more important when it comes to buying a product: the quality or the price? Why?

# Use of English

## Part 3 Word formation

**1** Look at the photos and discuss what 'bling' means. Does it appeal to you? Why/Why not?

**2** Read the text below, ignoring the gaps, to find out who is wearing 'bling' and who is making money from it.

**3** Complete gaps 1–8 with words formed from those next to the text. The tip box will help you.

# THE BUSINESS OF 'BLING'

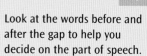

**tip**

Look at the words before and after the gap to help you decide on the part of speech.

A New Orleans rapper named 'BG' coined the term 'bling bling' to describe his taste in **0** ...flashy...
jewellery. Since then, it has certainly not gone **1** ............. as a fashion statement. In fact,
it's the byword for a **2** ............. , extravagant lifestyle. Bling means big money, so it's hardly
surprising people are keen on it. When footballer David Beckham wanted a gift for his wife, he
commissioned New York designer 'Jacob the Jeweller' to send a priceless pink diamond ring to Spain
to surprise her with the **3** ............. present.

| | |
|---|---|
| **0** | FLASH |
| **1** | NOTICE |
| **2** | GLAMOUR |
| **3** | EXPECT |

Other New York jewellers have client lists that are
**4** ............. made up of hip-hop and R&B stars. The
hip-hop industry is valued at an **5** ............. sum
of money annually. As with the world of fashion,
hip-hop stars are now joining in and **6** .............
creating jewellery lines of their own. And they face
fierce **7** ............. from those in the rap world. It
seems jewellery has become much more than just a
**8** ............. accessory.

| | |
|---|---|
| **4** | INCREASE |
| **5** | CREDIBLE |
| **6** | FEVER |
| **7** | COMPETE |
| **8** | BASE |

# Vocabulary

## Easily confused words (2)

**4** Use one of these words in the correct form to complete sentences a–h below.

> repute  notice  surprise  conserve
> suit  describe  dispute  compete

a What you're wearing is totally ......... for a formal event. It's far too casual.

b 'Bling bling' is considered by the rich and famous to be the ......... 'king' of jewellery.

c You will need to give the police a detailed ......... of the ring that you lost.

d This seemingly unappealing style of jewellery has become ......... popular recently.

e This new fashion designer is beginning to make quite a ......... for herself.

f I can see no ......... difference between this year's sales figures and last year's.

g To succeed in the tough world of fashion, you need to have a very ......... nature.

h My grandmother doesn't like modern jewellery. Her tastes are much more ......... than mine.

**5** For words a–k, identify the part of speech and then use the correct prefix to make each word negative.

> ab-  dis-  mis-  un-
> il-  im-  in-  ir-

a normal  .........
b possibility  .........
c understand  .........
d similar  .........
e logical  .........
f patience  .........
g attractive  .........
h responsibility  .........
i responsive  .........
j correct  .........
k lead  .........

**6** Write sentences of your own which include six of the words you made in 5.

**1** Use a dictionary to find the correct word in italics to complete each sentence.

a In some countries the *economic/economical* growth rate has been dramatic in recent years.

b It is company policy that the *personal/personnel* manager attends all interviews.

c One of my colleagues gets to work by walking or cycling on *alternative/alternate* days.

d At the monthly farmers' market they sell only locally grown *products/produce*.

e Most international businesses promote equal *opportunities/possibilities* for all employees.

**2** Decide which of the words not used in 1 are defined in a–e. Use a dictionary to help you.

a something that is private to you
b goods that have been manufactured
c the chances that something may happen
d something that saves you money
e another way of doing something

**3** Read the text and choose the most suitable word to correctly complete 1–10.

> It is **1** *scarce/scarcity/scarcely* surprising that Tricia Black, one of the country's leading businesswomen, is now a multi millionaire. She puts her success down to **2** *honesty/honest/honestly* and claims that people will simply stop dealing with you if you are **3** *trustworthy/untrustworthy/trusting*. And when it comes to her **4** *employment/employers/employees*, she is incredibly **5** *sense/sensible/sensitive* to their needs, and treats everyone **6** *fair/fairly/fairness*. She has also worked **7** *tirelessly/tiresomely/tiredly* for charity and has raised money for many good causes. Black tries to deal in products that are **8** *environmentally/environment/environmental* friendly. It seems that what she **9** *really/real/reality* wants in life is to become a **10** *height/highly/high* regarded member of the community.

# Writing Part 2 A report WG p162

**1** If you could choose to do work experience in any job for six weeks, what would you like to do and why? Would you be prepared to do any of the jobs shown in the photographs? Why/Why not?

**2** Read the exam task and model answer. Make brief notes on who the writer worked for and what he did. How did he feel about the experience?

> You are studying abroad. Recently your college sent you to do six weeks' work experience. Now your college principal has asked you to write a report. You should say
>
> - who you were working for and how you spent your time there
> - whether your experience was positive
> - whether you would recommend the experience to other students.

**3** Read the model answer and discuss questions a–e. Has the writer:

  a  included the important points?
  b  organised ideas into paragraphs?
  c  linked sentences and paragraphs?
  d  used the correct register?
  e  made a good impression through the layout of the report?

### Introduction

The aim of this report is to describe and evaluate my six weeks' work experience with RPC Music and to make recommendations for the future.

### About the company

RPC Music is one of the oldest record companies in the world, dating back to 1940. It employs around 5,000 employees worldwide and is represented in over 50 countries. The company records and publishes music of all types and represents many of the best-known recording artists in the world.

### My work experience

During my six weeks with RPC Music, I was assigned to three different departments.

#### Publicity

My first placement was in the publicity department. Here I learnt how CDs are promoted and helped write promotional literature for music magazines. I also helped to set up a TV interview with one of RPC's best-known rock artists.

### Sales

I spent two weeks in the sales department where I helped check stock and learnt how to process orders.

### Design

During my final fortnight I worked in the design department where I helped to arrange photo shoots. I also helped design a cover for a new CD.

## General comments

On the whole, I found my time with RPC Music extremely beneficial. The staff were very helpful and I obtained a good understanding of how each department functions. However, I believe I would have benefited more if my work experience had been for a longer period.

## Conclusion

To sum up, RPC are an ideal company with which to do work experience. I have no hesitation in recommending that we send other students to the company in future.

**4** Think of a job you know enough about to base the exam task on. Make notes on:

a  who you would work for and what they do.
b  what tasks you might do as work experience.

tip

If you don't have any work experience, use your imagination to plan your answer with enough information.

**5** Compare your notes from 4 with a partner, and discuss the positive and negative experiences you might have. Think about a–g below.

a  working hours          e  variety of tasks
b  location               f  colleagues
c  facilities available   g  future career
d  dress code

**6** Plan your introduction and think about your headings. Decide whether you would recommend your experience to others or not and give your reasons. Then write your **report** in **220–260** words in an appropriate style.

# Review

## 1 Complete the dialogues with suitable responses using expressions with the word *business*.

1  A: Do you know why the store closed?
   B: The number of people downloading music from the Internet put it ............... .

2  A: I haven't seen much of you recently – have you been away?
   B: I've been abroad for a month ............... .

3  A: Why won't you tell me what happened?
   B: It's rather personal and ............... .

4  A: Have you got everything for the gym?
   B: I'll get my trainers and we're ............... .

5  A: Shouldn't we begin our end-of-term project?
   B: Absolutely. Let's meet tomorrow afternoon and get ............... .

## 2 Write words which match the definitions in a–h. The first letter of each word is given.

a  look at but not buy goods: w........... s...........

b  buy a lot of things you don't really need: go on a s........... s...........

c  someone who is always shopping: a s...........

d  pay at a later date: buy o........... c...........

e  argue over the price of something: h...........

f  paper showing proof of purchase: a r...........

g  compare the prices of goods in different shops: s........... a...........

h  steal goods from a shop: s...........

## 3 Write the words in brackets in their correct form.

a  I'd like to say how ........... (gratitude) I am for all the help you've given me.

b  We plan to make some fundamental changes to the structure of the college at the ........... (early) opportunity.

c  I have little respect for politicians because they tend to be ........... (economy) with the truth.

d  It's cheaper to buy in bulk than to purchase items ........... (individual).

e  I think running regularly is very ........... (benefit).

f  We need you to write some ........... (promotion) literature to advertise the company.

g  This ring is thought to be very ........... (value).

h  More staff training will bring about greater ........... (efficient).

## 4 Complete sentences a–j with one of the adverbs below.

| plainly | hardly | utterly | simply |
| barely | fairly | exceptionally |
| highly | tirelessly | adequately |

a  I ........... can't understand how you could do such an unkind thing!

b  It takes an ........... brave person to risk their life to save others.

c  The law ........... states that it is illegal to drive when drunk.

d  None of us were ........... dressed for a cold day.

e  They were ........... astonished to learn that their neighbour had been arrested for spying.

f  It is ........... surprising that Gemma became a scientist. She always loved science.

g  In a recent survey, ........... half those interviewed could correctly name the capital of the USA.

h  Many thanks to all those who have worked ........... to organise this very special event today.

i  Mr Westfield, who died recently, was a ........... regarded member of our community.

j  He may be a strict teacher, but he treats all the students ........... .

## 5 Choose the correct words for 1–9 to complete this extract from a report.

The **1** *ambition/aim/goal* of this report is to evaluate the IT course I recently attended. Throughout the course, I was **2** *selected/assigned/chosen* to a personal tutor. As part of my studies, I was asked to **3** *turn/put/set* up and conduct an interview with other students. I **4** *passed/spent/filled* several hours doing this and **5** *on/in/over* the whole, I found it, and indeed the course itself, extremely useful. However, I would like to **6** *do/advise/make* one recommendation for the future. The course would have been of more **7** *good/benefit/advantage* if it had been for a longer **8** *period/interval/span*. Despite this, I have no **9** *doubt/hesitation/uncertainty* in recommending the course to others.

# 11
# Entertainment or art?

## Lead in

**1** Which of these do you consider to be 'art'? Why? What do you think makes 'good' art?

**2** Which of a–d do you think art should do? Does it have any other role? Give examples where possible.

   a  entertain          c  provoke
   b  stimulate        d  inform

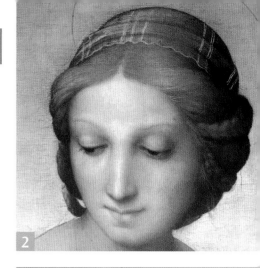

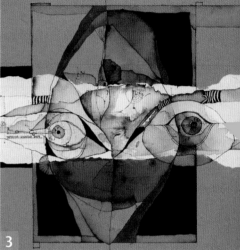

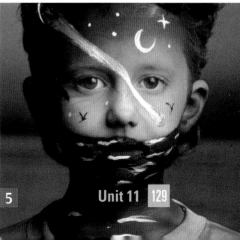

# GENIUS OR SHOWMAN?

Four writers comment on conceptual artist Damien Hirst's 'retrospective' exhibition at Tate Modern, in which we see a representative selection of the artist's work.

**A** This exhibition incudes Hirst's iconic sculpture depicting a dead shark floating suspended in a tank. It is superb. What seems at first to be an image of invulnerability, the killer about to devour its prey, is in fact
5 the opposite; the death-dealer has turned into a symbol of human death. Hirst's great drive was to express the terror of death, but he had done that so brilliantly by his late twenties that he had little room for manoeuvre thereafter. As you walk through the show you notice his compulsion
10 to go over the same ground twice; when a piece works, he makes it again or makes it bigger. It's hard to see the point of all this. You also realise that as Hirst's pay cheques have grown, his motifs have become ever more bling. Witness the diamond-encrusted skull, exhibited here
15 under tight security. It is sad to reflect how quickly Hirst went from being utterly brilliant to perfectly crass.

**B** Hirst was an exceptionally talented art student who is now perhaps the world's most ostentatious luxury brand. Again and again his work makes an undeniable claim
20 to the status of 'good art'. Take one of his early pieces featuring a shark suspended in a tank, included in this exhibition. With time it has gained a new significance; the bringer of painful death is transformed into an emblem of human death itself – the crusty remains of a once-
25 living being (you). Many detractors denigrate Hirst's art as tasteless and lacking in integrity, but viewed together here we can admire his works as the product of an artist with a clearly defined visual language.

## Reading Part 6 Cross-text multiple matching

**tip**

You can often ignore unfamiliar words or phrases but if this effects your ability to answer the questions, use the context to help work out the meanings.

**tip**

Use different colour highlighters to pick out the part of each text which links to the topic mentioned in each question. You can then compare them more easily.

1 Would you prefer to go to an exhibition of traditional painting or of modern, conceptual art? Why?

2 Quickly read the four reviews. What do they tell you about the most important theme in Hirst's art?

3 Read the texts again and answer questions 1–4. The reviews may be chosen more than once. The tip box will help you.

Which reviewer, A, B, C or D:

has a different opinion from the others on Hirst's artistic output? 1 ....
shares reviewer C's opinion on the repetitious nature of Hirst's works? 2 ....
takes a similar view to reviewer D on Hirst's commercialisation of his art? 3 ....
expresses a different view from the others regarding one of Hirst's most famous pieces? 4 ....

**C** Hirst's art centres on our inability to comprehend life's great
30 mysteries, especially death. In creating his early pieces – the dead
sheep, the fish and the cow's head – Hirst is giving a sense of
order to futility. It's this vision that gives his art power and humanity.
It's here in another early piece – a dead shark suspended in a
tank; death confronts us but remains impossible to comprehend.
35 Hirst's more recent work lacks this sense of creativity. His habit of
recreating successful pieces is tedious – he even delegates the
crafting of some works to an army of assistants, arguing that art is
conception rather than execution. His recent paintings revealed his
struggle with his own limitations, but they are not included in this
40 show. This is regrettable as the image of Hirst as a glib showman
isn't the complete picture. He is a more challenging, fallible and
interesting artist than is on show here.

**D** Writing a straightforward review of Hirst's work is almost
impossible. The glass display case containing a cow's head was
45 made decades ago, yet seen in this exhibition, is still extremely
powerful. Not all his early pieces have stood the test of time,
however. The shark suspended in a tank seems here to have
shrunk so that it looks more like a laboratory specimen than an
open-jawed threat. The quality of Hirst's art has diminished with the
50 creation of ever more decadent and overblown artefacts. Maybe he
is pandering to the vulgarity of super-rich collectors, or maybe he
thinks he is giving us what we deserve: an art of spectacle and the
tokens of wealth, such as his diamond-encrusted platinum skull.
My problem with Hirst is not the money, nor the vulgarity he has
55 opted for, but his capitulation as an artist. He could have been so
much better.

Tate Modern

**4** Discuss the meaning of these phrases from the text.

    a  to have (little) room for manoeuvre (l.8)
    b  to go over the same ground twice (l.10)
    c  to see the point of something (l.11)
    d  to pander to someone or something (l.51)
    e  tokens of wealth (l.53)

**5** Match adjectives a–f from the text with meanings 1–6.

    a  iconic (l.1)
    b  crass (l.16)
    c  ostentatious (l.18)
    d  tedious (l.36)
    e  glib (l.40)
    f  fallible (l.41)

    1  vulgar, inelegant, unaware of other people's feelings
    2  spectacular, showy, intended to attract attention
    3  imperfect, likely to make mistakes
    4  insincere, lacking in intellectual depth
    5  very boring, lasts too long
    6  very well known, famous, representative of its type

# Vocabulary

## Art and entertainment

**1** Find the odd one out in word groups a–g. What is the theme of the new group?

| | | |
|---|---|---|
| a | soundtrack | subtitles | easel |
| b | canvas | plot | chapter |
| c | lyrics | tune | sketch |
| d | clip | premiere | gallery |
| e | stage | landscape | rehearsal |
| f | palette | cast | extra |
| g | performance | show | watercolour |

**2** Choose the most suitable word to complete a–f.

a This stunning self-portrait was painted in oil on *palette/canvas/easel*.

b Do you know who wrote the *extras/lyrics/chapter* for this musical?

c Some people aren't keen on films with *soundtracks/subtitles/special effects* because they find them distracting.

d A convincing thriller needs a strong *landscape/tune/plot*.

e A new *gallery/landscape/sketch* is planned to showcase local artists' works.

f A bad dress *show/rehearsal/performance* could foretell a successful opening night.

**3** Use a dictionary to find definitions for words from 2. In pairs, give a definition to your partner and ask them to guess the word. Then swap roles.

**4** Discuss the following questions.

a Which is more important: the lyrics or the tune of a song?

b How important to a film is the soundtrack?

c What kind of films often need extras?

d Would you consider a career in the entertainment industry? Why/Why not?

e What significant changes have already happened or are likely to happen in the entertainment industry?

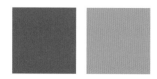

# Grammar GR p180–182

## Comparatives and superlatives

**1** Correct the errors with comparatives and superlatives in sentences a–i.

a Michael Schumacher invariably drove more fastly than the other Grand Prix drivers.

b The longer I live in this city, more I like it.

c The Pyramids are among the ancientest structures in the world.

d My job interview wasn't nearly as rigorous than I had expected.

e What an awful film! It had by far the less convincing ending I think I've ever seen.

f Summers in Australia tend to be much more hot than in Britain.

g He did a great deal more badly in the athletics competition than his teachers had expected.

h You may think you know the answer but I'm afraid you couldn't be wronger.

i Both of my brothers are considerably elder than me.

**2** Correct the spelling errors with the adjectives in a–e.

a Repairing my motorbike was slightly trickyer than I'd anticipated.

b Many of us would like to be a bit slimer but dieting too strictly can be dangerous.

c This year has already been much weter than the whole of last summer.

d Meteorologists say that this summer has been dryer than any other summer on record.

e What is the very lattest time we can arrive at the party?

**3** Discuss the answers to a–d, using comparative and superlative forms of the words in brackets.

a Put these planets in order of distance from the Earth: Mars, Venus, Jupiter (far/near)

b Put these inventions in order of age: transistor radio, electric guitar, portable calculator (old/recent)

c Put these oceans in order of size: Pacific, Indian, Atlantic (large/small)

d Put these in order of number of calories they contain: bread, chocolate, lettuce (little/much)

**4** Match a–d with a sentence of similar meaning from 1–4.

a  It's *slightly* safer.
b  It's *far* safer.
c  It's *just* as safe.
d  It isn't *nearly* as safe.

1  It's *no more* dangerous.
2  It's *much* more dangerous.
3  It's *nowhere near* as dangerous.
4  It isn't *quite* as dangerous.

**5** Which italicised words and expressions in 4 above could be replaced with a–e?

a  a bit
b  a great deal
c  a little
d  a lot
e  nothing like

**6** Complete these sentences using the expressions from 4 and 5.

a  The standard of living in Northern Europe is .......... higher than in most African countries.
b  As you can imagine, crossing the continent in a bumpy old truck is .......... as comfortable as travelling by plane.
c  I thought things would be cheaper in the market but the trainers I bought there were .......... as expensive as the ones in the shop.
d  A five-star hotel should be .......... luxurious than a four-star hotel.
e  Temperatures in the south of my country are .......... warmer than in the north, but the difference isn't very great.

**7** Choose the correct word to complete each of a–g.

a  The film was *enough/so/too* scary that my little brother had nightmares after watching it.
b  I like the idea of bungee jumping but I don't know if I'd be brave *so/such/enough* to do it.
c  The painting had to be restored because it was in *enough/so/such* a bad state of repair.
d  Elaine has *very/so/too* little talent for singing that it's no wonder she was dropped from the choir.
e  Tim had *too/so/such* great a shock when lightning struck his plane that he swore never to fly again.
f  My neighbour auditioned for a big musical but they said he was *enough/too/so* old for the part.
g  Our local bus service is *very/such/so* unreliable that I prefer to walk.

**8** Complete sentences a–e using *as* or *like*.

a  I've been working .......... a volunteer in the local hospital.
b  What on earth's the matter? You've gone as white .......... a sheet!
c  You look .......... a film star in that outfit.
d  I'm not so much angry .......... disappointed at what the council have decided.
e  Mrs Lyons was built .......... a bus but her son was small and rather weedy.

**9** Compare two places in your country, using a variety of comparatives and superlatives. Use the prompts to help you.

- popularity with tourists
- weather
- which you would rather visit
- attractions
- cost

# Listening Part 2 Sentence completion

1 Look at the picture and answer the questions below.

a What does this picture represent to you?
b Would you like to take part in an activity like this? Why/Why not?
c What, in your opinion, makes events like these so popular?

2 🎧 Listen to a radio programme about a fiesta (festival) which takes place in the Spanish town of Catoira. Before you listen, read through sentences 1–8, then as you listen, complete the sentences.

## THE TORRES DE OESTE FIESTA

The festival has been an annual event since
1 ............................ in this part of Spain.

The festival commemorates the 2 ...........................
of the ancestors of local people.

Crowds are entertained by 3 ............................ at two
different venues.

Visitors to the 4 ............................ are warned not to
arrive late.

The highlight of the festival is when the town's
5 ............................ is captured by the so-called Viking
invaders.

The arrival of the Viking ship is preceded by
6 ............................ on the rocks.

The Vikings wave their 7 ............................ about in a
dramatic way.

The 8 ............................ which are cooked over bonfires
are bigger than those many people might be used to.

3 Complete the expressions in a–h with the words below to match the meanings
on the right.

| remembrance | dedicated | ordinary | known |
| delight | mill | building | familiar |

a out of the ......            = very unusual
b run of the ......            = not at all unusual
c in ...... of                 = in memory of
d be ...... to                 = be named in memory of
e crowds start ...... up       = crowds start gathering
f be ...... as                 = be called
g much to the ...... of        = much to the amusement of
h be ...... with               = to know quite well

# Speaking Part 2

1 Discuss what a–e have in common. Say which ones can be used to talk about each photo in 1–4, and when you would use each of the others.

a spectator    c witness    e viewer
b audience    d observer

2 🎧 Read the exam task above the photos, then listen to part of what one candidate said while doing the task and note down all the link words she uses.

- Why might the people have chosen to watch these kinds of entertainment?
- How different might the people's reactions to the entertainment be?

3 With a partner, each choose one pair of photos and take it in turns to do the task in 2, talking for a minute each. Then look at each other's photos and decide which people are most enjoying what they are watching.

# MUSIC TO THEIR EARS

Standing at a bus stop or on a railway station platform and feeling intimidated **0** ....by..... a group of noisy youths is not uncommon. Some expensive solutions **1** ............ this problem have been tried but now playing classical music is gradually becoming adopted **2** ............ a low-cost answer. All that is needed is the required licence to play music and a few speakers and the problem seems to just disappear.

One railway station had experienced problems with youths hanging around, **3** ............ getting up to criminal activities but engaging in anti-social behaviour, **4** ............ as using bad language and annoying passengers.

Passengers complained and the authorities responded by introducing classical music, a solution **5** ............ completely eliminated the problem. Music is an important part of our identity. If we are forced to listen to music we don't like, we will react and move **6** ............ from it. Now the passengers not **7** ............ say they don't see youths hanging around, but they also no **8** ............ feel uneasy when travelling.

# Use of English

## Part 2  Open cloze

**1** Read the text opposite quickly, ignoring the gaps, to find out how music is being used at a railway station and with what results.

**2** Read the text again and complete each of gaps 1–8 with one suitable word.

## Part 4  Key word transformation

**3** Rewrite the second sentence in a–f keeping the meaning the same. Use three to six words including the word given.

a   I'm afraid I now find myself unable to attend the meeting tomorrow.
   **LONGER**
   Unfortunately, I am ............................ to attend the meeting tomorrow.

b   If listening to music is forced on people, they react against it.
   **MADE**
   If people ............................ music, they react against it.

c   Eliminating a problem is difficult if you don't know what's causing it.
   **RID**
   It's not easy to ............................ a problem when you don't know what's causing it.

d   Perhaps he has forgotten about the rehearsal again.
   **SLIPPED**
   Maybe the rehearsal ............................ again.

e   What the boys were doing at the station is a mystery to me.
   **GETTING**
   I have no idea what the boys ............................ at the station.

f   I don't think I can continue to play tennis as it's too time consuming.
   **UP**
   I think I'll have ............................ tennis as it's too time consuming.

**4** Would the idea described in the text work where you live? Why/Why not?

# Vocabulary

## Three-part phrasal verbs GR p182–183

**1** Complete the three-part phrasal verbs in a–g with the missing particle, then match them with similar meanings 1–7.

a I don't want to *fall* .......... *with* you but I really can't agree with what you're doing.

b I think the reason the car's stopped is that we've *run* .......... *of* petrol.

c We had to *put* .......... *with* the noise in our hotel because nowhere else had any rooms available.

d Sam bought me a bunch of flowers to *make* .......... *for* hurting my feelings.

e My father doesn't *get* .......... *with* his new boss so he's looking for another job.

f One of the marketing team has *come* .......... *with* a good idea for a new advertisement.

g The factory has decided to *do* .......... *with* the old computers and install a new system.

1 tolerate
2 get rid of
3 have a good relationship with
4 argue
5 compensate for
6 use all of something
7 think of

**2** Form three-part phrasal verbs in a–f using *out*, *up*, *in* or *on* and complete the sentences appropriately. Use a dictionary to help you.

a You'll have to walk .......... . I can't *keep* .......... *with* you.

b What's got into Clare? She *came* .......... *with* a very .......... remark at breakfast this morning.

c If Jack's wife keeps *going* .......... *at* him all the time he's likely to .......... .

d If you don't *stick* .......... *for* your rights, people will .......... you.

e His wife *walked* .......... *on* him, leaving him to .......... on his own.

f The reason Tina's so .......... is that her parents *give* .......... *to* her all the time.

**3** Correct any mistakes with the phrasal verbs in these sentences.

a Ben fell down with his father some years ago and they haven't spoken to each other since.

b Do you know which writer first came away with the term 'robotics'?

c Could you talk more slowly please? I can't keep up to what you're saying.

d I'd like to find a solution but I'm afraid I've run away of ideas.

e Don't let anyone bully you – stick up to yourself!

f My parents keep going on with me to study harder.

# Writing Part 2 A review WG p160

**1** What is the most recent film you have seen? What made you decide to see it?

**2** Which of a–e might be included in a film review?

   a  a summary of the plot
   b  comments on special features
   c  a biography of the lead actors
   d  a description of the costumes
   e  a recommendation about whether or not to see the film

**3** Read the exam task and the model answer below and answer these questions.

   a  Does the answer address all parts of the task?
   b  Does the information given help you decide whether you would want to see the films?

> You write for an international student magazine. The editor has asked you for a review recommending two films, one for adults and the other for a younger audience. You should comment on the plot and the acting and explain why the films are suitable for each age group.
>
> Write your **review** in **220–260** words in an appropriate style.

*Life of Pi* and *Django Unchained* are both highly enjoyable movies. However, they will appeal to very different audiences.

*Life of Pi* is an outstanding fantasy adventure story about a boy whose father manages a zoo in India. When times get bad they are forced to emigrate and ship their animals to Canada. But the ship is wrecked in an atrocious storm. Pi survives on a lifeboat, with only an unpredictable tiger for company! The pair endure 227 days at sea, visited by spectacular creatures like flying fish and luminous jellyfish. The cinematography is stunning. The animals, ocean and sometimes even the boy are digital creations, but they seem utterly convincing. Children will love it!

**4** Find adjectives in the model answer which mean the same as a–h.

*Life of Pi*
a  extremely good/exceptional
b  terrible/awful
c  visually wonderful/impressive

*Django Unchained*
d  unconventional/weird
e  wicked/cruel
f  very funny
g  believable
h  magical/charming

**5** Tell a partner what you thought of the last film you saw, using some of these ideas.

a  It's a gripping/slow-moving/action-packed story.
b  The plot is far-fetched/intriguing/predictable.
c  The final scenes are thrilling/spine-chilling/spectacular.
d  The script is witty/natural/awkward.
e  The acting is wooden/uninspired/unconvincing.
f  The lead actor/actress gives a tremendous/mediocre/fantastic performance.
g  The special effects are amazing/stunning/disappointing.

**6** Decide whether adverbs a–i are strong, medium or weak adverbs. Then say which of the adjectives you chose in 5 they can modify.

a  rather        d  extremely      g  completely
b  slightly      e  really         h  totally
c  utterly       f  absolutely     i  fairly

**7** Choose two suitable films to review for the exam task. For each one make notes on:

• the plot and the acting
• any other notable aspects
• who they are suitable for and why.

**8** Write your review including:

a  an introduction naming the films and their genre
b  a conclusion summarising who they are suitable for.

*Django Unchained* is a much more adult film, being an action-packed revenge story set in Texas in the year 1858. The plot concerns a slave, Django, who is part of a chain gang. An eccentric German buys Django and promises him freedom in return for his help. He also agrees to help find Django's wife Brunnhilde, who is a slave on a plantation and has been abused by her owner, the villainous Calvin Candie (played by Leonardo DiCaprio). Some scenes are full of tension; in others, the dialogue is hilarious. The characters are well developed and the friendship between slave and rescuer is both credible and compelling.

Either of these films would make a great evening's entertainment. *Life of Pi* is an enchanting film that is suitable for children, but *Django Unchained*, with its adult themes and violence, is definitely not for the kids!

# Review

1 Complete sentences a–g using the verb in brackets in the passive form and an appropriate ending from 1–7.

**Example**

*A plot is thought up by an author.*

a ~~A plot (think up)~~
b A soundtrack can (hear)
c Extras (often/hire)
d Tunes and lyrics (write)
e An easel can (find)
f A premiere (organise)
g Rehearsals (always/hold)

1 on a film.
2 for crowd scenes in films.
3 ~~by an author.~~
4 to publicise a film.
5 before a show's first night.
6 for musicals.
7 in an artist's studio.

2 Complete the words in a–f which refer to people looking or watching. The first letter of each one is given.

a A crowd of curious o.......... had gathered around the street performer.
b I didn't actually take part in the debate as I'd simply been sent along as an o.......... .
c Police are appealing for w.......... to the accident to come forward and give statements.
d At the end of the match the players thanked the s.......... for the fantastic support they had given throughout the tournament.
e I gather there's some a.......... participation in this play, so if you don't want to join in, don't sit near the front of the stage!
f TV controllers desperate to win back v.......... have vowed to cut the number of repeats as ratings reach an all-time low.

3 Rewrite the second sentence in a–e keeping the meaning the same. Use three to six words including the word given.

a Is the government considering getting rid of low-level income tax?

DOING

Is the government thinking ............ low-level income tax?

b Brian and Susan have surely had an argument because they aren't speaking to each other.

FALLEN

Brian and Susan ............ because they aren't speaking to each other.

c The Smiths lived with the noise of traffic in the city for years before they moved to a small village.

PUTTING

After years ............ the noise of traffic in the city, the Smiths moved to a small village.

d He forgot my birthday and I couldn't forgive him, because he did nothing to show he was sorry.

MAKE

I would have forgiven him if he'd tried ............ my birthday, but he did nothing to show he was sorry.

e We couldn't think of a better idea for improving the traffic problems.

COME

We were not ............ a better idea for improving the traffic problems.

4 Rearrange the letters in brackets (1–7) to form adjectives to complete this article.

When Alexandre Dumas wrote his (thingrill) ............1 classic, *The Man in the Iron Mask*, he said it combined two driving forces of life: love and action. The musical based on the novel, however, captured none of its charisma and turned a (pingprig) ............2 story into a (spaceratcul) ............3 failure. The critics hated it. In addition to slamming its (wardkaw) ............4 lyrics and (ringspinuni) ............5 music, they criticised members of the cast for their (nedoow) ............6 acting. Visually, the production may have looked attractive and no doubt entertained some of the audience, even if for all the wrong reasons. The show's producers blamed (pointingpasid) ............7 attendance figures throughout theatreland, but the real reason for its sudden end, just two days after its premiere, were some of the most scathing reviews of recent times.

# A changing world

**12**

## Lead in

**1** Read the extract below and discuss these questions.

a  What arguments do you think those in the energy industry and environmentalists would use for and against opening up the Wildlife Refuge?

b  Do you think decisions like these are inevitable in the long run?

c  What threats are there to other areas of outstanding beauty?

It is described as the last great American wilderness and has been the battleground between America's most powerful oil interests and environmentalists for more than two decades. But the giants of the energy industry are celebrating a significant victory and looking forward to the chance to move into one of the most lucrative oil fields left in the US, following the decision to open up the pristine Arctic National Wildlife Refuge in northern Alaska.

**2** Read these ideas for saving energy then discuss questions a–c below.

- Turn down your thermostat by one degree.
- Replace an ordinary lightbulb with a low energy one.
- Turn off TVs instead of leaving them on standby.
- Turn off lights in unoccupied rooms.
- Only boil enough water in a kettle to meet your needs.

a  Which of the above have you ever done, or do you do regularly?

b  Do you think the suggestions could make a significant difference?

c  Who should be responsible for protecting our resources – governments or the individual?

# Reading Part 8 Multiple matching

**1** Read the text opposite about five places under threat (A–E), and match them with areas 1–5 on the map below.

**2** Underline the key words in questions 1–10 in the exam task below. Where possible, think of other ways of expressing the same information.

Example   *plants and animals = wildlife/ecosystems/flora and fauna/ vegetation/creatures*

In which section, A–E, are the following mentioned?

| | |
|---|---|
| the potential disappearance of huge numbers of <u>plants and animals</u> | 1 .... |
| a system which relies on the direct effect of temperature on water | 2 .... |
| a geographical feature that may face almost total destruction | 3 .... |
| a substance which provides vital nourishment for sea creatures | 4 .... |
| an area where extreme temperatures protect the Earth | 5 .... 6 .... |
| a harmful effect equivalent to decades of man-made pollution | 7 .... |
| the damaging effect that rainfall could have on temperatures | 8 .... |
| a possible increase in the number of destructive insects | 9 .... |
| an area where evidence of its past can be seen at certain altitudes | 10 .... |

**3** Read each section A–E carefully one at a time. Identify which of 1–10 are mentioned in each, leaving any difficult ones until last.

**4** Do you think we have a duty to preserve the Earth as it is? Why/Why not?

# CHANGING PLACES

Five parts of the world where global warming could have dramatic consequences for the environment.

## A The Amazon Forest

The Amazon forest is one of the most biodiverse regions on Earth. Models suggest that global warming will cause a decrease in Amazonian rainfall, leading to the gradual
5 death of the forest and collapse of the myriad ecosystems it supports. The extinction of species is only one consequence of a warmer planet. Carbon dioxide is a greenhouse gas and scientists have long warned about the levels
10 produced when we burn fossil fuels. As the trees of the Amazon die off, fall and rot, they too will release carbon dioxide. The quantities of gas emitted could, at worst, be of the same order of magnitude as from the 20th century's total fossil
15 fuel output.

## B The Sahara Desert

The vast Sahara desert is expected to shrink as more plentiful rain brings vegetation to its southernmost reaches. The fertile land will be a boon for some, but the Sahara plays a broader
20 role in the health of the planet. The dry dust whipped up by strong winds contains crucial nutrients that seed the Atlantic and may even help fertilise the Amazon. As the desert shrinks, the flux of these nutrients into the ocean is
25 expected to drop, restricting food for tiny creatures called plankton. As the number of plankton falls, so does food for aquatic creatures further up the food chain. Plankton also lock up the greenhouse gas $CO_2$ from the atmosphere
30 and so help counter global warming. With fewer plankton, the oceans will take less of the gas from the Earth's atmosphere. If rains return to the Sahara, disease and crop damage from pests could soar too.

## C Greenland

35 The Greenland ice sheet holds about 6% of the planet's supply of fresh water and it is imperative that this water remains frozen. If global warming sees temperatures rise by more than about 3°C, Greenland ice is likely to begin to melt, steadily releasing all that water into the North Atlantic Ocean. A more drastic temperature
40 increase could see the Greenland ice sheet all but disappear, causing a dramatic rise in sea level. And this is not the only danger. The Arctic tundra is a storehouse for decaying vegetation that has been buried for thousands of years. If the permafrost melts, carbon and methane stored in this vegetation will be
45 released. These greenhouse gases will cause a further increase of temperatures.

## D The North Atlantic

The North Atlantic current works like a conveyer belt. Surface water in the North Atlantic Ocean is first cooled by westerly winds from North America, making the water more dense and
50 salty so it sinks to the ocean floor before moving towards the equator. Driven by winds and replacing the cold water moving south, warm water from the Gulf of Mexico moves upward into the Atlantic. The effect of the current on climate is dramatic. It brings to Europe the equivalent of 100,000 large power
55 stations' worth of free heating. Computer models predict that as global warming increases, so will rainfall in the North Atlantic. Gradually, the heavier rains will dilute the sea water and make it less likely to sink, which could bring the whole conveyer belt to a gradual halt. This would hit Iceland, Scotland and Norway most,
60 where temperatures could drop 10°C or more.

## E The Tibetan Plateau

The Tibetan plateau spans one quarter of China's entire landmass and reaches 6,000 metres above sea level. Many millions of years ago the entire region lay beneath the sea – fossils of marine animals can
65 be found in mountain ridges now standing more than 4,000 metres above sea level. The area is of global ecological importance, and is one of our planet's last great wildernesses. Permanently buried under snow and ice, the region acts as a giant mirror, reflecting the sun's rays back
70 into space. The effect is to keep a lid on global warming, at least locally. In a warmer world the white of the Tibetan plateau will slowly turn to brown and grey as the snow retreats to reveal the ground beneath. As well as contributing to a rise in global temperatures, these changes could effect global
75 jet streams, disrupting weather patterns right across the world.

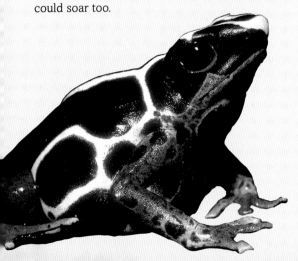

# Vocabulary

## Expressions with *earth, world* and *ground*

**1** Complete sentences a–i with *earth, world* or *ground*.

a Carmen's designer shoes must have cost the .......... ! Where did she get the money, I wonder?

b Now I've passed my driving test, I feel on top of the .......... .

c The government hoped a lot of people would vote in the election but they were very thin on the .......... .

d My grandfather is always telling me that if I graduate from university, I will have the .......... at my feet.

e I fell behind at college last term and now I have a lot of .......... to make up.

f Nothing on .......... would persuade me to swim with a shark.

g My sister's boyfriend's a bit boring – I don't think he's going to set the .......... on fire.

h Now that my dad's new business has got off the .......... , it's bringing in good profits.

i Politicians are always trying to set the .......... to rights.

**2** Complete sentences a–f to illustrate the meaning of the phrases in italics.

a The food in that hotel is *out of this world*. I really …

b A break will *do him the world of good*. He's …

c Jane's *in a world of her own* today so …

d Believe me, I wouldn't hurt you *for the world*. On the contrary, …

e Her husband *thinks the world of her*. Recently …

f Where *on earth* have you been? You …

**3** Discuss questions a–d below. A dictionary will help you.

a Have you ever bought anything that cost the earth? Was it worth it?

b If you were a politician for a day, what would you do to set the world to rights?

c In a perfect world, what would your town be like?

d Do you know anyone without a care in the world?

# Grammar

## Emphasis GR p182

**1** Use an appropriate word to complete the inversions in a–h.

a *No sooner* ......... the firemen extinguished one forest fire than another started.

b *Never before* ......... I been so petrified as when I did a parachute jump.

c I suspect that *only* much later from now ......... we find out the cause of the explosion.

d *Little* ......... we know at the moment where the ability to clone humans might lead.

e *Under no circumstances* ......... passengers permitted to smoke on the flight.

f *At no time* ......... you leave your luggage unattended at airports.

g *Rarely* ......... anyone have witnessed such an amazing sight as the view from space.

h *Not until* they were sure that everyone was safe ......... the soldiers leave the building.

**2** Correct the errors with word order in a–h. You may need to change more than one aspect of the sentence.

a Scarcely the band had announced their world tour when they were forced to cancel it.

b The planet not only is becoming polluted but it is getting warmer too.

c In no way the lorry driver was to blame for the crash.

d No sooner the prince arrived in the ski resort than he was besieged by reporters.

e Little Shakespeare's contemporaries can have guessed how enduring his plays would prove to be.

f Nowhere in the world they serve such delicious food as in Italy!

g Not until a few years ago anyone knew about the existence of the buried treasure.

h Botanists only by chance discovered the rare plant growing under a rock.

**3** Rewrite the information in a–h using the emphasising structures from 1 and 2.

a  We drove off to the coast and got a puncture almost immediately.

b  I couldn't find a pencil anywhere in the house.

c  When she went to work that day she didn't know what lay in store.

d  It was pure luck that we were passing by as the boy fell down the cliff.

e  The mistake wasn't your fault at all.

f  This flat is damp and draughty as well.

g  It's only recently that we found out his true identity.

h  They'd only just got to the summit when a thick fog descended.

**4** Talk about things currently in the news, using a–g for emphasis.

a  It's a real shame …

b  It came as something of a shock …

c  It wasn't much of a surprise …

d  It will be interesting to see …

e  It isn't the first time …

f  It angered a lot of people …

g  It was embarrassing …

**5** Join the pairs of sentences in a–h starting with the information shown.

**Example**

*I love visiting foreign countries. I particularly like trying out exotic food.*

*What I particularly like about visiting foreign countries is trying out exotic food.*

a  I know you went to the disco last night. I'm curious to know who you went with.
What I'm curious to know is …

b  I don't like gardening in general. The job I hate most is mowing the lawn.
Mowing the lawn …

c  I think John and Clare are too young to get married. I've suggested that they wait for another year.
What …

d  Of course a cruise would be wonderful. I'm just worried about how much it would cost.
All …

e  You told me English was a useful language. You didn't tell me the grammar would be so hard.
The thing …

f  It wasn't me who upset your mother. It was you.
The person …

g  I had to leave work early today. I'm holding a dinner party for twenty people tonight.
My reason …

h  You need a gorilla suit for the fancy-dress party tomorrow? You won't get one anywhere but a joke shop.
The only …

**6** Complete dialogues a–e with your own ideas.

a  I really like getting out and about at weekends.
Really? All I …

b  My favourite films tend to be romantic comedies.
Actually, what I …

c  I'm learning languages because I want to travel.
Are you? The reason …

d  I'm going to visit some old friends this evening.
That sounds good. What I'm …

e  I quite enjoy doing homework.
Really? Doing homework …

# Listening Part 4 Multiple matching

**1** Discuss the advantages and disadvantages of producing energy in the four different ways shown. Think about:

- cost
- safety
- renewable energy
- local residents

**2** 🎧 Listen to five people talking about nuclear power. Which of the advantages or disadvantages you discussed in 1 do they mention?

**3** 🎧 Listen again twice and do the exam tasks below.

For 1–5, choose from A–H how the people felt initially about the building of nuclear power stations.

A  I was determined to fight to stop them building one.
B  I felt that research had proved it was a cleaner form of energy.
C  I felt I knew too little about it to form an opinion.
D  I regarded it as an unavoidable necessity.
E  I believed the alternatives would not produce enough energy.
F  I wasn't bothered where my power supply came from.
G  I felt we already had more nuclear power stations than we need.
H  I strongly objected to it.

| Speaker 1 | | 1 |
| Speaker 2 | | 2 |
| Speaker 3 | | 3 |
| Speaker 4 | | 4 |
| Speaker 5 | | 5 |

For 6–10, choose from A–H what concerns the people have now about nuclear power stations.

A  Local people aren't kept up to date with developments.
B  They put people off moving into an area.
C  They create very few jobs in an area.
D  They are too costly a method of providing energy.
E  They pose a threat to the very existence of the planet.
F  We still don't know what their long-term effects might be.
G  There are alternatives we should explore first.
H  They eventually become a health and safety hazard.

| Speaker 1 | | 6 |
| Speaker 2 | | 7 |
| Speaker 3 | | 8 |
| Speaker 4 | | 9 |
| Speaker 5 | | 10 |

**4** What action could you take to protest against something you disagreed with?

# Speaking Parts 3 and 4

**1** Look at the Part 3 task below and for each prompt, think of two examples of the kinds of problems these things are creating in the world today. There is an example for one of the prompts.

   a  an expanding population: *not enough food to go around/housing is expensive and inadequate*
   b  economic recession
   c  species becoming extinct
   d  climate change
   e  energy resources becoming depleted

**2** 🎧 Listen to two students doing the Part 3 task and note down what problems they mention for prompts c–e.

**3** With a partner, do the Part 3 task below. Take two minutes to discuss all of the prompts. Try to use some of the phrases below.

    Suggesting alternatives

      You have a point, but …

      That's true, but don't you think … ?

      I'm not sure if I agree with you. What about … ?

      I can see what you mean but …

      Yes, but on the other hand …

      I agree with you up to a point, but …

**4** With the same partner, take one minute to decide which of the five threats would be the easiest to deal with effectively, then compare your decisions with those of another pair.

**5** In small groups, discuss these Part 4 questions.

   a  Would you agree that in some countries nowadays, eating too much food is a bigger problem than finding enough food for an expanding population? (Why/Why not?)
   b  How likely do you think it is that we might find alternative sources of energy on other planets? (Why?)
   c  Some people say that the world would be a better place without money. What's your view?
   d  What can sometimes prevent global problems from being solved?

> **tip**
>
> If you don't know or can't remember a particular word in English, don't worry. Use other words to explain what you mean.

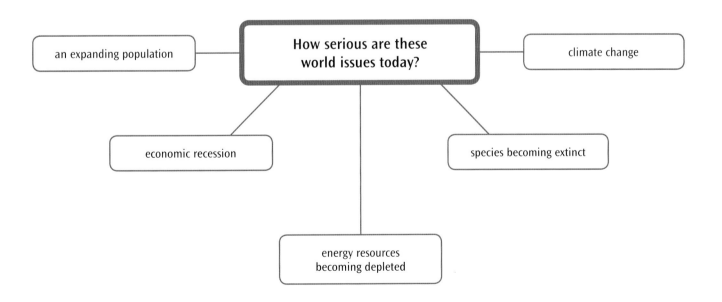

an expanding population

How serious are these world issues today?

climate change

economic recession

species becoming extinct

energy resources becoming depleted

# Use of English Part 1 Multiple-choice cloze

**1** What do you think the pieces of art shown are made from?

**2** Read the leaflet below about a recycling project, then decide which answer (A, B, C or D) best fits each gap.

| | | | | |
|---|---|---|---|---|
| 0 | A increase | B lift | C raise | D growth |
| 1 | A distributing | B discarding | C disposing | D dumping |
| 2 | A share | B assist | C enter | D participate |
| 3 | A bearing | B cutting | C holding | D backing |
| 4 | A levels | B grades | C layers | D stages |
| 5 | A direction | B course | C attempt | D aim |
| 6 | A transmitted | B transformed | C translated | D transported |
| 7 | A communicated | B informed | C instructed | D acquainted |
| 8 | A venture | B affair | C speculation | D offer |

# Turn trash into treasure

## The facts

The amounts of annual household waste are on the 0 ...A... .
Consequently, **1** ......... of such large amounts is becoming a problem which needs addressing.

## How to recycle ... with a difference

Our recycling for art programme, 'Turning trash into treasure', is currently one way of tackling this problem. This is a great way of producing original works of art such as mosaics and collages, which are inexpensive to make. Projects may vary from area to area, but everyone is eligible to **2** ......... .

## Why recycle?

Recycling has many advantages, such as **3** ......... down on landfill space and limiting environmental damage. This leads to a reduction both in energy use and pollution **4** ......... , but it can also encourage people to be creative. Paper, magazines and broken pottery and glass can all be recycled. Our main **5** ......... in recycling these materials is that they can be **6** ......... into exciting new creations.

## FURTHER INFORMATION

Our website will keep you **7** ......... of the progress of our new and exciting **8** ......... .

**3** Read the article below, then decide which gap 1–8 relates to each group of four words below the text.

### Can cardboard change the world?

A cardboard bicycle has the **1** ......... to change transportation habits, its Israeli inventor says. Izhar Gafni, 50, is an expert in designing automated production lines. He is an amateur cycling enthusiast who has now **2** ......... the idea of making a bicycle from cardboard. He told Reuters during a recent **3** ......... that his latest prototype had now proven itself and **4** ......... production would begin in a few months.

Nimrod Elmish, Gafni's business partner, **5** ......... recycling cardboard in this way could bring a major change in current production norms. Grants would only be given for local production and there would be no financial **6** ......... from making bicycles where labour is cheap. 'This changes the way products are manufactured and shipped. It **7** ......... factories to be built everywhere instead of moving production to cheaper labour **8** ......... ,' Elmish concluded. The bicycles are not only very cheap to make, they are light, need no adjustments and have solid reconstituted rubber tyres that will never get a puncture.

.... exhibit  showing  demonstration  illustration
.... powers  makings  potential  likelihood
.... thought up  thought over  come up  come out
.... said  quoted  uttered  mentioned
.... fields  markets  zones  countries
.... quantity  bulk  block  mass
.... causes  results  provokes  effects
.... aids  assets  benefits  boons

**4** Now decide which one of the four options best fits each gap 1–8.

**5** Choose one word which is not the answer from each of the groups in 3 and use them in sentences of your own.

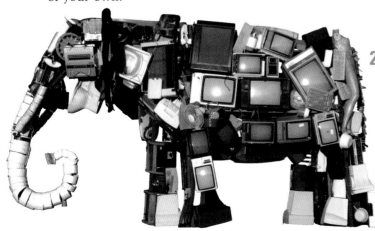

# Vocabulary
## Adverbs and their meanings

**1** Put the adverbs below into pairs with similar meanings. Then choose one adverb from each pair and use it in a sentence to illustrate its meaning.

Example
*a  annually*          *j  yearly*
*Glastonbury is a famous music festival held annually in Britain.*

a  annually          f  rarely
b  increasingly      g  occasionally
c  infrequently      h  presently
d  currently         i  progressively
e  irregularly       j  yearly

**2** Which of b–i in 1 have the same meaning as a–f below? There may be more than one possible answer.

a  now and then
b  from time to time
c  hardly ever
d  more and more
e  almost never
f  at the moment

# Writing Part 1 An essay WG p154

**1** How 'green' is your school or workplace? List the measures it has taken to protect the environment, e.g. recycling procedures, fitting solar panels. Should any more measures be taken, in your opinion? Describe them.

**2** Read the writing task and input text and underline the key information. How many methods must you include in your essay? How must you compare them?

You have just taken part in a panel discussion on the state of the environment. The discussion focused on the methods international organisations should use to persuade companies in countries around the world to become 'greener'. You have made the notes below.

Methods international bodies could use to persuade companies in different nations to become 'greener':

- legislation
- individual protests
- government boycotts

Some opinions expressed in the discussion:

'There should be precise laws about all this, and they should be strictly enacted.'

'It's up to all of us, not just international bodies, to protest if companies damage the environment.'

'If international bodies refuse to do business with "bad" companies, then maybe these companies will have to listen.'

Write an essay discussing **two** of the measures in your notes. You should explain **which measure you think is more important** for international organisations to consider, **giving reasons** in support of your answer.

You may, if you wish, make use of the opinions expressed in the discussion, but you should use your own words as far as possible.

Write your **essay** in **220–260** words in an appropriate style.

**3** Discuss the three methods mentioned in the exam question and list points you could make about each. Then choose the two you have most to write about. Which of those two is more important, do you think? Give reasons.

**4** Read the first two paragraphs of the model essay opposite and find examples of the following:

a   rhetorical questions
b   varied sentence patterns
c   a direct appeal to the reader
d   appropriate linking words
e   high-level vocabulary including collocations and set phrases
f   a clearly expressed opinion

**5** Read the third paragraph of the model. What has the writer forgotten to do?

**6** Rewrite paragraph 3 in an appropriate way. Consider the features a–f in exercise 4. Would any of them be useful for your paragraph?

**7** Now write a concluding paragraph for the essay. The tip box and the phrases below will help you.

■ Concluding

To sum up, …
All in all, …
In conclusion, …
As we have seen above, …

> **tip**
> The conclusion of an essay usually contains a brief summary of what has been said, plus a comment that 'rounds off' the essay. Develop this paragraph in the same way as the preceding paragraphs. Avoid one-sentence conclusions.

**8** Now write your own answer to the exam task in 2, using the ideas you made in 3. The how to do it box will help you.

## Making companies greener

1 Over the past century we have inflicted a huge amount of damage on our environment. Although some national companies are doing their best to 'green up', plenty are not; instead they continue with practices that are harming our planet. This has to stop!

2 So how can international bodies force national businesses and corporations to look after our world? In my opinion, their biggest priority should be to introduce wider legislation and then enforce it far more strictly than is the case with current laws. As I'm sure you agree, too many companies still pollute air, land or sea – and get away with it. Until international organisations prove that they mean what they say, and impose huge fines or even prison sentences, the worst companies will never mend their ways.

3 Another way to encourage change would be for these bodies to boycott offending companies. By refusing to deal with these companies or to offer them contracts, international organisations could make it impossible for them to survive. Fear of this would surely make most companies think twice about their ways of working.

4 ...

## how to do it

Don't just discuss the two methods – compare them and say which is more important.

Give reasons for your opinion.

Use your own words.

Remember the 'three Ps' – Plan, Paragraph, Punctuate!

# Review

**1** Complete the phrases in sentences a–l with *earth*, *world* or *ground*.

a That new restaurant was excellent but the place never really got off the ............ .

b That outfit I bought for the wedding was stunning but it cost the ............ .

c The studio's latest film is uninspiring. It's certainly not going to set the ............ on fire.

d After my illness last month I had a lot of ............ to make up at work.

e The mountain walks in this area are out of this ............ . You'll love them.

f Everyone had hoped for a huge turnout at the film premiere but fans were thin on the ............ .

g I suffer from vertigo, so nothing on ............ would make me go bungee jumping!

h A few days' rest will do you a ............ of good. You haven't been your usual cheerful self lately.

i I felt on top of the ............ when I got engaged but the wedding day was a disaster!

j It's the tennis final this weekend and I wouldn't miss it for the ............ .

k What on ............ have you done to your hair? It looks absolutely dreadful!

l What's on your mind? You seem to be in a ............ of your own at the moment.

**2** Replace the words in italics in a–h with verbs 1–8 below in the correct form.

a Police are hoping the witness will *make available* more information about the robbery.

b A radical change of image is needed if we are to *help sell* the rock band's new tour.

c Does anyone know what *led to* the accident last night?

d Thanks to their new advertising campaign, they have *produced* huge interest in the product.

e Susan's parents made every effort to *persuade* her to go to university.

f Will scientists ever really find out how the universe *was formed*?

g What was already a difficult situation was *negatively affected* by media interference.

h We need to *produce material to be used by* people with different learning styles.

| | | |
|---|---|---|
| 1 cause | 4 worsen | 7 generate |
| 2 provide | 5 promote | 8 encourage |
| 3 cater for | 6 create | |

**3** Write one word which is the opposite of the words in a–j. More than one answer may be possible.

a increase ............
b fertile ............
c shrink ............
d broader ............
e fall ............
f retreat ............
g appear ............
h permitted ............
i descended ............
j frequent ............

**4** Write adverbs with the same meaning as phrases a–e. Some letters are given to help you.

a more and more: inc...
 pro...

b from time to time: irr...
 occ...

c hardly ever: ra...
 in...

d every twelve months: an...
 y...

e at the moment: pre...
 cur...

**5** Rewrite the information in a and b using as few words as possible, beginning with the words shown.

a It would be a very good idea to try and persuade people to recycle things like old mobile phones they do not want any more.

 People ...

b It would really make a lot of difference to create some parks and it would make the whole area a much more pleasant place for local inhabitants to live in.

 Creating ...

# Appendix

## Unit 1 What are you like?

### Lead in

**2** Add up your points for each separate section: a = 1, b = 2, c = 3. Then look below to see which category you are in.

**Head or Heart:** If you got 3–5 points you're Head; 6–9 points you're Heart.

**Extrovert or Introvert:** 3–5 points you're Introvert; 6–9 points you're Extrovert.

**Facts or Ideas:** 3–5 points you're Facts; 6–9 points you're Ideas.

Now find your combination of answers in the table (e.g. Head, Introvert, Ideas) to see what it says about your personality and the careers that might suit you.

| Combination | Personality type | Possible careers |
| --- | --- | --- |
| Heart, Introvert, Facts | methodical, conscientious, friendly and sensitive | nurse, teacher, doctor, librarian |
| Heart, Extrovert, Facts | energetic, fun-loving, sociable and caring | teacher, designer, child-care worker, office manager |
| Heart, Introvert, Ideas | committed, faithful, sceptical and inventive | psychiatrist, writer, artist, entertainer |
| Heart, Extrovert, Ideas | fun-loving, optimistic, passionate and facilitative | writer, musician, editor, designer |
| Head, Introvert, Facts | dependable, practical, realistic and analytical | accountant, computer programmer, engineer, mechanic |
| Head, Extrovert, Facts | adventurous, high-energy, tough, ambitious | marketing manager, supervisor, purchasing agent |
| Head, Introvert, Ideas | independent, clear-thinking, logical and insightful | architect, lawyer, judge, manager |
| Head, Extrovert, Ideas | flexible, innovative, decisive, energetic | photographer, journalist, doctor, administrator |

## Unit 6 Would you believe it?

### Lead in

**1**
a  T
b  F  The word simply comes from 'new'.
c  T
d  F  It takes no longer to digest than anything else, i.e. a few hours.
e  F  The number of people alive today is estimated at 7 billion. 6.5 billion are estimated to have lived since the building of the Pyramids, and probably about 60 billion in total in the 40–45,000 years humans have been around.
f  T  A 20-cm stalk contains about six calories. More are burnt off during digestion – not chewing – but you would have to eat a lot of celery to make any real difference to your weight.

# Writing Guide

## Essays

You have just listened to a local radio discussion programme about ways in which your town could be improved. You have made the notes below.

Which facilities should the town council support if they are to improve our town?

- cultural venues
- shopping centres
- sports clubs

Some opinons expressed in the discussion:

'Not everyone likes theatre, ballet or opera.'

'Shops are crucial if we are going to bring prosperity to the town.'

'Keeping fit should be a top priority for everyone.'

Write an essay discussing **two** of the facilities in your notes. You should **explain which facility is more important** for the town council to support, **giving reasons** for your answer.

You may, if you wish, make use of the opinions expressed in the discussion, but you should use your own words as far as possible.

Write your **essay** in **220–260** words in an appropriate style.

1　Make a plan before you start by listing your points and putting them in a logical order.
2　Summarise the subject clearly in the introductory paragraph.
3　Organise your ideas into paragraphs.
4　Use linkers to make your writing flow.
5　Use a variety of sentence structures.
6　Reword phrases from the input text where possible.
7　Express your opinions clearly and give reasons to justify choosing one option above the other.
8　Use appropriate phrases to compare and contrast ideas.

Our town used to be a thriving place but over the past decade it has become very run down. It is therefore (4) important that we think carefully about how to prioritise any planned improvements. (2) (3)

One of the major problems in the town is our lack of good sports amenities. (6) The present gymnasium is very small and the equipment is out of date and very unreliable. As I am sure most people would agree, fitness plays an essential role (6) in the health and happiness of all the inhabitants of our town and that is why I believe (7) it should be our top priority. (3)

Of almost equal importance (8) is the need for adequate cultural venues in our town. Although (4) the town boasts a well-established theatre, a new art gallery or cultural centre would make a significant contribution to the educational opportunities available to local people, as well as (4) offering another place of entertainment and recreation. Nevertheless, (4) it is likely fewer people will take advantage of these facilities than will use the sports club and for that reason (7) I believe they should take second place. (8)

To sum up, to enhance our town we eventually need both the new sports facilities and the cultural venues. Given the need to prioritise, however, (4) it seems clear that sport should come first. Having attended to that area, we can later turn our minds to the cultural venues we so desperately need. (3)

## phrase bank

**Sequencing points in an argument**
Take, for example …
In the first place/To start with, …
Secondly, …
Finally, …

**Prioritising/comparing**
I believe X should be our top priority.
It is my opinion that X should take second place.
It seems to me that X must come first.

**Justifying opinions**
The reason I think this is because …
… and that is why I believe …
… and for that reason I think …

**Conclusions**
In sum/To sum up, …
In conclusion, …

# Informal letters and emails

You have received a letter from an English friend, Steve. Read part of the letter and then write your letter to Steve.

Guess what? I've passed all my exams with top grades! As you know, I didn't expect to do so well, so instead of enrolling at university, I decided to backpack round the world next year. Now my family are urging me to rethink and go to uni after all. I'd really like your advice please. What are the pros and cons of each, and which should I choose? Or maybe you think it's possible to do both?

Write soon.

Best wishes

Steve

**Write your letter in 220–260 words in an appropriate style.**

1  Begin informal emails/letters with 'Dear ...' or 'Hi'.

2  Finish with 'Best wishes' (or 'Love' for very close family or friends).

3  Use an informal style that is in keeping with the relationship you have with the reader of your letter.

4  Group similar ideas together and develop them to form paragraphs.

5  Use linking phrases where appropriate.

6  Start a new paragraph when you change topic.

7  Close your letter with a set phrase.

Dear Steve, (1)

Congratulations on passing your exams, you clever thing! You must have been delighted when you got the news. Hope you've been celebrating hard!

Now, about your two options for next year. (5) They both sound great so I'm not surprised you're having trouble deciding what to do.

The idea of travelling round the world is really exciting and of course we probably need to do these things while we're still young. Having said that, (5) I think you need to bear in mind that going to university could change your whole future. Just think – with the grades you've just got, you could study something brilliant, like medicine. Do you want to jeopardise your chances of doing that? Somehow I don't think so.

(4) If you really have to choose one option over the other, university has to come first – it's a no-brainer, as far as I can see. But I do have an alternative suggestion. Why don't you apply for uni but ask for a year off before taking it up? That way you can have the best of both worlds – travel and university. What do you think?

Anyway, Steve, I hope my suggestions make sense to you and that they help with your decision.

Best of luck with (7) your dilemma and don't forget to write and tell me the outcome.

Love, (2)

Laura

## phrase bank

**Opening and ending your letter/email**
Dear John/Maria
Hi John/Maria
Love = (very informal)
Best wishes = (neutral)
Regards = (neutral/a little more formal)

**First lines**
Congratulations on … !
It was great to hear from you and get all your news.
I was really pleased to get your recent letter/email.

**Giving advice**
I think you need to bear in mind that …
Why don't you … ? That way, you could …
Have you thought about … ?
Just think … !
Do you really want to … ? Somehow I don't think so.

**Final lines**
I hope my suggestions help you to …
Don't forget to write and tell me …
Best of luck with …
Keep in touch.
Hope to hear from you soon.
Looking forward to hearing from you.

# Formal letters and emails

You have seen the following announcement on the 'Young World' website:

**Wanted: TV presenter**

We are an international TV company planning to make a series of programmes, in English, about issues of interest to young people around the world. Could you help to present the show? If you think you are the right person for the job, write to me, John Finch, giving reasons for this. You should also explain which issue you think we should highlight in our first programme, and why.

Write your **letter** in **220–260** words in an appropriate style.

1 Use formal language when writing to a person in authority such as the head of a company, the editor of a newspaper, or a college principal.

2 Open with 'Dear ...' and use the person's name if known, otherwise use 'Dear Sir/Madam'.

3 Start by giving your reason for writing.

4 Group similar ideas together and develop them to form paragraphs.

5 Link sentences and paragraphs carefully using appropriate linking phrases.

6 Start a new paragraph when you change topic.

7 Use a good range of vocabulary and structures.

8 Make sure your grammar and punctuation are correct.

9 Close your letter with a set phrase.

10 End with 'Yours faithfully' if you don't know the person's name, or 'Yours sincerely' if you do.

Dear Sir or Madam (2)

I have seen your announcement on the 'Young World' website and am writing to apply for the post of presenter for your forthcoming series. (3)

(4) I am twenty years old and, as you will see, I have a great deal of appropriate experience. (5) First, I am a trainee journalist and have been taking care of the 'Young People Today' section of my local newspaper for the past few months. In this role, I spend a lot of time interviewing young people on issues they find important, which ties in well with the post you are offering. (5) Secondly, I belong to an amateur drama group. Having played many acting roles, I would be very much at ease in front of an audience. (5) Last but not least, I am well able to present the series in English since my mother comes from the United Kingdom and I am bilingual.

(6) The issue I suggest we focus on, given the age of our target audience, (7) is emotional relationships. Young people have many difficulties in this area, whether it be in forming new friendships, boy–girl relationships, dealing with break-ups or coping with family upheavals. (7) A programme that illustrated typical problems and offered advice on dealing with each of these would, I am sure, be seen as extremely helpful and could even become essential viewing. (7)

I hope I have shown that I would be an ideal presenter and that you like my ideas for the programmes.

I look forward to hearing from you. (9)

Yours faithfully (10)

Miranda Jiménez

## phrase bank

### Starting your letter
Dear Sir/Madam,
Dear Mr/Mrs … ,

### Reason for writing
I am writing to apply for …
I am writing to you about/with regard to …
I am writing in response to …
I am writing to enquire /complain about …
I would like to apologise for …

### Giving personal information
I've been studying … for the past two years.
I currently work as a … so I am used to …

### Making suggestions
The issue I suggest we focus on is … . This is because …
I propose we begin with … . The reason for this is that …
My first suggestion would be to … . Let me explain why.

### Concluding remarks
I hope my application will meet with your approval.
I hope I have shown that …
I hope you will find this information of use.
I trust you will look into this matter fully.
I hope you understand my concern about this matter.
I would be very grateful for your help in this matter.
I look forward to hearing from you.

### Signing off
Yours faithfully,
Yours sincerely,

# Reviews

The editor of a local newspaper has asked you to write a review of *two* quite different places where young people can meet up for a drink or a meal in your town.

Write your **review** in **220–260** words in an appropriate style.

1  Remember that reviews can include criticism as well as praise.

2  Divide your review into paragraphs with a clear introduction and conclusion.

3  Give a clear, concise description of the place you are reviewing.

4  Start each paragraph with a topic sentence.

5  Keep your opinions/recommendations for the final paragraph.

# review

There are many places for young people to eat together and socialise in our town, but two have become very popular. Keen to discover whether they live up to their reputations, I went along this week to sample what was on offer. (2)

The first on my list was *Hollywood Rock*. (4) Step inside this restaurant and you feel as if you've been transported into the past. The interior is a series of small rooms, each dedicated to legendary rock performers like Elvis or the Beatles. The walls are decorated with rock guitars and record covers and other memorabilia. (3) As you eat, rock music booms out around you. The menu is predictable (1) – the usual choice of pizzas, burgers and fries – but it offers good value for money.

My second visit was to *Gigi's*, a riverside café in the student quarter. (4) This is a very cosmopolitan venue, attracting students from all over the world. In good weather, customers can eat outside and enjoy the marvellous river views. The menu is limited (1), with an emphasis on seafood, but it is reasonably priced and the quality is good. There is live music at weekends, but noise levels are kept low.

So which of the two restaurants should you choose? (4) While *Hollywood Rock* is original and will appeal to certain music fans, it is noisy, which makes conversation difficult. (1) If you prefer to socialise outdoors or in a slightly quieter setting, I suggest you try *Gigi's*. (5) But go early – tables fill up quickly, especially at weekends.

## phrase bank

**Making positive points**

It offers good value for money.
It is reasonably priced.
The quality is good/excellent.
Its facilities are impressive/stylish.
It will appeal to …

**Making negative points**

Unfortunately, the … is a bit predictable.
Disappointingly, the menu/range/service is limited.
It is noisy/disappointing/not up to standard.

**Comparing and contrasting/Weighing up the pros and cons**

While … , sadly …
Taking into account … , I suggest …
Either of these would be a good choice, but …

**Giving advice**

Go early!
It is probably best to go early.
If you would rather … , I recommend that you …

# Reports

You are on the student committee at your college. This year you helped the English Department organise a three-week study trip to the UK. The principal of the college has asked you to write a report on the trip.

You should explain what was successful about the trip, describe any problems, and suggest improvements for future trips.

Write your **report** in **220–260** words in an appropriate style.

**Possible plan**

Intro: aim of this report

Accommodation: host families helpful but elderly – younger ones next time?

Sports/social programmes: v. good (give details) – keep next year

Language classes: teachers friendly but we need more speaking and listening practice next time

Conclusion: recommend repeat the trip with improvements

1   Use appropriate linking words.

2   Use appropriate phrases to make suggestions and recommendations if appropriate (also see page 165).

3   Organise your report into sections with headings.

4   Include a clear introduction and conclusion.

5   Write clear and concise sentences

6   Use a formal style.

### Introduction (4)
The aim of this report is to assess the success of this year's study trip to the UK and to recommend any changes.

### Accommodation (3)
Students appreciated the hospitality offered to them by their host families and the help they gave them with their language practice. However, (1) some of the host families were rather elderly. It would be preferable (2) if younger host families could be found for our next trip.

### Sports and social programme (3)
Students were highly enthusiastic about this side of the trip, which offered them the chance to compete against British students in various sports and also learn about British culture while mixing with British students. They were able to visit art galleries and museums and the programme included a hit show and some rock and pop events. I propose that (2) we repeat this type of programme next year.

### Language classes (3)
While (1) most students got on well with the teachers, they would have liked more chance to improve their speaking and listening skills. I suggest we request that more class time is spent on communicative skills next year.

### Conclusion (4)
To sum up, (1) this year's trip appears to have been enjoyed by most students despite the reservations mentioned above. If the suggested changes are implemented, I have no hesitation in recommending (2) that we send other students on the trip next year.

## phrase bank

**Introduction**
The aim of this report is to …
This report describes/outlines/deals with …
This report is based on …

**Making recommendations**
It would be a good idea to …
It might be advisable to …
It would be preferable to …
I suggest/propose/recommend that we (should) …

**Conclusion**
To sum up, …
In conclusion, …
I have no hesitation in recommending …

# Proposals

Your college has been awarded a large sum of money. The college principal has asked the student committee to write a proposal explaining which areas most need improving and why, and how the money should be spent.

Write your **proposal** in **220–260** words in an appropriate style.

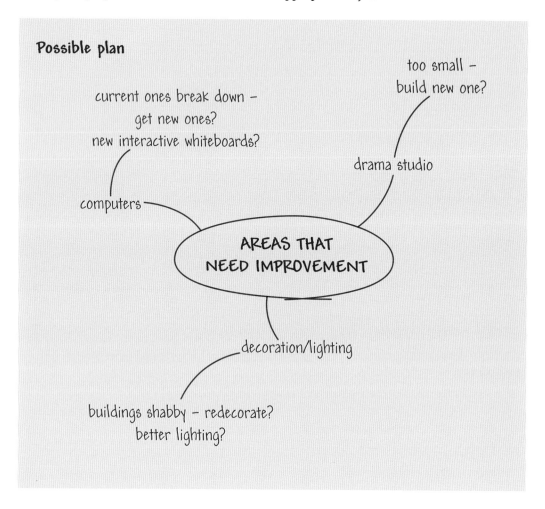

Possible plan

current ones break down –
get new ones?
new interactive whiteboards?

too small –
build new one?

drama studio

computers

AREAS THAT
NEED IMPROVEMENT

decoration/lighting

buildings shabby – redecorate?
better lighting?

1  Use appropriate language for making suggestions and recommendations (also see page 163).

2  Use linkers to sequence points.

3  Set out your text so that it looks like a proposal and not a letter.

4  Divide your proposal into sections with headings.

5  Include a separate introduction and conclusion.

6  Be clear and concise.

7  Use an impersonal tone.

### Introduction (5)

The purpose of this proposal is to outline areas which need improving and to make recommendations as to where money should be spent.

### Equipment (4)

Many students pointed out that the computers currently in use are becoming dated and are apt to break down quite frequently. I would therefore recommend (1) that we buy new, state-of-the-art computers. Additionally, (2) it was felt that the existing basic whiteboards were outdated. I therefore propose that we invest in interactive whiteboards.

### Buildings (4)

Many students are unhappy with the size of the drama studio, which is too small to house major productions. I suggest (1) we consider a new building as this would allow us to provide much better facilities and to stage much bigger shows.

### Decoration and lighting (4)

Several students pointed out the fact that the college is badly in need of redecoration. Others were worried about their personal safety due to the fact that the college is poorly lit. My recommendation is (1) that we redecorate the entire premises, inside and out, and that we install effective lighting in the college grounds.

### Conclusion (5)

In conclusion, (2) I believe that the areas identified in this proposal are the ones that are most in need of improvement. If the recommendations above are followed, I believe they would have the support of all our students.

## phrase bank

**Introduction**
The aim/purpose of this proposal is to …
This proposal relates to …
This proposal describes/outlines …

**Suggestions and recommendations**
I recommend/propose/suggest/
believe (that) we (should) …
We could also …
If we … , we could …

**Conclusion**
To sum up, I believe that …
In conclusion, I would say that …
On balance, we are of the opinion that …

# Grammar Reference

## Present and past tenses

### Present simple

Use the present simple:

1 to talk about habitual events and fixed truths:

*Most authors write about 1,000 words a day.*

*Violins have four strings.*

2 to talk about how often you do something. Frequency adverbs (*always, usually, often, sometimes, never*) are often used:

*Carla checks her text messages every few minutes.*

3 for states that imply permanence or for those that are true for a long time:

*The President of the United States works in the White House.*

### Present continuous

Use the present continuous:

1 for temporary states:

*He is acting as manager while his boss is away.*

2 to talk about an activity that is taking place when you speak or around the time of speaking:

*Listen! This computer is making a strange noise.*

*He's studying at evening class at the moment.*

### Past simple

Use the past simple to express an event that took place at a definite past time. Past time words are often used to fix the action or state in the past. For example, *when, yesterday, last week, three months ago*, etc:

– *When did you last write a letter by hand?*

– *I think it was about a year ago.*

When there are no past time words, the context often places the action or event in the past (either the recent past or the more remote past):

*Where did you learn to do those magic tricks?*

*Karl Benz invented the first motor car.*

The action can either last for a period of time in the past or finish at a fixed time in the past:

*Henry ran 15 kilometres every day for 60 years.*

*He gave up running in June and died in July.*

### Past continuous

Use the past continuous:

1 to talk about things that were in progress in the past. They may or may not be finished:

*Last week, the police were watching the house on the corner.*

2 to talk about a background activity:

*We were lying on our backs looking at the stars.*

A single past event often interrupts the background activity, so the past continuous and the past simple are used together:

*We were lying on our backs looking at the stars when a comet flew across the sky.*

But when two or more past events happen consecutively, the past simple is used for both:

*The* Titanic *hit an iceberg and sank a few hours later.*

Note: Don't use the past continuous to talk about past habits or to say how often something happened in the past. Use the past simple:

*They phoned the zoo three times yesterday.*
(Not: *They were phoning …*)

### Present perfect simple

Use the present perfect simple:

1 when there is a connection between the past and the present. The connection can either be implied or obvious. The exact timing is not important:

*The explorers have just reached the North Pole.*

*He's lost a lot of weight in the last few months.*

2 for things that have just happened or when the event is still relevant or is still 'news':

*Oh, no! The wheel has fallen off!*

You must use the present perfect simple form when you mention the number of times:

*That train has broken down three times so far this week.*

The event might have started at some time in the past and still continues:

*I have known about the problem for a long time, but I haven't done anything about it yet.*

3   to give general news or information. This is followed by more detail using the past simple:

*A new zoo for endangered species has opened in the Lake District. It took five years to build and runs entirely on solar energy.*

## Present perfect continuous

Use the present perfect continuous:

1   for events that began in the past and continue into the present. Like the present perfect simple, it is often used with *since* ( + starting point), *for* ( + period of time) and *how long*:

*They have been going out with each other since Christmas.*

*That dog has been chasing its tail for about ten minutes.*

2   to talk about long or repeated actions that have just finished, but where the consequence is still clear:

– *You're late for the meeting!*

– *Sorry! I've been trying to park my car.*

## Past perfect simple

Use the past perfect to talk about what happened before a certain point in the past:

*The robber had run away by the time the police arrived.*

## Past perfect continuous

Use the past perfect continuous to emphasise a longer action. This action continues up to the time of the main action (expressed by the verb in the past simple):

*I wasn't surprised that Dave and Amy emigrated. They had been thinking about it for years.*

But use the past perfect simple to say 'how many times':

*By the time he was 25, he had already been married twice.*

## Used to *and* would

Use *used to* ( + infinitive) to talk about past habits:

*Believe it or not, but people used to write letters by hand and send them to their friends.*

To ask questions, use *did* + name/pronoun + *use to* (not *used to*):

*Did your parents use to allow you to ride a motorbike?*

The negative form is *didn't use to* (not *didn't used to*):

*Policemen didn't use to carry firearms.*

It is sometimes possible to use *would* instead of *used to* when talking about past personal habits, but usually only in the positive. *Would* is quite a literary style and is often found in continuous narrative:

*When we were young we would go to the river and throw stones in the stream, then go to a little teashop and buy some cakes.*

Use *used to* for past situations and states that no longer exist or are no longer true (*would* cannot be used).

*In the 1930s that bar used to be a very famous little theatre.*

*Did Shakespeare use to live in London?*

Note: Don't use *used to* to say how long something lasted in the past. Use the past simple:

*I did the national lottery for a long time, but I didn't have any luck.* (Not: *I used to do …*)

# Future forms

## Present simple

Use the present simple to express future events that are timetabled or part of a calendar:

*The directors' meeting starts at 3 o'clock on Friday.*

*Hurry up. The plane leaves in half an hour.*

The present simple is used when the timetabling or arrangement is impersonal (someone else has made them or they are part of a natural law):

*The next college term starts on 8th September.*

For personal arrangements, where the speaker or another person has made the decision, the present continuous is usually used:

*I'm starting a new course in biology next term.*

## Present continuous

The present continuous is used to express the future when definite plans or arrangements have been made:

– *What are you doing next Saturday?*

– *I'm taking my driving test.*

You can use the present continuous tense with verbs of motion, even if no fixed arrangements have been made:

*You had better hurry up and get ready, because we're leaving very soon.*

### *Going to* and *will*

**Use *going to*:**

1  when you have made a decision to do something:

*Could you please let me know if you are going to accept the job?*

2  when you have made some *basic* plans:

*I'm going to buy an old barn and do it up.*

But when more definite plans are in place, use the present continuous:

*We've signed the contracts and we're moving into the building on Monday.*

3  to say what someone is just about to do:

*I won't be a minute. I'm just going to say goodbye to my colleague.*

4  for predictions when there is clear evidence that an event is about to take place:

*Based on the first page, I think I'm going to enjoy reading this book.*

For 'neutral' predictions that are based on personal belief, rather than clear evidence, see *will* below:

**Use *will* and *won't*:**

1  to ask for and give information about the future, which is often a simple matter of fact:

*The train standing at platform 3 will stop at Oxford.*

*'The work won't take long,' the builder said.*

2  to express the near future when there has been no conscious planning or premeditation. For example, on-the-spot decisions:

*I'll have a mushroom omelette and a green salad.*

– *Will you marry me?*

– *No, I won't.*

3  to predict what you think will happen in the future, based on what you believe or guess will happen:

*Soon, we will all pay our bills by mobile phone.*

*Video machines won't be available in a few years.*

But when there is clear evidence about what is going to happen, use *going to*:

*The builder looked at the old house and said, 'I'm sorry, but it's going to fall down.'*

## Future continuous

Use the future continuous to talk about an event that will be in progress at a certain time in the future:

*This time next week I'll be lying on a beach.*

Future time phrases are common with this tense:

| | |
|---|---|
| *In a few months' time* | |
| *Before long* | *we'll be travelling* |
| *This time next year* | *around South America.* |
| *By December* | |

The question form of the future continuous is often used for polite requests as it avoids the urgency of other tenses:

*Will you be checking out of your room by noon?*

## Future perfect simple

Use the future perfect to talk about things that will have happened by a certain time in the future. It is often used with a phrase starting with *by* to emphasise completion before a certain future time:

| | |
|---|---|
| *By Monday* | |
| *By lunchtime* | *he will have finished* |
| *By this time next year* | *his report.* |
| *By the time you read this* | |

## Future perfect continuous

Use the future perfect continuous to talk about how long things will have been happening by a certain time in the future (and perhaps beyond that time). It is often used with a phrase starting with *for* to emphasise duration:

*Next month he will have been working at the factory for 25 years.*

## The future in the past

Use the following 'future in the past' structures when you are talking about the past and want to say that something was still in the future at that time:

1 past continuous or *was/were going to* (+ infinitive):

*Danny waited outside the station. He was meeting his daughter at 2 o'clock and they were going to watch the Cup Final.*

The planned or expected future action often doesn't happen:

*He was planning to sell the house, until it caught fire.*

2 *would* (+ infinitive):

*None of us thought the exam would be so easy.*

3 *was/were to* (+ infinitive):

*A politician was to give a speech, but she didn't turn up.*

Use *was/were just about to* in the same way:

*They were just about to disappear round the corner when they saw me waving.*

## Time clauses in the future

Use the present tense in many future subordinate clauses. Use a future form in the main clause:

*He is going to Barcelona, when he gets a ticket.* (Not: *when he will get …*)

*As soon as he arrives he's going to buy a weekly travel ticket.* (Not: *As soon as he will arrive …*)

Conjunctions that introduce these clauses include:

as soon as    when    once    by the time

Use the present perfect after *as soon as* or *when* to express completion:

*James is going to have a party as soon as his parents have gone away.*

*I'll check your work for you when you have finished.*

Use the present continuous after *while* to show that the action still continues:

*I'll stop drilling while you are trying to work.*

# Non-continuous verbs

Many English verbs express a state rather than an activity, so they are not normally used in any of the continuous tenses. These verbs fall into several groups:

1 Verbs that describe wants and likes and preferences, e.g. *want, like, prefer, hope, wish.*

2 Verbs that describe thought processes and opinions, e.g. *think, believe, know, remind, understand.*

3 Verbs for the senses, e.g. *hear, see, taste, smell, touch, feel.* But 'sense' verbs that describe an active, deliberate use of the senses are used in the continuous tenses, e.g. *watch, look, stare, listen.*

4 Verbs for belonging and containing, e.g. *own, possess, belong.*

Many of the verbs above and other 'stative' verbs can sometimes describe 'actions', with a change of meaning. With the new meaning it is usually possible to use continuous forms. Remember that continuous forms imply a temporary action:

*She is usually quite honest.* (a permanent characteristic)

*She isn't being very honest.* (a temporary condition)

*I think you're unreliable and over-ambitious.* (= have the opinion)

*I'm thinking of changing my solicitor.* (= consider)

*He appears to be quite mature, but he's actually quite the opposite.* (= seem)

*Several comedy acts will be appearing at The Palace Theatre during the summer.* (= take part in)

*I don't expect you'll like this, but I'm leaving the company.* (= think)

*I've been expecting you to arrive since 8 o'clock this morning.* (= anticipate)

*I don't have much experience of negotiating prices.* (= possess)

*I'm having dinner with the Prime Minister after the meeting.* (= eat)

*This is how you should present your CV. Do you see what I mean?* (= understand)

*How long have you been seeing a psychiatrist?* (= consult)

# Passives

## Form and structures

Most active sentences have a corresponding passive. All transitive verbs (verbs that take a direct object) can have a passive form. Intransitive verbs like *die, arrive, sleep,* etc. cannot have a passive form.

The object of an active sentence is the subject of the corresponding passive sentence:

**Active:** *We have counted all the votes, and we can now announce the winners.* (all the votes and the winners are the objects)

**Passive:** *All the votes have been counted and the winners can be announced.* (all the votes and the winners are the subjects)

You can form passives from all tenses, future forms, and also modals such as *can, must,* etc. A passive is formed with the appropriate tense of *be* + the past participle:

**Present simple:** *People who want a visa are required to complete long application forms.*

**Present continuous:** *The plane is being prepared for take-off.*

**Present perfect:** *I can't phone you. My phone has been stolen.*

**Past simple/past perfect:** *The man wasn't allowed to see his solicitor until after he had been interviewed by the police.*

**Past continuous:** *The children were being taught how to use a computer.*

**The future:** *You are going to be taken to prison, where you will be given a haircut and overalls.*

**Modals:** *Credit cards can be used to confirm the hotel booking.*

*The evidence mustn't be touched after it has been put into the plastic bags.*

*The prisoners should be allowed to make a phone call to their solicitors.*

*All the rules here have to be obeyed.*

There are various passive structures that use the infinitive and are often used in news reporting. For example:

*The ringleader of the gang **is thought** to be Spanish.*

*Plans for the new sports centre **are said** to be under threat.*

*Negotiations **are believed/rumoured** to be coming to a conclusion.*

Use *have* + past participle in the past:

*The ringleader of the gang is thought to have fled to Spain.*

*Plans for the new sports centre are said to have been shelved.*

Use *to* + infinitive in the passive structure after the verbs *see, hear, make* and *allow*:

*Three very suspicious men were seen to leave the building carrying black sacks.*

*A young boy at the back of the hall was heard to laugh during the Prime Minister's speech.*

*One thing he hated about prison life was being made to peel potatoes.*

*The passengers were not allowed to get off the plane.*

Note: When the verb *let* is used in an active sentence, *allow* must be used in the equivalent passive sentence:

**Active:** *The police didn't let him phone his lawyer.*

**Passive:** *He wasn't allowed to phone his lawyer.*

When more than one verb is used in the passive, the auxiliary verb *be* does not have to be repeated:

*Forensic evidence will be collected, sent to a laboratory and analysed.*

You can change the subject of a passive sentence midway through the sentence. Again, the verb *be* does not have to be repeated:

*Fingerprints are taken and the results (are) fed into a computer.*

## When to use the passive

Passive structures are used when the action is more important than who did it (the 'agent'). The most important information in English often comes at the beginning of a sentence, and new information or more details come at the end.

The passive is often used:

1 in advertising, because the product becomes the focus of attention:

*Our sportswear is tested by robots and worn by world champions.*

2 in formal, impersonal texts:

*Your application has been received and you will be informed of our decision in due course.*

3 in scientific texts, official writing and newspaper headlines:

*Many breakthroughs in the fight against cancer have been made over the past few years.*

4  when the agent is unknown or is not important or is obvious from the context:

   *The wheel was invented about 5,000 years ago.*

5  to avoid the overuse or repetition of personal pronouns or vague words such as *people*:

   *The M25 motorway is being repaired and should be avoided for the next two weeks.*

You can mention the agent in a passive structure if it is important. Use *by* + name or noun:

   *The boxer was knocked out in the first round.*
   *(The agent is not named, so we assume it wasn't anything remarkable.)*

   *The boxer was knocked out in the first round by a rock thrown from the spectator's area.*

### *have/get something done*

Use the structure *have* + noun/pronoun + past participle when someone else does something for you. For example, your car needs a service, your eyes need to be tested, etc:

   *Sorry, I can't talk. I'm just having my hair cut.*

You can use this structure to refer to things that are done by someone else and are beyond your control:

   *The boy had his locker broken into and his camera stolen.*

You can often use *get* with the same structure, but it is often more informal or more urgent:

   *I must get those documents signed.*

# Gerunds and infinitives

### verb + *to* + infinitive

Certain verbs are often followed by *to* + infinitive of another verb:

| | | |
|---|---|---|
| deserve | expect | hope |
| manage | offer | promise |
| refuse | threaten | want |

   *It's a pity he lost the race, because he deserved to win.*
   *What did you expect to find when you opened the box?*

*To* can stand alone to avoid repeating the verb or phrase:

   *I'm not sure I'm going to pass my driving test first time, but I certainly hope to.*

With many verbs, an object comes before *to*:

   *The sales director asked the editor to give an outline of the proposal.*

### verb + object + *to* + infinitive

The verbs that use this construction fall roughly into two groups:

1  Verbs that convey the idea of asking, telling, compelling, allowing, forcing:

| | | | |
|---|---|---|---|
| advise | allow | ask | expect |
| forbid | force | permit | persuade |
| teach | tell | warn | |

2  Verbs that convey the idea of wanting, needing, etc:

| | | | |
|---|---|---|---|
| want | need | prefer | would like |

Note that '*that* clauses' are not possible with the verbs in this group:

   *I really don't want ~~that anyone misunderstands~~ me.*

### verb + infinitive

The infinitive without *to* is used after:

1  *had better* and *would rather*:

   *There's a storm coming. We had better go home.*
   *I would rather not sit in the back of the car.*

2  the verbs *make* (meaning 'force') and *let* (meaning 'allow'):

   *You can't make me do anything that I don't want to do.*
   *If you let me borrow your car, will you expect me to pay for the petrol?*

   Note that *make* in the passive is followed by *to* + infinitive:

   *The soldiers were made to stand for hours in the sun.*

3  the objects of verbs of perception (*see*, *hear*, etc.):

   *When she was walking through the car park, she heard someone call her name.*

### verb + *-ing* form

Certain verbs are only followed by the *-ing* form of another verb. (That is, the *-ing* form of the second verb acts as a gerund, the object of the first verb.) Verbs that take *-ing* forms often convey likes and dislikes:

| | | |
|---|---|---|
| can't stand | detest | don't mind |
| fancy | feel like | enjoy |

Other verbs convey the idea of saying, thinking, describing:

> admit    consider    deny    describe
> imagine    suggest

Other common, miscellaneous verbs are also followed by an *-ing* form:

> avoid    deny    finish
> miss    practise    risk

Note that verbs that follow prepositions are always in the *-ing* form:

> *Don't apologise for arriving early. It's great to see you.*
>
> *He would probably get more done if he was better at working at night.*

### verb + infinitive/-*ing* form

A few verbs can be followed by an infinitive or an *-ing* form, with little or no change of meaning. For example:

> begin    continue    start

> *When the limousine drove past the crowd, some people began to throw/began throwing flowers onto the roof.*

Some common verbs can be followed by an infinitive or an *-ing* form, but with a change of meaning, e.g.:

> *remember*: I don't care how busy you are, you must remember to pay your credit card bill. (= remember to do something in the future)
>
> *I remember going fishing a lot when I was a boy, but I don't remember catching many fish. (= remember doing something in the past)*
>
> *regret*: I regret to inform you that I am resigning as company secretary. (= be sorry for a present or future action)
>
> *Neither of my parents regret getting married when they were so young. (= regret doing something in the past)*
>
> *stop*: 'Come on,' said the man in the museum. 'If you stop to look at all the paintings, we'll never get round.' (= stop one thing to do another)
>
> *He went to China last month and he hasn't stopped talking about it since. (= give up doing something)*
>
> *try*: She tried to reach the book on the top shelf, but it was too high. (= make an effort)
>
> *Have you ever tried doing a martial art? (= try out as an experiment)*

*mean*: Oh, I meant to tell you something. But I've forgotten what it was. (= intend)

*Buying this house means paying a higher mortgage. (= become necessary)*

# Relative clauses

## Defining relative clauses

Defining relative clauses are a vital part of the meaning of a sentence. They identify the subject or object or add vital information about them. Therefore you can't leave them out. They define *who* or *what* you are talking about. The vital information can come in the middle of a sentence or at the end:

> *The children that he knew would succeed were those who were motivated.*
>
> *Can you give me a good reason why you need to borrow so much money?*

**Relative pronouns:**

| | |
|---|---|
| *who/that* for people | *when* for time |
| *that/which* for things | *where* for place |
| *whose* for possession | *why* for reason |

*Who, that, which* are often omitted when they refer to the object of the sentence (not the subject).

> *Have you ever had one of those days that starts badly and gets worse? (that refers to the subject: 'one of those days')*
>
> *The mistake (that) he made was silly. (that refers to the object: 'the mistake')*

You can't omit *whose*. You can omit *when* if it refers to the object:

> *Sit down and tell me the exact time (when) it happened.*

You can omit *where*, but only if you add an appropriate preposition:

> *The old fisherman's hut (where we stayed) we stayed in was small and warm and it smelt of fish.*

You can omit *why* when it refers to the object:

> *Tell me the exact reason (why) you want to leave.*

You can omit the relative pronoun and the auxiliary verb, but only when the relative pronoun refers to the subject:

> *Buildings (that were) constructed before 1960 will be demolished.*

## Non-defining relative clauses

'Non-defining' relative clauses are quite formal and mostly found in written or literary styles. They add extra information that is not vital to the meaning of a sentence. They can usually be omitted without losing the sense of the main sentence. This extra information can come in the middle of a sentence or at the end:

> *Manatees, which are sometimes called 'sea cows', can be found in the warm waters around Florida.*

> *The trees were full of large, black birds, all of which made a tremendous noise.*

### Relative pronouns:

*who* for people
*which* for things (not *that*)
*whose* for possession

*when* for time
*where* for place

*Whom* is a formal relative pronoun that refers to the object:

> *The young artist, whom we had heard so much about, stumbled onto the stage to collect the prize.*

To identify a certain number of people or things from a group use *none/one/two/most of whom*:

> *She walked into a room that was full of teenagers, none of whom looked up from their work.*

You cannot omit relative pronouns in non-defining relative clauses.

# Direct and indirect speech

## Tense changes

When you report what someone said, you often 'move back' the speaker's verb tense:

| | | |
|---|---|---|
| *'I feel dreadful.'* | ⇒ | *He said he felt dreadful.* |
| *'I am swimming about ten kilometres a week.'* | ⇒ | *The girl said she was swimming about ten kilometres a week.* |
| *'I was the athletics captain at school.'* | ⇒ | *He said he had been the athletics captain at school.* |
| *'I have just become a vegetarian.'* | ⇒ | *She said that she had just become a vegetarian.* |
| *'We have been planning the trip for a long time.'* | ⇒ | *He said they had been planning the trip for a long time.* |
| *'I was travelling in Thailand when I heard the news.'* | ⇒ | *She said she had been travelling in Thailand when she heard the news.'* |

If you move back the tense, then the speaker's words were true when they were spoken but not necessarily true when they were reported. Don't move back tenses if the situation is still true or still relevant:

| | | |
|---|---|---|
| *'Bob and Anna are learning Russian,' he said.* | ⇒ | *He said that Bob and Anna are learning Russian.* (they are still learning it) |
| | | *He said that Bob and Anna were learning Russian.* (they may have stopped) |

A reporting verb can be in the present tense (e.g. *says*), in which case the speaker's verb tense does not change:

| | | |
|---|---|---|
| *'The medicine is working.'* | ⇒ | *My doctor says the medicine is working.* |

## Modal verbs

These modal verbs change for reported speech:

| | | |
|---|---|---|
| *will* | ⇒ | *would* |
| *may* | ⇒ | *might* |
| *can* | ⇒ | *could* |
| *must* | ⇒ | *had to* |

| | | |
|---|---|---|
| *'You will feel better by Friday.'* | ⇒ | *The doctor said I would feel better by Friday.* |
| *'You won't lose weight unless you do some exercise.'* | ⇒ | *She said I wouldn't lose weight unless I did some exercise.* |
| *'You must train every day if you want to be a champion.'* | ⇒ | *He said I had to train every day if I wanted to be a champion.* |

These modal verbs do not change for reported speech:

| | | |
|---|---|---|
| would | could | might should |
| ought to | used to | had better |

| | | |
|---|---|---|
| *'You should/ought to see a good sports psychologist.'* | ⇒ | *He said I should/ought to see a good sports psychologist.* |

## Other changes

When reporting, make logical changes to pronouns and possessives:

| | |
|---|---|
| 'My personal trainer has helped me build up my confidence.' | ➡ She said her personal trainer had helped her build up her confidence. |
| 'I sometimes speak to myself.' | ➡ He said that he sometimes spoke to himself. |

Make logical changes to 'place' words:

| | |
|---|---|
| 'I'm coming over there to see you.' | ➡ She said she's coming over here to see us. |

The words *this, that, these, those* are usually reported as *the*:

| | |
|---|---|
| 'This diet doesn't seem to be working.' | ➡ She said the diet didn't seem to be working. |

When *this, that, these* or *those* are used as subjects, they usually change to *it* or *they*:

| | |
|---|---|
| 'This/that is an incredible amount of money.' | ➡ He said it was an incredible amount of money. |
| 'These/Those are very difficult problems to solve.' | ➡ He said they were very difficult problems to solve. |

Make logical changes to 'time' words:

| | |
|---|---|
| an hour ago | ➡ an hour before/previously |
| last year | ➡ the previous year |
| yesterday | ➡ the day before |
| tomorrow | ➡ the following day |
| in a week's time | ➡ a week later |
| next month | ➡ the following month |
| 'I had a heart attack a couple of years ago.' | ➡ He said he had had a heart attack a couple of years before. |
| 'I'm going to take up yoga sometime next month.' | ➡ He said he was going to take up yoga sometime the following month. |

## Questions

Reported questions are not real questions. The word order is the same as for statements. They do not have question marks. Verb tenses, modals, etc. change in the same way as reported statements.

Yes–No questions are usually introduced by *if* (or sometimes *whether*):

| | |
|---|---|
| 'Have you ever worked abroad?' | ➡ He asked me if I had ever worked abroad. (not: *He asked me had I ever …*) |
| 'Would you like a hand with your luggage?' | ➡ The taxi driver asked me if I would like a hand with my luggage. (not: *The taxi driver asked me would I like …*) |

To report *wh- questions*, use the *wh- word* followed by the reported clause:

| | |
|---|---|
| 'How long have you been working in the sports centre?' | ➡ He asked me how long I had been working in the sports centre. (not: *He asked me how long had I been …*) |
| 'When did you first feel a pain in your back?' | ➡ The doctor asked me when I had first felt a pain in my back. (not: *The doctor asked me when had I …*) |

## Summarising verbs

There are a large number of verbs which summarise what people say, rather than report the exact words. These verbs are followed by various constructions. Some verbs have more than one construction. For example, *suggest* is not used with an object (*I suggested him to go.*), it is followed by an *-ing* form or a *that* clause:

He suggested training hard and running the London marathon.

His coach suggested that she should rest for a couple of days.

**verb + *that***

| | | | |
|---|---|---|---|
| admit | mention | protest | complain |
| realise | explain | suggest | |

**verb + object + *that***

| | | |
|---|---|---|
| advise | warn | remind |
| persuade | tell | |

**verb + object + *to* + infinitive**

| | | |
|---|---|---|
| beg | order | advise |
| forbid | warn | ask |
| remind | persuade | tell |

**verb + *to* + infinitive**

| | | |
|---|---|---|
| threaten | refuse | agree |
| promise | offer | |

**verb + *-ing* form**

| | | |
|---|---|---|
| deny | recommend | suggest |
| admit | propose | |

**verb + preposition + *-ing* form**

| | | |
|---|---|---|
| apologise (for) | insist (on) | speak (of) |
| boast (about) | congratulate (on) | |

**verb + object + preposition + *-ing* form**

| | |
|---|---|
| accuse (of) | blame (for) |
| praise (for) | discourage (from) |

# Modals

There are ten modal verbs:

| | | | |
|---|---|---|---|
| can | could | should | ought to |
| must | will | shall | would |
| may | might | | |

These five verbs and expressions act in the same way:

| | | |
|---|---|---|
| be able to | have to | need to |
| had better | used to | |

## Ability: *can/could/able to*

Use *can* to describe an ability in the present:

> *Professor Smith can speak five languages but he can't remember his name.*

Don't use *can* to describe ability in the past or future. Use *could* or a form of *be able to* for the past and *be able to* for the future:

Use *could* for general ability only in the past:

> *Max could write before he could read.*

Use *was able to/were able to* for one particular action concerning ability in the past:

> *They had to travel first class because they weren't able to get cheap tickets.*

Use *couldn't* for specific or general lack of ability in the past:

> *When I asked Professor Smith what his name was, he couldn't remember.*

Use *will be able to* for ability in the future:

> *After six months of intensive training you will be able to fly a helicopter.*

Note: You have to use a form of *be able to* after verbs or phrases that are followed by the infinitive or *-ing* form:

> *I would like to be able to swim every day, but I don't have time.*

## Permission: *can/could*

Use *can* to ask for and give permission in the present. In formal situations, *may* can also be used:

> *Can I ask you a personal question?*

> *You may now turn over your examination papers and you may start.*

*Could* is also a polite way of asking for permission. But *can* is used in replies:

> – *Could I use your dictionary for a moment?*

> – *Yes, of course you can.*

*Could* and *was/were able to* are used to talk about permitted activities in the past:

> *The schoolchildren could/were able to wear casual clothes on the last day of term.*

*Will be able to* is used for the future:

> *I'll be able to drive without 'L' plates when I pass my test.*

## Possibility: *might/may*

Use either *might* or *may* to express possibility in the future:

> *If we leave before midnight, we might/may arrive in time for breakfast.*

Present possibilities can also use *might/may* when you are making a deduction based on current knowledge:

> *Due to the heavy defeat in the recent election, some party members might/may now be unhappy with their leader.*

Use *might/may* + past participle to talk about a possibility in the past. It implies some uncertainty about whether the action happened or not:

> *I'm not sure, but I might/may have read this book when I was young.*

## Necessity: *need (to)*

Although *need* is often used as a normal verb, it can also act like a modal verb to express a necessity (usually one that the speaker feels). In the present positive use *need to* + infinitive to express present or future necessity:

> *You need to apply for a new passport if you've lost yours. You can't simply get a replacement.*

Use *needn't/don't/doesn't need to* to say that something is not necessary in the present or future or wasn't necessary in the past:

> *You needn't/don't need to put your seatbelts on yet. We have to wait for one more passenger.*

In the past, there are two negative forms:

*didn't need to* ( + infinitive)

> *I didn't need to send my CV.* (Perhaps I did send a CV, but it wasn't necessary, or I didn't send it and it didn't matter.)

*needn't have* ( + past participle)

> *I needn't have sent my CV.* (I sent it, but it wasn't necessary.)

## Obligation: *must/have to*

Use *must* or *have to* to express a positive obligation in the present or future. *Must* is often used when the speaker feels an obligation himself/herself:

> *I must lose a bit of weight before I go on holiday.*

*Have to* is used when the speaker feels an obligation from outside (a rule, law, regulation) or is just expressing a fact:

> *We have to put the paper to be recycled in the green box.*

*Mustn't* is used to express negative obligation (an obligation not to do something):

> *You mustn't park on the side streets during normal working hours.*

## Advice and recommendation: *should/ought to*

Use *ought to* and *should* for strong advice and recommendations. They are very similar in meaning:

> *When you go skiing on your own you should/ought to tell someone where you're going, in case you have an accident.*

> *If you're not a strong swimmer you shouldn't/ oughtn't to go out of your depth.*

## Assumptions/Deductions: *must be/can't be, must have/can't have*

Use *must* for a logical deduction about the present, when you want to express certainty:

> *It must be very boring to live in a small village where nothing happens.*

The opposite of *must* in this case is *can't*:

> *The letter can't be from your Aunt Harriet. It's got a Chinese stamp on it.*

Use *must have* + past participle and *can't have* + past participle to make logical deductions about the past:

> *The burglars must have got in through the little kitchen window.*

> *Dave can't have played football yesterday. He broke his leg last week.*

Use *may have/might have/could have* + past participle to make assumptions that you are not entirely sure about:

> *I was expecting a package today, but it hasn't arrived. I suppose it may/might/could have got lost in the post.*

# Reduced clauses

Use reduced clauses:

1   to simplify sentences:

*When the runner finished the race he was gasping for breath.*

*The runner finished the race gasping for breath.*

2   to reduce two sentences to one sentence:

*He's broken his arm. He'll have to watch the match from the sidelines.*

*Having broken his arm, he'll have to watch the match from the sidelines.*

Sentences with reduced clauses can often sound quite formal. Some uses would not normally be used in everyday spoken English:

*Being the richest person there, Fiona paid for the meal.* (formal)

*Fiona was the richest person there, so she paid for the meal.* (informal and usual)

When you use reduced clauses like adverbs they give more information about the *main verb*. For example: they may describe *the way* someone walked, *how* someone acted, someone or something's general manner or behaviour, etc. The main clause would normally come first:

*The marathon runner came into the stadium waving at the crowds.*

3   in written dialogues:

*'You're just in time to check in,' he said, looking at the clock on the wall.*

4   to talk about two things happening at the same time:

*Sam and Millie sat on the jetty talking about their future.*

If one long action is 'interrupted' by another shorter action, the longer action usually comes at the end of the sentence. The word *while* (meaning 'when' or 'at the time') can often be used:

*The aid worker died peacefully in a remote African village, (while) doing the job he loved most.*

5   to talk about two actions that happen within a short time period:

*The fire swept through the Australian town, leaving burnt out houses behind it.*

Often the second action is a direct consequence or *result* of the first action:

*The film has been a runaway success, paving the way for five or six sequels.*

Sometimes there is an obvious sequence – one action then another action. The reduced clause would normally come at the beginning:

*Taking off his heavy overcoat, he sat down on the red leather sofa.*

6   to imply a reason:

*Not knowing where he was, he stopped and checked the map.* ( = because he didn't know where he was)

Note: verbs that can't normally be used in continuous tenses can have a present participle form.

Prepositions are always followed by the present participle:

*On hearing the news, they started to celebrate.*

*Before getting on the plane, the President and his wife waved and smiled at the small crowd.*

Participles after a *noun* give more information about the noun. They are like shortened relative clauses in which the relative pronoun and the auxiliary verb have been omitted:

*Ruby Stone, smiling and waving to the crowds, got out of the limousine. (who was smiling and waving …)*

Note that the structure noun + present participle indicates an activity in progress:

*The man sitting over there wearing …*

If there is no activity in progress, you can't use a reduced clause:

*The scientist ~~inventing~~ the robotic washing machine will win a prize.*
*The scientist who invented the robotic washing machine will win a prize.*

With passive relative clauses, use the past participle:

*The meeting, scheduled for 10 o'clock, has been cancelled. (that was scheduled)*

These can often imply a condition:

*Watered once a day, the plant will grow really well. (if it is watered)*

# Conditionals

## Zero conditional

| If-clause<br>Present simple | Main Clause<br>Present simple |
|---|---|

Use the zero conditional to talk about scientific facts, constant laws of nature, unchangeable rules, customs and personal routines. Either *if* or *when* can be used in the *if*-clause.

*If/When it is lunchtime in London, it is breakfast time in New York.*

## First conditional

| If-clause<br>Present simple | Main Clause<br>will/won't + infinitive |
|---|---|

In the first conditional the **present** tense usually refers to possible/probable conditions in the **future**:

*If there is much more rain, the whole village will probably get flooded.*

*If Real Madrid's captain doesn't play, they won't win the game.*

Don't use *will/won't* in the *if*-clause:

*If there ~~will be~~ much more rain, the whole village will probably get flooded.*

Use the first conditional for threats or warnings involving direct action:

*If you don't go away, I'll call the police. ( = Go away or I'll call the police.)*

You can use an imperative in the main clause:

*If you hear the fire alarm, walk quickly to the nearest fire exit.*

*If you are frightened of heights, don't go up there.*

You can use the present continuous or the present perfect instead of the present simple:

*If you are doing your violin practice, I'll phone later.*

*If you have read my CV, you will know all about me.*

## Second conditional

| If-clause<br>Past simple | Main Clause<br>would/wouldn't + infinitive |
|---|---|

In the second conditional the past tense refers to 'unreal' or 'hypothetical' conditions in the present or future:

*If I had a daughter, I would teach her Russian.* (unreal present)

*If I started my own business, I wouldn't work on Friday afternoons.* (hypothetical future)

Don't use *would/wouldn't* in the *if*-clause:

*If I ~~would start~~ my own business, I wouldn't work on Friday afternoons.*

Use the second conditional to give advice to other people:

*If the solicitor was rude to you, I'd complain to his manager.*

You can use the past continuous instead of the past simple:

*If they were looking our way, they would see us.*

The past tense in second conditionals distances meaning from reality (in the same way that the past is distanced from the present). Compare first and second conditionals:

First conditional: *If I become President, I will increase taxes for high earners.* (spoken by a Presidential candidate)

Second conditional: *If I became President I would spend more money on after-school clubs.* (spoken by a schoolgirl)

## Third conditional

| If-clause<br>Past perfect | Main Clause<br>would have/wouldn't have<br>+ past participle |
|---|---|

Use the third conditional for past events that are untrue:

*If you had listened to the instructions, you would have known what to do.*

*If there hadn't been an earthquake, there wouldn't have been a tsunami.*

Don't use *would have/wouldn't have* in the *if*-clause:

*If there ~~wouldn't have been~~ an earthquake, there wouldn't have been a tsunami.*

You can use the past perfect continuous instead of the past perfect:

*If they had been looking more carefully, they would have seen the signpost.*

You can use *could (not) have* instead of *would have* to express possibility:

*If Sally had been a centimetre taller, she could have become a police officer.*

You can use *might (not) have* instead of *would have* to express 'perhaps/perhaps not':

*If he had known the film wasn't very good, he might not have gone to see it.*

## Formal forms

In first conditionals, you can use *should* before the infinitive in the *if*-clause to add uncertainty or increase politeness:

| | |
|---|---|
| *If he has a problem with his visa,* *If he should have a problem with his visa,* | *I'll sort it out for him.* |
| *If you need any help,* *If you should need any help,* | *I'll be in that office.* |

In second conditionals, you can use *were to* like *should*, above:

| | |
|---|---|
| *If we complained about the lack of clean water,* *If we were to complain about the lack of clean water,* | *what would you do about it?* |

## Alternatives to *if*

You can usually use *provided* (or *providing*) and *as long as* instead of *if*:

*Jim will land safely on the ground provided/as long as his parachute opens.*

*Supposing* (or *suppose*) means 'what if'. It can replace *if* in questions and comes first in the sentence:

*Supposing you missed the plane, what would you do?*

*Unless* can be used to mean 'if … not':

| | | |
|---|---|---|
| *You can't join the swimming team* | *if you can't/ unless you can* | *swim 100 metres in less than 75 seconds.* |
| *Don't sell your shares* | *if there isn't/ unless there is* | *a sharp fall in prices.* |
| *You can sit in a first-class seat* | *if nobody else/ unless someone else* | *wants it.* |

# Mixed conditionals

Mixed conditional sentences are formed from two clauses with different time references. The most common 'mixed' conditionals involve a clause from a second conditional and a clause from a third conditional. The *if*-clause can state the 'cause' or 'reason' and refers to the past (third conditional), with the 'result' in the main clause referring to the present (second conditional):

       (3rd)          (2nd)
1 *If Sally hadn't tuned her violin … it wouldn't sound very nice.*

       (3rd)
2 *If Tom had read the instructions more carefully, …*
  (2nd)
  *he would know what to do.*

These conditionals answer the question 'why?':

1 *Why does Sally's violin sound okay? Because she tuned it.*
2 *Why doesn't Tom know what to do? Because he didn't read the instructions very carefully.*

Mixed conditionals of this type often express regret (or satisfaction) in the present for something that happened in the past:

*If I hadn't married Tom, I wouldn't be living in Australia.*

They can express present possibilities based on past events:

*If you had kept the receipt, we would give you your money back.*

The modals *might* or *could* can be used:

*If I had started my own business ten years ago, I might be better off by now.*

*If she had studied languages at university, she could be a translator.*

The time reference of the clauses can be reversed. The *if*-clause (the cause or reason) can refer to the present (second conditional), the main clause (the result) can refer to the past (third conditional):

     (2nd)        (3rd)
*If his eyes weren't so bad, he would have seen the road sign.*

(He didn't see the road sign because his eyes are bad.)

     (2nd)        (3rd)
*If Anna wasn't so clever she wouldn't have known how to take my blood pressure.*

(Anna knew how to take my blood pressure because she is clever.)

In mixed conditionals of this type, the reference to the present makes it clear that the situation exists now. In 'pure' third conditionals, the time reference only refers to the past.

        (2nd)           (3rd)

*If Jack wasn't interested in people, he wouldn't have studied sociology at university.*

(Jack was and still is interested in people)

        (3rd)           (3rd)

*If Jack hadn't been interested in people, he wouldn't have studied sociology at university.*

(Jack was interested in people, perhaps he still is, but we are not sure)

# Wishes and regrets

Use *wish* + past simple for situations in the present that you would like to be different:

*I wish I didn't get so many unwanted emails.*

You can often use *were* instead of *was*, particularly in formal English:

*The young man is so unhappy that he often wishes he were somewhere else.*

Use *wish* + the past modal *could* (not *would*) to express a regret about a personal lack of ability:

*I wish I could swim further without taking a rest.*

Use *wish* + the past modal *didn't have to* to express lack of enthusiasm about an obligation:

*I wish I didn't have to carry my identity papers with me everywhere I go.*

You can use *wish* + *would* to criticise other people or an aspect of the present situation that you are unhappy with:

*I wish she wouldn't keep talking about her children.*

*I wish this computer would stop crashing.*

You can also use *wish* + *would* to talk about future situations that you want to change:

*I wish someone would fix the central heating..*

You can use *wish* + past perfect to express regrets about the past:

*I wish the advertising agency had thought of a better brand name.*

You can often use *if only* instead of *I wish*. But the result is more a thought than a voiced regret:

| | |
|---|---|
| *I wish/* | *I didn't have to commute to work every day.* |
| *If only* | *I could get a job in advertising.* |
| | *English spelling was easier.* |
| | *credit card companies wouldn't keep sending me their offers.* |

# Comparatives and superlatives

## Comparatives

Use *as … as …* to say that two elements are equal in some way. There are several structures you can use. The words *just* and *nearly* often come before the first *as*:

| | | |
|---|---|---|
| *as* | *adjective* | *as* |
| | *adverb* | |
| | *much/many + noun* | |

*He plays tennis nearly as well as his girlfriend.*

*I get paid just as much money as you.*

*There are just as many cafés in London as (there are) in Paris.*

Object pronouns, nouns and clauses can follow the second *as*:

*That car is nearly as old as me.*

*The food in Le Select is just as good as it was ten years ago.*

*Walking in London is often just as fast as taking a bus.*

Use the opposite structure *not as … as …* to talk about two elements that are unequal in some way. The words *nowhere near*, *nothing like* and *not quite* often come before the first *as*:

*The sports car was nowhere near as fast as I had expected it to be.*

*I can play the piano, but not quite as well as (I can play) the guitar.*

*Flying in a hot-air balloon was nothing like as frightening as I thought it would be.*

Use comparatives to compare people, groups and things. Use a comparative adjective (*healthier, more exciting*, etc.) or adverb (*earlier, more carefully*, etc.):

*You won the silver medal but Emma Dean beat you with a much faster time.*

*Would you like to have your interview where there is a greater degree of privacy?*

Use *than* to make comparisons between two different things of the same type:

*The weather in many countries is now warmer and wetter than it used to be.*

*Fiats are less expensive than Ferraris.*

You can qualify the comparative with these words and expressions:

| a bit | a little | much | a great deal |
|-------|----------|------|--------------|
| slightly | a lot | far | |

*Driving in a Mercedes is a great deal more comfortable than riding a scooter.*

*Book 2 in the series is slightly longer than Book 1.*

*She always does a bit better at English than maths.*

You can also use the expression *no (more) ... than* in the same way as *just as ... as*:

*The film was no more frightening than the book. The book was just as frightening as the film.*

You can use the following structure to talk about two things that happen together:

*the* + comparative clause + *the* + comparative clause:

*The bigger the waves the better it is for surfing.*

*The heavier the boxer the slower he moves round the ring.*

## Superlatives

Use superlatives to compare one member of a group with the whole group. Always use *the* with a superlative:

*the best film    the most exciting journey*

You can qualify a superlative with these words and expressions:

| among | one of | two of |
|-------|--------|--------|

*Shane Walker is among the best young writers in the country.*

*Crossing the icy ridge was one of the most difficult parts of the expedition.*

## Degree: *enough, too, so, such, as, like*

### *enough*

Use *enough* (with the meaning of 'sufficient/ sufficiently') after adjectives and adverbs:

*His exam results were okay, but they weren't good enough to get him his university place.*

*You're playing well enough to be in the team, but not well enough at the moment to be team captain.*

You often use *to* + infinitive after *enough*:

*I know you're physically fit but are you resilient enough to keep going?*

### *too*

Use *too* (with the meaning 'more than enough') before adjectives and adverbs:

*Sally auditioned for a part in a Broadway play, but they said she was too small for the part.*

*He tried to take a photo of the Tour de France cyclists, but they rode past far too quickly.*

You often use *too ... to* + infinitive:

*It was 38 degrees in the shade yesterday. Far too hot to sunbathe.*

*I ran out of time. I wrote too slowly to finish all the questions.*

### *so* and *such*

Use *so* before adjectives or adverbs, but not when a noun follows:

*There probably are other planets, but they are so far away that astronomers can't see them.*

*The trains are so unreliable (that) it's no wonder commuters get angry.*

Note that you can use *so much* or *so many* with a noun:

*'You've got so many problems,' said the psychologist, 'I hardly know where to start.'*

Use *such* before a noun (with or without an adjective):

*I haven't been to the cinema for such a long time (that) I can hardly remember the last film I saw.*

*Advertisers always want us to think they have such wonderful products, whereas most of it is such rubbish.*

### *as* and *like*

Use *as* as a preposition to mean 'in the role of':

*Mr Potter has been working as an accountant for twenty years.*

But use *like* as a preposition when it means 'similar to':

*Mr Potter doesn't look like an accountant. He's built more like a professional athlete.*

You also use *as* with adjectives to make comparisons:

*Nothing seems as frightening the second time you do it.*

# Emphasis

## Inversion

Use the word order you use for questions to give emphasis:

*I have never heard such a frightening noise.*

*Never have I heard such a frightening noise.*

You can use inversion:

1   after certain 'negative' adverbials:

| | | |
|---|---|---|
| never | hardly | scarcely |
| rarely | little | not for one minute |
| not since | not until | never before |

*Hardly had he sat down when he started to talk.*

*Scarcely had she got home when the phone rang.*

*Little did they expect so many supporters to write to them.*

2   after expressions with *only* or *no*:

| | |
|---|---|
| only when | not only |
| the only | in no way |
| on no account | under no circumstances |
| at no time | no sooner |

*The only way to get anywhere quickly is to fly.*

*Although the trip wasn't very pleasant, at no time did I feel in any danger.*

You can use inversion to replace *if* in conditional sentences that include *should*, *were* or *had*:

*If you should need any help with your bags, please let the receptionist know.*

*Should you need ...*

*If you were to stop messing around with your mobile phone, you might learn a bit more.*

*Were you to stop ...*

*If you hadn't tried to do three things at once, this would never have happened.*

*Had you not tried ...*

## Emphatic structures with *it* and *what*

You can use *it is ... / it was ...*, etc. to emphasise a particular part of a sentence:

*There were five members of the climbing team, but it was Bill who reached the summit first.*

*It was very disappointing that I didn't reach the top.*

Use *what is ... / what was ...* to emphasise the subject or object of a sentence:

*What they saw when they reached the summit was a French flag fluttering in the wind.*

There are various other expressions that can be added to the start of a sentence for emphasis:

*The reason I'm here today is to tell you about art.*

*The thing I like most about Harry is his generosity.*

*All he could talk about was his work.*

## *-ing* forms as subject of a sentence

You can use an *-ing* form as the subject of a sentence to give emphasis:

*Arguing with traffic wardens is a waste of time.*

# Phrasal verbs

## Adverbial phrasal verbs

Adverbial phrasal verbs are made from a verb + an adverb. Some phrasal verbs are intransitive (they have no object):

*The witness broke down when he was asked about her husband.*

*He packed his rucksack and set off.*

Transitive phrasal verbs (those with objects) are 'separable'. If the object is a noun, it can go:

1   between the verb and the particle:

*The police broke the demonstration up.*

*Can you set your ideas down in writing?*

2   or after the particle:

*The police broke up the demonstration.*

*Can you set down your ideas in writing?*

But if the object is a pronoun, you must put it between the verb and the particle:

*The police broke it up.*

*If you have any suggestions, please set them down in writing.*

## Prepositional phrasal verbs

Prepositional phrasal verbs are made from verbs + a preposition. The verb and the preposition are 'inseparable', so all objects whether they are nouns or pronouns must follow the particle:

*You should turn off the motorway at junction 2.*

*We've received your complaint and we'll look into it.*

Adverb particles can have several different meanings. For example, *off* can suggest:

1  a beginning of some kind:

*Go to bed early because we are setting off at dawn.*

2  finishing or delaying:

*We're going to finish off the lesson with a quiz.*

*I'm busy. I'll have to put the meeting off until tomorrow.*

3  some kind of separation or disconnection:

*Workmen closed off the road to do maintenance work.*

*Come in and take off your wet jacket.*

*My phone has been cut off because I didn't pay the bill.*

The particle *in* can suggest:

1  some kind of participation:

*Bob never joins in the fun.*

2  some kind of deception:

*She was too clever to be taken in by the salesman's smooth talk.*

3  some kind of collapse/retirement due to pressure:

*'Do you give in?' asked the wrestler, twisting the man's arm.*

Some phrasal verbs change their meaning when used with or without an object. For example, the particle *out* can suggest:

1  failure:

*My old car made a horrible noise and gave out five kilometres from the garage.*

2  distribution:

*She stood in the market and gave out leaflets about her new shop.*

## Three-part phrasal verbs

A few phrasal verbs have three parts: verb + particle + preposition. You cannot separate the verb from the other parts. All objects must come after the preposition:

*He's going to do away with all his old mobile phones.*

*Is he going to completely get rid of them?*

*I've just run out of time.*

# OXFORD
## UNIVERSITY PRESS

Great Clarendon Street, Oxford, OX2 6DP, United Kingdom

Oxford University Press is a department of the University of Oxford.
It furthers the University's objective of excellence in research, scholarship,
and education by publishing worldwide. Oxford is a registered trade
mark of Oxford University Press in the UK and in certain other countries

© Oxford University Press 2014

The moral rights of the author have been asserted

First published in 2014

2018  2017

10 9 8 7

ISBN: 978 0 19 451250 3

Printed in China

This book is printed on paper from certified and well-managed sources

ACKNOWLEDGEMENTS

*The authors and publisher are grateful to those who have given permission to reproduce the following
extracts and adaptations of copyright material*: p.9 Adapted extract from "What are you
like?" by Rachel Porter, *Daily Express*, 1 September 2004. Reproduced by permission of
Express Newspapers. p.11 Adapted extract from "What are you like?" by Maureen Rice,
*The Observer*, 28 March 2004. Copyright Guardian News & Media Ltd 2004. pp.12, 24,
60, 72 Definitions from Oxford Advanced Learner's Dictionary, 8th Edition. © Oxford
University Press 2010. Reprinted by permission. p.16 Text adapted from "Do you feel
lucky? (punk)" by Susan Aldridge, published in *BBC Focus Magazine*. © Immediate Media
Company Bristol Ltd. p.22 Extract from "The remotest festival on earth" by Beatrice
Newbery, www.geographical.co.uk, June 2004. Reproduced by permission of *Geographical*,
the magazine of the Royal Geographical Society (with IBG). p.26 Adapted extract from
"Indigenous History: Native Americans get national museum", http://www.reuters.com,
22 September 2004. Reproduced by permission of Reuters Ltd, a Thomson Reuters
Company. p.28 Adapted extract from "Deep in the heart of the Amazon rainforest,
*Geographical* discovers…a particularly painful rite of passage" by Patrick Cunningham,
www.geographical.co.uk, April 2004. Reproduced by permission of *Geographical*, the
magazine of the Royal Geographical Society (with IBG). p.34 Adapted extract from
"Investing in Our Future: Does Investing in Space Exploration Help or Hinder Progress
Towards Prosperity?" by Richard Garriott de Cayeux, *Huffington Post*, 5 September 2012.
Reproduced by permission of Richard Garriott de Cayeux. p.40 Adapted extract from
"Shh… your real age is an open secret" by Sarah-Kate Templeton, *The Sunday Times*,
24 October 2004. Reproduced by permission of News Syndication. p.46 Adapted extract
from "More than just a pretty face" by John Elliott and John Gerritsen, *The Sunday Times*,
28 November 2004. Reproduced by permission of News Syndication. p.53 Adapted
extract from "Will these creatures one day stalk the Earth?" by John Triggs, *Daily Express*,
26 August 2004. Reproduced by permission of Express Newspapers. p.57 Adapted extract
from "100 ways to get fit" by Andy Darling, *The Guardian*, 15 January 2005. Copyright
Guardian News & Media Ltd 2005. p.59 Adapted extract from "Is it possible to be too fit?"
by David Adam and David Munk, *The Guardian*, 10 June 2003. Copyright Guardian News
& Media Ltd 2003. p.100 Adapted extract from "Revealed – the meaning of life" by Julian
Baggini, *The Guardian*, 20 September 2004. Copyright Guardian News & Media Ltd 2004.
p.107 Adapted extract from *Writing Crime Fiction* by Lesley Grant-Adamson, Teach Yourself
Books, (2003). Copyright © 2003 reprint edition by Lesley Grant-Adamson. Reproduced by
permission of Hodder and Stoughton Limited. p.112 Adapted extract from "Is personal
freedom a thing of the past?", *The Guardian*, 25 September 2004. Copyright Guardian
News & Media Ltd 2004. p.118 Adapted extract from "Everything must go" by Simon
O'Hagan, British Airways' *Business Life*, October 2004. Reproduced by permission of Simon
O'Hagan. p.124 Adapted extract from "bling-bling" by Ekow Eshun, British Airways'
*Business Life*, October 2004. Reproduced by permission of David Godwin Associates. p.141
Adapted extract from "The oil under this wilderness will last the US six months. But soon
the drilling will begin" by John Vidal, *The Guardian*, 18 March 2005. Copyright Guardian
News & Media Ltd 2005. p.143 Adapted extract from "Pressure points" by Ian Sample, *The
Guardian*, 14 October 2004. Copyright Guardian News & Media Ltd 2004. p.149 Adapted
extract from "Cardboard bicycle can change the world, says Israeli inventor" by Ori Lewis
and Lianna Gross, www.reuters.com, 15 October 2012. Reproduced by permission of Pars
International. All rights reserved. Republication or redistribution of Thomson Reuters
content, including by framing or similar means, is expressly prohibited without the
prior written consent of Thomson Reuters. Thomson Reuters and its logo are registered
trademarks or trademarks of the Thomson Reuters group of companies around the
world. © Thomson Reuters 2012. Thomson Reuters journalists are subject to an Editorial
Handbook which requires fair presentation and disclosure of relevant interests.

*Sources*: p.34 www.nasa.gov. p.33 www.bbc.co.uk. p.34 http://news.discovery.com.
p.34 www.airspacemag.com. p.64 *The Guardian*, 18 September 2004. p.83
www.truthinscience.org.uk.

*The publisher would like to thank the following for permission to reproduce photographs*: Alamy
pp.14 (Girl with camera/Chris Leschinsky/Glasshouse Images), (mosaic/BRYANT
Nicolas/SAGAPHOTO.COM), 26 (gallery/Alex Segre), 27 (Armistice Parade/Colin
Underhill), 28 (Brazilian boys/Sue Cunningham Photographic), 33 (Graph/Paul Gibbs),
38 (Stonehenge/Mark Baigent), 38 (Stonehenge new visitor centre/Christopher Jones),
39 (Architect/Jacky Chapman/Janine Wiedel Photolibrary), 45 (Fin/David Fleetham),
45 (Tiger/Profimedia.CZ s.r.o.), 45 (toucan/Steve Bloom Images), 47 (Dolphins/
Brandon Cole Marine Photography), 54 (Pond dipping/Jason Smalley Photography),
54/55 (Volunteers/Jim West), 56 (toucan/Steve Bloom Images), 59 (Ranulph Fiennes/
Royal Geographical Society), 75 (Boy/Popperfoto), 87 (Battle reenactment/By Ian Miles-
Flashpoint Pictures), 90 (Stocktrek Images, Inc.), 98 (Jeff Morgan), 105 (Dennis Hallinan),
111 (library sign/Jeff Greenberg 3 of 6), (quiet zone sign/Lynch Creative Ltd), (security
signs/Credit/), (prohibited signs/Caro), 112 (CCTV/David Stares), 116 (Dennis Hallinan),
117+128 (Market/Peter Adams Photography), 135 (Punch and Judy/Ron Sutherland/
The Garden Picture Library), 143 (Frog/Jim Zuckerman), 146 (Oil rig/G P Bowater),
pp.151 (Think green lightbulb/Cienpies Design); Bridgeman Art Library Ltd p.86 (Vice
Admiral Sir George Anson's (1697-1762) Victory off Cape Finisterre, 1749 oil on canvas),
Scott, Samuel (c.1702-72)/Yale Center for British Art, Paul Mellon Collection, USA); Corbis
UK Ltd pp.19 (Woman/Steve Prezant), 19 (Man/Rick Gomez), 21 (Tomato festival/Reuters),
26 (totem pole/Jason Reed), 27 (Graduates/Reuters), 27 (Olympics), 30 (Aborigine men/
Free Agents Limited), 30 (Kylie Minogue), 30 (Surfer/Paul A. Souders), 33 (Horse racing/
Steve Boyle/NewSport), 33 (Microscope/Michael Pole), 39 (Winner/DiMaggio/Kalish),
45 (Tail/Paul A. Souders), 45 (Ibex/Steve Kaufman), 45 (Talons/W. Perry Conway), 45 (Tusks/
Martin Harvey; Gallo Images), 50 (cheetah/Frans Lanting), 50 (photographing sharks/
Jeffrey Rotman), 58 (Swimming triathlon/Douglas Peebles), 58 (Running Triathlon/
Rick Doyle), 58 (Cycling triathlon/Lucy Pemoni/Reuters), 75 (Opera singer/K.M.
Westermann), 75 (Scooby Doo, Chicken and Red Head/Frank Trapper), 75 (Rupert
Bear/Helen Atkinson/Reuters), 81 (Sphinx/Roger Wood), 81 (Proportions of face/
Alinari Archives), 81 (Vietnam/Tim Page), 81 (Helen Statue/Mimmo Jodice), 81 (Cave
Paintings at Tassili N'Ajjer/Kazuyoshi Nomachi), 87 (Manuscripts/Michael Freeman),
87 (Momentos/Jim Cornfield), 87 (Archeologist/Richard T. Nowitz), 87 (Tourists/Roger
De La Harpe/Gallo Images), 88 (Fresco/Bojan Brecelj), 88 (Egyptian painting/Charles &
Josette Lenars), 92 (Cave Paintings at Tassili N'Ajjer/Kazuyoshi Nomachi), 107 (Images.
com), 111 (builder/Construction Photography), (no parking/Markos Berndt/First Light/
Corbis, 112 (Iris scan/Varie/Alt), 114 (man in prison/moodboard), 119 (Bear/Kim Sayer),
124 (Julio Donoso SYGMA), 126 (Flamingos/Enrique Marcarian/Reuters), 126 (Chef/Gary
Houlder), 127 (Window cleaner/John Gress/Reuters), 127 (Racing/Sam Sharpe), 129 (Face
with Two Moods/Images.com), (Face with Two Moods/Images.com), (David statue/Tony
Gentile/Reuters), (Virgin Mary/Francis G. Mayer), (boy with painted face/Bob Sacha),
134 (Viking Festival/Salvador Sas/epa), 135 (Ampitheatre/Mimmo Jodice), (Basketball/
Greg Fiume/NewSport), 141 (Arctic/Paul A. Souders), (Oil spill/Lowell Georgia), (Highway/
Paul A. Souders), 142 (Robert van der Hilst), 143 (Yak/Craig Lovell), 146 (Wind farm/
Owaki - Kulla), 149 (cardboard bicycle/Baz Ratner/Reuters), 152 (Highway/Paul A. Souders);
Getty Images pp.10 (ink blot/spxChrome), 11 (inkblot/spxChrome), pp.21 (Tomato/Robert
Earnest/Stone), 22/23 (Yann Latronche/Gamma-Rapho), 23 (Yann Latronche/Gamma-
Rapho/Afel Bocoum and Damon Albarn), 26 (carousel/Hiroshi Watanabe), 32 (Tomato/
Robert Earnest/Stone), 50 (Arctic fox/Tom Walker), 62 (sleeping/Tara Moore), 66 (gym/
Gary John Norman), 67 (yoga/Tim Platt), 71 (X-Men:First Class 2011/Murray Close), 78 (gift/
Asia Images), 79 (hugging/Dimitri Otis), 81 (Battle against the Rutuli, miniature from
the Aeneid, by Virgil (70 BC-19 BC), with Servius' commentary, manuscript 493, vellum,
1469. France, 15th century. Dijon, Bibliothèque Municipale De Dijon (Library) (Photo
by DeAgostini), 114 (Judge/Michael Kelley), 117 (auction/Michael Kelley), 117 (man on
laptop/MECKY), 129 (Ceramic plate Painting by Tatsuya Kodaka/Kei Uesugi), 130 (Damien
Hirst/Mark Robert Milan/FilmMagic), 131 (Tate Modern/Justin Lightley), 136 (Frankfurt
train station/Robin MacDougall), 141 (polar bear/David Trood), 141 (Lightbulb/jml5571),
146 (hydroelectric dam/John Moore); Hemera Technologies pp.76, 118, 119 (Handbag),
119 (Books); Illustration Source p.65 (businesswoman graphic/James Endicott); NASA/JSC
p.91; Nature Picture Library p.28 (Wasp/Premaphotos); Ogilvy & Mather p.122 (toothpaste/
Erick Sulistio), (hotwheels/Javier Cresp); Oxford University Press pp.30 (Sydney Opera
House/Photodisc), 31 (Uluru/Ayers Rock/Photodisc), 33 (storm/Stockbyte), 34 (astronaut/
Photodisc), 39 (play/Comstock) 44 (storm/Stockbyte), 117 (clothes shop/Punchstock/
Photodisc green); Press Association Images p.135 (Ronnie O'Sullivan/Empics); Rex
Features pp.14 (Singing/Image Source), 14 (Paint balling/Sipa Press), 21 (Cat festival/
Christophe Potigny), 70 (Superman/Everett Collection), 70 (Spider man/c.Columbia/
Everett), pp.74 (Beyoncé/Rex), 82 (Bill Bryson/Ray Tang), 94-95 (I Robot 2004/Moviestore
Collection), 138 (Life of Pi 2012/20th Century Fox/Everett), 139 (Django Unchained 2012/
Weinstein/Everett); Science Photo Library pp.64 (mosquito/Volker Steger), 82 (Big Bang
artwork/Henning Dalhoff); 124 (Jim Smeal/BEI), 148/149 (Tess Peni), 148 (Weee man/Tony
Kyriacou), 148 (Elrington sculpture 1/John Wright); Ronald Grant Archive pp.71 (Universal
Pictures), 87 (Sydney Street); Science Photo Library p.146 (Nuclear power station/
Colin Cuthbert); The Future is Wild pp.52 (Ocean fish), 52 (Megasquid), 53 (Toraton),
53 (Snowstalker); Shutterstock pp.14 (car restoration/Hurst Photo), 16 (clover/Lionel
B), 33 (geese/Ana Gram), 33 (bees/Han maomin), 35 (Mars/James Steidl), 39 (researcher/
PhotoSky), 62 (mature man/auremar), 62 (ophthalmologist/Iakov Filimonov), 79 (mouse/
Alexander Kalina), 82 (evolution/Andre Jabali), 89 (dinosaur/Robert Adrian Hillman)

*Illustrations by*: Gill Button 13, 49, 72, 100, 102 103 121; Rod Clark/Art Market 93, 104;
Melvyn Evans p.101; Oliver Gaiger 41 96; Stephane Gamain 57, 68; Brian Grimwood pp.9,
20, 69, 80; Sarah Nyler/NB pp.17,29, 42-43; Ali Pellat pp.15, 25, 36-37, 61, 85, 97, 109, 133,
145; David Tazzyman pp.113, 137.

*Grammar reference by*: Ken Singleton

*Although every effort has been made to trace and contact copyright holders before publication, this
has not been possible in some cases. We apologise for any apparent infringement of copyright and,
if notified, the publisher will be pleased to rectify any errors or omissions at the earliest possible
opportunity.*